The Heart of Captain Cook Country

by

Queenie F. R. Ward

Queenie F. R. Ward

TABLE OF CONTENTS

PREFACE   5

Chapter 1	Our Ancestors	9
Chapter 2	The Coming of the Normans and Monks	25
Chapter 3	The Middle Ages	35
Chapter 4	In Tudor and Stuart Times	49
Chapter 5	The Landscape Changes	59
Chapter 6	The Progressive 18th Century	73
Chapter 7	The 18th Century Textile Industry in Cleveland	101
Chapter 8	Culture and Religion in the 17th and 18th Century	109
Chapter 9	Life on the Banks of the River Tees in Early 19th Century	131
Chapter 10	The Coming of the Railway	143
Chapter 11	The Coming of the Iron-Masters	155
Chapter 12	The Twentieth Century	173

Acknowledgements and grateful thanks are extended to the authors of the books below. On behalf of the communities living in the present county of Cleveland and its borders, appreciation is expressed for the tireless research among old documents which their writing has entailed.

These include:

"The Story of Cleveland" by Minnie Horton (1979).
"History of Guisborough before 1900" edited by B.J.D. Harrison and G. Dixon (1981).
"Stokesley Selection" collection of papers of local historical interest by Alec Wright and John Mawson (1982)
"Great Ayton" by Dan O'Sullivan (1983).
"The Birth and Growth of Middlesbrough" (c.1967)
"The Story of Eston" by Maurice Wilson.
"A Visual History of Great Ayton" by Ruth Gaudie.
"The Story of Nunthorpe Church & Village" (1976) a leaflet.
"Cleveland Village" by Robert Kettlewell - reprint of old records of Great Ayton and Ormesby.

The classical histories of the area in their times covering the whole Wapentake of Langbarugh which comprised the North Riding of Yorkshire.

"History Cleveland" by Rev. John Graves (1808).
"History and Antiquities of Cleveland" by John Walker Ord (1846).

For the history of the River Tees and it's difficult navigation:
"The Story of the Tees Pilots" by D.S. Hellier.

For a comprehensive study of the North York Moors, their geological structure, the significance of the stones found there and the people who erected them:
"The North York Moors" by Stanhope White (1979).

For research on a wider field in the study of local history:
"The Folk Museum at Hutton-le-Hole" - brochure.
"The North-East in Early Times 69AD-1464AD" Eye witness Series edited by Edwin Miller.
"The Common Stream" by Roland Parker (1976).
"The Making of the English Landscape" by W.G. Hoskins (1955).
"English Social History" by G.M. Trevelyan.
"The Lost Villages of Britain" by Richard Muir (1981).
"Who was Who in 19th Century Cleveland" by David M. Tomlin and Mary Williams (1987).
"Yorkshire Wit Character and Custom" by Richard Blakeborough (1896).
"Witches in Old North Yorkshire" by Mary Williams.
19th Century Parish Magazines of St. Cuthbert's Church, Marton.

AROUND CLEVELAND IN BYE-GONE DAYS
A Social History of Nunthorpe and the Surrounding District.

PREFACE

This account of the once village, now suburb of Nunthorpe and its surroundings attempts to catch glimpses in the lives of those men and women who once lived on the same patch of Mother Earth which we have now inherited. It will be concerned principally with the common folk so that it may at times appear as if we are taking a "worm's eye" view. For example when examining the effect of the Civil War on the area, the concern will not be with Prince Rupert, riding his fine horse and followed by his famous war-dog but with the poor housewife who has his unruly troops of the Royal Army billeted on her!

If at times we use our sympathetic imagination in trying to understand the many trials which our forebears underwent, there is a sound historical basis for this view. It must be understood that until the mid-19th Century and the industrialisation of Victorian England was launched into this area, Nunthorpe consisted only of Nunthorpe Village, a small agricultural community largely dependent on Great Ayton and Stokesley. After the coming of the railway in 1853 houses were built near the station for business men to commute to Middlesbrough and elsewhere. Since 1957 these houses have been augmented by housing estates until now Nunthorpe has come to be regarded as a suburb of Middlesbrough.

The story of the small community founded more than a thousand years ago embraces the history of its larger neighbours of Great Ayton, Stokesley and Guisborough, and the neighbouring villages of Ormesby and Marton, for they were all part of the pattern of rural life in this corner of the North Riding of Yorkshire. This pattern has now been broken and the commercial interests of modern Tees-side now dominate but it makes a fascinating study to look back to a pre-industrial age and see how the landscape and lives of people till the present time has developed.

Now Nunthorpe Village which is cut off from the main road by a by-pass, with no shop, post-office or ale-house, the school closed, her own small chapel in the Hall grounds unused, the Hall itself a home for Senior Citizens. "Grey Towers" the home of her last Squire, was a large hospital now closed, is like a modest old lady living in retirement, enjoying peace and quiet. Our imagination may go further and say that her daughter at

Nunthorpe Station has been married to her neighbour Marton's son and together they have produced a family of estates, shops, schools and roads! She has her memories of very bad times but also some very prosperous periods too. She takes satisfaction in the knowledge that she has survived when so many of her neighbours perished long ago. She knows that the name she has passed on is in good hands. She does not like to think of herself as a Clevelander when only a short distance away is her Yorkshire mother of Great Ayton. Yet she consoles herself with the thought that in these newcomers veins runs the same English blood that has given courage, strength and joy to all her sons and daughters down the ages.

The school boy James Cook must have known Nunthorpe well when he went to visit his friends in Marton, then partially situated at the top of the slope in Stewart's Park. He would have to pass through a Nunthorpe of thatched cottages and may have seen horses and carriages outside the village inn. He probably watched the blacksmiths at work shoeing a horse or fixing an iron on a cart wheel. A hundred years later three blacksmiths worked at the smithy at the end of the village street.

The "Heart of Captain Cook Country", Ormesby, Marton, Nunthorpe, Ayton, Stokesley, situated as they are, can be said to be by geography the heart of the area now known as Captain Cook Country but the title has another implication. The living heart of any area is its people and the animals and plants who share this planet with us. In the following pages the reader will find plenty about the people who lived in this area, something of the horses and other animals they kept and glimpses of the trees and flowers of this lovely countryside.

AUTHOR'S NOTE

The author wishes to pay tribute to two outstanding local historians who provided a great deal of the research upon which this book is based. Mr W.P. Baker was a W.E.A. lecturer from Leeds University who gave lectures in Middlesbrough in the 1960's. Mr Alec Wright, the Stokesley artist whose work is so much appreciated these days also gave lectures on local history and was an ardent conservationist. They both left behind the fruits of their labour but did not live long enough to embody their knowledge of local history in a book.

Mr Alec Wright bequeathed his printing blocks to "Studio Prints" at Guisborough and their permission has been granted to use some of his prints in illustrating this book.
Finally the author wishes to express her gratitude and appreciation of the help she received from Miss Grace Dixon, the local historian of Guisborough, and the late Mary Williams of Marske, in producing valuable research material.

A very special word of thanks must be given to Mrs Joan Brunton of Nunthorpe who tirelessly typed the text and without whose help and encouragement this book would never have been published. Thanks and tribute must be given to Mr Tom Pearce as well as Mrs Joan Brunton for maps and photographs used and Mr Norman Moorsom for his permission to use his pictures as well as his encouragement.

Life is made of joy and woe
And when this we rightly know
Safely through the world we go

William Blake

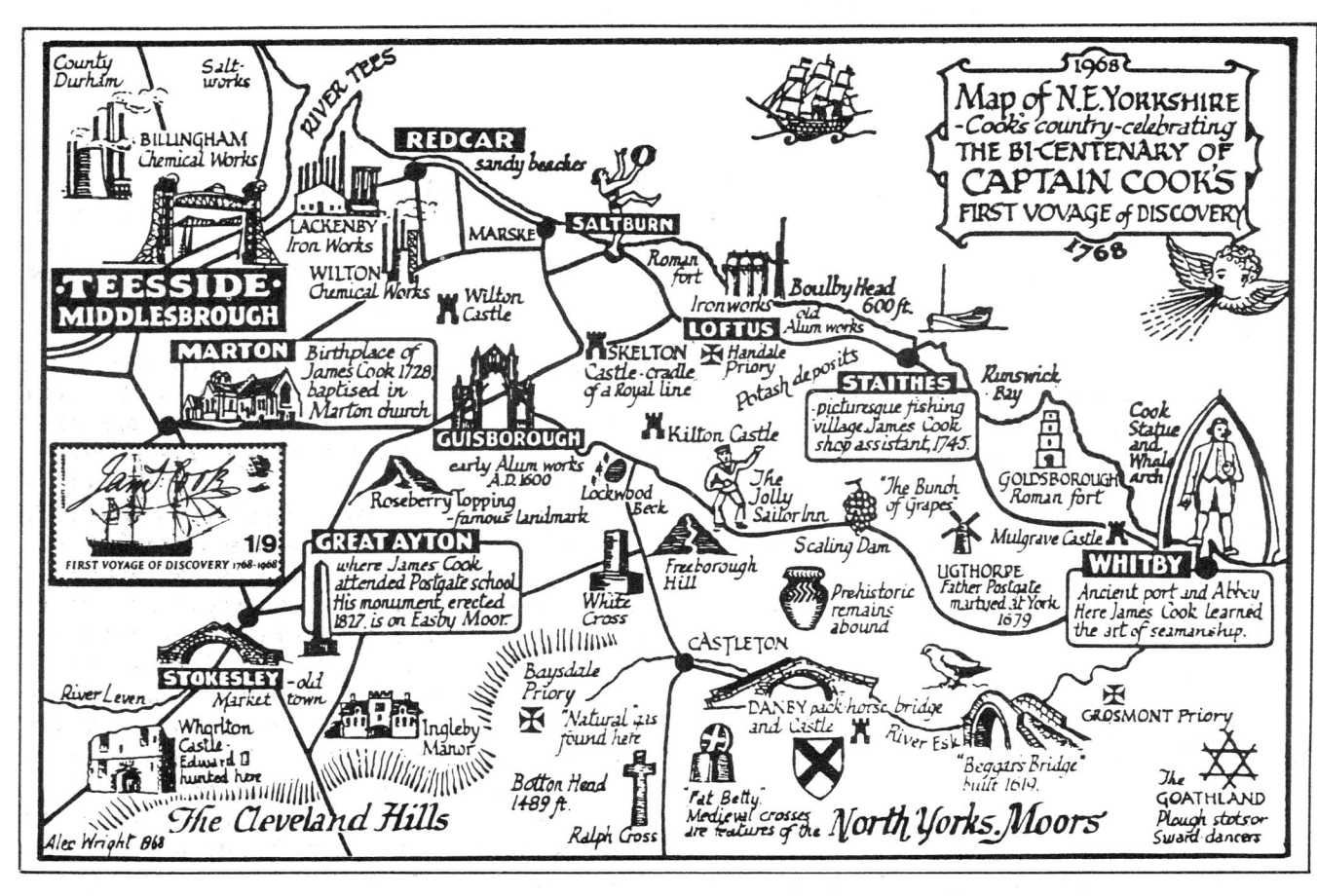

Map of N. E. Yorkshire.

CHAPTER 1

Our Ancestors

Greedy blue eyes gazed westwards over the calm sea which stirred gently in an easterly breeze. A picture of a shelving sandy beach directly over the sea on the opposite shore came into the mind of that chief of an Angle tribe, standing tall and strong on the sandy shore in Northern Germany. It was ideal weather for beaching his ships in a raiding assault on that distant shore and he thought of the gold, wheat and slaves that could be theirs for the taking. But - this was the beginning of the fifth century and the land the Romans called Britannica was carefully guarded now. This particular beach was overlooked by a signal station on a high cliff (Huntcliff). Moreover Roman soldiers guarded the valuable salt-pans further along the beach (Coatham) not far from that river which the Romans Called Teisa.

No! it was not wise to attempt the raid - yet!.........

Thus in imagination begins the story of the coming of our ancestors. Not long afterwards our Angle chief received the news that the Romans had left Britannica in order to defend their own land and our Angle chief lost no time in setting off with his men to raid the defenceless coast. The strong fair-haired warriors landed ship-load by ship-load; carrying their weapons they marched inland along the Roman minor roads and ancient tracks through the woodland and marshes, so convenient for their purpose. These were not the great military Roman roads - the great "motor-ways" of their age, but the smaller transport roads. As the Angles and the later Danish and Viking invaders passed along these minor roads they unconsciously determined the pattern of the villages of the area from that time on.

The best road for them was the Roman salt-road. It ran directly from the salt-pans at Coatham to the great Roman Camp at Catterick and it still does more or less to this day. The names of the villages along it give us their origin - the "ham" and "ton" of the Anglo-Saxons and the "by" ending of the Danes and Vikings - Coatham, Wilton, Eston, Marton alternating with Lazenby, Normanby, Ormesby, Tollesby and so on. Compared with the Roman villas, camps and towns like York and Malton further south, the Roman presence in this area was not very significant. Coins have been found dating from the first to fourth centuries chiefly near the salt-road and at Guisborough and a perfect Roman soldier's helmet was found on the south side of Barnaby Moor. A silver vase containing Roman coins found near Swainby at Whorlton Moor is a prize exhibit in the British Museum. Historians believe that in the flatter parts of the region there were Romans-British farms supplying wheat for the troops stationed further south, but no remains of such a farm have been found. Guisborough has always been regarded as the site of a small Roman fort but no evidence of Roman building has been found. Historians argue that the ending "borough" meaning fortified place and the roads radiating from the market cross seem to confirm its Roman connection. Judging by the names of the villages through which these roads pass, it is evident that first the Angles and later the Viking invaders marched along these ancient tracks.

The "gate" most interesting to the people of Nunthorpe is Westgate, for from it branched two routes westward. The bottom of the Guisborough valley at this time was very marshy, possibly a shallow lake. After leaving Guisborough it is conjectured the road did not go far before it turned up the hill-side, probably near where the drove road leaves the present road near the farm at Woodhouse. Then it passed along the southern side of Eston Hills, past the sites of the two "lost" Saxon villages of Barnaby and Upsall. The track came out near the south end of Flatts Lane, continued along the well-marked ancient track leading to near the top of Ormesby Bank. This continued till a few years ago across the field into what is now Rothesay Grove and so leads into Gypsy Lane which was a very ancient, possibly prehistoric pathway. This eventually led via Gunnergate Lane to the old Roman salt-road. Frank Elgee, the Cleveland historian and archeologist writing in "Romans in Cleveland" (1923), states that the Romans paved these ancient trackways and "traces of such paving are still found in Gypsy Lane" (that is before the lane was metalled).

The other route leading from the Westgate in Guisborough ran along the foot of the hills, going through Hutton and Newton-under-Roseberry, then turning via Great Ayton to Whorlton. Passing along it one day in the fifth or sixth century some of our ancestors ended their journey there beside the river at Ayton. Here they founded a settlement which was to influence the people of this corner of Cleveland for a thousand years.

Although the Angles and Saxons came in the first place to rob and pillage the land, they were also farmers and knew good fertile soil when they saw it. When the chiefs and their men saw this lovely countryside with its fine woodland and streams of pure water flowing down the hillsides, they decided to colonise this good land leaving behind their own barren country with its marshes and sandy earth. Having overcome what opposition there was their next task was to bring their families here and establish their own type of village. We can imagine an Angle chief with one or two shiploads of fair-haired warriors having walked along the forest track at the foot of the hills coming upon the lovely River Leven for the first time with a suitable flat area beside it and deciding to settle there, making their own "tun". They gave it the name "Ayton" which means a settlement by a "farm or enclosed meadow" by the side of a river.

Their first task would be to build a "hall" by selecting, cutting down and trimming the great oak trees which then grew in abundance in this area. Once built this would be where they would live until the ground around it had been cleared for the three great fields in which to grow their future food supply. One can imagine that these men gloried in their strength as they wielded great axes with arms grown powerful by pulling oars. Game in the woods there would be in plenty and they could live off the land. At night round a great camp-fire or later in the hall each would boast of his mighty deeds and a minstrel would sing a saga of heroes of old - a truly masculine assembly. In the summer some would return home to fetch the families while others built a stout stockade to keep out intruders. It was a tough pioneer life for this first generation of Anglo-Saxons even used as they were to supplimenting their farming with raiding overseas, but in a comparatively short time they settled down to a domestic village life, for the soil in the fields was good and rewarded their labour. The women, too were strong and resourceful as they brought up their families in the new land.

From now on the hall, home of the chief and his household was the centre of village life. It was like a large log cabin with a raised dias at one end where the chief and his household sat to dine. A fire burnt on a stone hearth in the middle, above which was a hole through which the smoke from it would gradually emerge. Boards and trestles provided tables for meals and all except the chief and his wife would sit on forms. Thus when these were stacked at the sides the space provided could be used as needed. The floor was strewn with rushes. Curtains partitioned off the private sleeping rooms of the chief and his family but the servants and retainer's slept on the floor with the dogs.

The married men of the village had each built for himself a house with wooden frame and "wattle and daub" walls. To make these walls basketwork of pliable thin branches and twigs of hazel and willow were fastened to the wooden frame of the house. To keep out all draughts, soft clay was beaten into the spaces and left to harden. Then thatch was firmly fixed to the latticed roof.

All worked with a will in the community, ploughing the common fields with oxen, tending the pigs in the surrounding oak-forest, the sheep on the higher land, and the hens and geese on the village green. Among their number were clever craftsmen to serve the community. The smith in his forge with his skill in shaping and repairing tools and weapons would be held in high esteem; a skilled carver in stone who could cut the large round mill-stones might serve several villages; the miller would set up his mill beside the stream; the wood-worker would be in constant demand making the simple wooden implements for farm and kitchen as well as those trestles, tables and forms for the hall; simple earthenware pots would have to be baked and each woman would be expected to at least spin, if not weave the wool from the sheep into cloth.

But there would have been times when all would gather in the Hall to listen to the sagas sung by the minstrel as they feasted off venison and wild boar at the long trestle tables. As the night went on, the walls would ring with merriment as the mead flowed.

They were a democratic people for the most part and village affairs were settled by their chief and a council of elders meeting on the village green. In this way the Angles settled down and grew to love their new land. Because the cliffs of the coast and the steep-sided scarps of the hills contrasted so sharply with the flat plains of Northern Germany they had left behind, they called the district Cliff-land - now Cleveland.

From time to time a King or overlord would send a messenger or the chief would be summoned with others to meet the ruler of the province which was known as Deira, later to become part of the kingdom of Northumbria. However the villagers of this busy community were usually little concerned with the rumours of quarrels among the Anglo-Saxon nobles and Kings but one day there came a stranger who was to have a great influence on their lives. He would travel along the same old tracks and news of his coming may have preceded him. Undoubtedly they would welcome this gentle monk who spoke with such conviction and resolution. He was one of those astonishing Celtic saints who brought their Christian message to convert the whole of the North East England before going to the rest of our land and the Continent itself. It is quite possible that this saint was St. Cuthbert himself for the neighbouring churches of Marton and Ormesby are both dedicated to St. Cuthbert and are of Saxon foundations. Early records of all the churches in the area have been lost. The old Great Ayton church is dedicated to All Saints which was quite a usual Saxon dedication but unusually it was mentioned in Domesday Book. Another local church mentioned in the Domesday Book was that at Acklam (village of the great oak trees). In the olden days up to the birth of modern Middlesbrough, Acklam parish extended southwards to the boundaries of Marton Parish and northwards to the river including the hamlets of Ayresome and Leventhorpe (Linthorpe), Newport and Middlesbrough. Nothing of the original church remains today for with the growing population it has been rebuilt and extended to cater for their needs. But it is interesting to note that on June 28th 1838 the people of the infant town of Middlesbrough marched all the way in a grand procession with bands to Acklam church to celebrate the Coronation of Queen Victoria. Another local church although not mentioned in the Domesday Book may have an even older origin. In the once beautiful cemetery at Eston is St. Helen's Church. It was until recently used as a Chapel-of-Ease chiefly for funeral services but is dedicated to St. Helen, the patron saint of the Roman Army and mother of the Emperor Constantine. Canon Stevenson, Vicar of Eston 1937-1946 suggested it may originally have been a garrison chapel of the Roman Legions as it is near the old salt-road, a military road to be guarded from invaders. Ord gives us a description of it before being "improved" by the later Victorians who covered up its old zig-zag mouldings. In the south east corner is a very old window probably Tudor, depicting St. Helen and a companion finding the true cross, which St. Helen holds. There were two bells, one with the inscription "Saint Helena, ora pro hobis" which was sold because it was cracked and the other, cast in 1725, having the inscription "Jesus be our speed" now hangs in Christ Church, Eston.

Part of the evidence for believing that All Saints, the old church at Great Ayton is of such an early foundation is because of the stones which have been found in the churchyard there. Writing in 1846 Ord tells us in his History of Cleveland *"According to Graves (1808) four fragments of stone (now in All Saints Church) found in the churchyard date to within two hundred years of Easter. Even in the year 627 when King Edwin was baptised by Bishop Paulinus at York. These stones are of great interest, because they are fragments of an empty cross, the emblem of the Resurrection of our Lord.*

It was an early custom to erect crosses and crucifixes in churches like the broken fragment in Ayton Church of which Mr Ibbotson (Vicar of Ayton and Nunthorpe 1827-1878) informs me it was found in the south wall of the church. It was covered with grass and never perceived till last summer (1843). The lower stone seems to be the socket to receive some upright pillar or shaft, probably of an ancient cross".

These fragments found in the 19th century were evidently parts of an old Northumbrian Celtic Cross. Such large beautifully carved crosses were erected by the Celtic saints where they founded a Christian Church. They were thrown down and smashed by the invading Vikings and remained buried for centuries. Several are exhibited in the Victoria and Albert Museum like the almost perfect one found buried until a few years ago in the churchyard of Wensley Church in Wensleydale.

Even if it were not St. Cuthbert but one of his fellow Celtic Monks who brought the Gospel from Holy Island, it is quite possible that Cuthbert visited the new Christians as was his wont. The Venerable Bede gives us such a vivid account of his missionary work that we seem to see him as he speaks to them on the village green.

"He often used to leave the monastery on horseback but

Gt. Ayton Church

Nunthorpe was in the Parish of Ayton till 1926. For a thousand years this old church with its Saxon foundation was the parish church of the people of Nunthorpe. Its site is recorded in the Doomsday Book. The present building dates from the 12th Century but the remains of a Celtic Cross and Saxon stones have been found. The font is of the 12th Century. In the late 18th Century it was restored by the the Marwood family in the style known as "Churchwarden Gothic". Round headed large windows were put in, a three-decker pulpit, box pews and a musician's gallery at the back. The gallery was removed because it was considered unsafe but there are Georgian style marble memorials on the walls. A tower was also added in 1788 but it was demolished in 1880 to make way for burials. The Solitary figure is Rev. Joseph Ibbetson, who was a friend of John Walker Ord, the historian and son-in-law of Thomas Simpson who built Nunthorpe Hall.

(Captain Cook's father is buried here.)

"Hunters Cremation".

A drawing by M. Maitland Howard from the book "Ancient Britons".
Published by: John Baker, an imprint of A. & C. Black (Publishers) Ltd.

more frequently on foot and visit the neighbouring towns (village settlements) where he preached the way of Truth to those who had gone astray. In those days whenever a clerk or priest visited a town, English folk always used to gather at his call to hear the Word, eager to hear his message and even more eager to carry out what they heard and understood. But Cuthbert was so skilful a preacher and had such a light on his angelic face and such a love for proclaiming his message that none presumed to hide his inmost secrets. He used mainly to visit and preach in the villages that lay far distant (from Lindisfarne) among high and inaccessible mountains, which others feared to visit and whose barbarity and squalor daunted other teachers. Cuthbert, however gladly undertook this pious task and taught with patience and skill to guide the peasants heavenward by his teachings and virtuous example".

The Venerable Bede, writing his "Life of St. Cuthbert" only about fifty years after the saint's death tells of an incident which might easily have taken place on our North York Moors or along the Esk Valley if he were making his way to Whitby Abbey. It was his custom to take a boy with him on his travels. As they walked over the rough tracks, they would recite the psalms together and the boy would learn daily the Christian way of life. This particular day was a fast-day, possibly a Friday and they had set out long before the evening meal. Evening was coming on as they were crossing the lonely moor and they were hungry. Then St. Cuthbert said "Let us ask God to supply our needs". They stood with arms outstretched and eyes raised towards heaven. Then as they gazed they saw an eagle (osprey?) swoop down out of the sky, towards the river. As it rose again they saw a large salmon in its mouth. It then flew towards them and dropped it at their feet. The boy picked it up and St. Cuthbert said "Cut it in two for the bird needs its share too". Having done that the saint then said "Let us take this to the next house we see. It can then be cooked and we can share it with others who are hungry too". In the eyes of the Celtic saints all God's bounty must be shared among all God's creatures whether animals or humans.

Even if St. Cuthbert himself did not visit Ayton in his lifetime there is evidence that his body was brought here to this district. When the Vikings raided Lindisfarne in 793 St. Cuthbert's tomb was not disturbed but when there was a further threat in 875 the monks decided to leave, taking with them among other things, St. Cuthbert's coffin and the famous Lindisfarne Gospels. They wandered from place to place for several years until they reached Chester-le-Street in 883. There they remained until 995. Prior Wassington of Durham writing in the 15th Century named a number of places in the North Riding of Yorkshire where they rested in their travels, among them Kildale, so close to Ayton, Kirkleatham, Wilton, Ormesby and Marton, all of whom have churches dedicated to him and it may be assumed that their foundation must date at least, if not before, then.

The moors over which the Celtic saints walked carrying the Christian message about thirteen centuries ago would have looked very much as they do today. Mr Stanhope White has described them as a "man made desert" and the people who were responsible for their deforested state were the Bronze Age people. He writes in his book "The North York Moors".

"The North York Moors is a man made desert, man made in the sense that it was our distant ancestors who destroyed the natural cover and allowed the growth of bog and heather to give the largest heather moor in England".

The Moors abound in pre-historic remains and the one nearest to Nunthorpe - Barnaby Moor with Eston Nab

15

(i.e. NEB - nose) is - or was - rich in remains. It is the site of a Bronze Age Settlement and a Celtic Iron Age hill fort. From about 1200BC - 700BC the Bronze Age farmers had villages on the hill tops. The weather was much warmer than in later centuries and they were able to grow crops there and keep sheep and goats. Their wooden ploughs were not able to till the heavy clay of the valleys. They cleared the tops of the hills of trees and their grazing animals prevented regeneration of the forests. About 700BC great climatic changes took place and it was no longer possible to cultivate the lighter sandy soil which had become exhausted. At the same time the Celtic tribes of the Iron Age people invaded the country but their iron tipped ploughs were able to till the heavy soil of the valleys so the hill tops were abandoned and left to become the moors we know today.

To the uninitiated the only visible remains of these prehistoric Bronze Age people are the large round mounds with a hollow in the middle - the tumuli. A tumulus is an ancient burial place. Over the North York Moors there are many hundreds of several different types which form a study of their own. About fifty years ago on the top of Eston Hills there was evidence of a large round pond with a causeway near which stone rings of Bronze Age date were found. These were used as weights for fishing nets and are now in the Dorman Museum. The most important part of the prehistoric village seems to have been Court Green, a flat area to the east of the stone tower now on the Nab where according to Ord there used to be a stone circle. It was the amateur antiquarian Victorian owners, possibly hoping to find buried treasure, who despoiled the tumuli and made it impossible for further investigation. Ord in his "History of Cleveland" (1846) gives us a full account of a day spent opening one of these tumuli, he writes:

"*On Thurs. Nov. 11 1843, through the kind permission of the Rev. M. Stapylton, we proceeded to explore the contents of two fine tumuli on Barnaby Moor near Eston Nab, about two hundred yards from the famous encampment there, and not more than forty yards distant from each other. The circumference of each barrow was thirty yards, the length across north and south nine feet eight inches and the breadth east and west nine feet six inches.*

The morning was clear, serene and beautiful, a sharp brisk invigorating breeze blowing from the west, the air bright and transparent and the heavens a deep brilliant azure, seemed to smile propitiously upon our undertaking....

At nine o'clock we commenced with the first tumulus and removed the first crust of turf and ling which entirely enveloped the surface. Beneath this lay a thin deposit of vegetable substance, the dust of the inner rind of turf. Underneath and within an inch or two of the extreme surface, we arrived at a mass of small stones, divided into compartments by large masses of sandstone placed at regular distances round the base of the tumulus. The removal of these occupied about five hours, four workmen being actively engaged during the whole of that time, assisted alternately by the parties present. After the removal of several tons of loose stone, the workmen struck upon a large ponderous slab, the enormous size of which and the hollow sounding noise of the pickaxes, excited the most pleasing prognostications of success, and we began already to anticipate visions of rich sepulchral vases, ancient ornaments or arms and perchance the gaunt remains of some grim old chieftain reposing in the dust.

This stone lay east and west, measured seven feet three inches in length, four feet three inches in breadth and eleven inches in thickness and proved to be considerably more than a ton in weight. After clearing away all

Eston Hill

The first ironstone was found on Eston Hills in 1850. It was mined there till 1949 and this was their appearance during that time. The watch-tower is plainly seen.

earth, rubbish and loose stones, the huge mass was raised sideways through the united efforts of the whole party, aided by an artificial fulcrum. The interior exhibited a perfect kist-vaen (stone chest or coffin of most ancient date) about a yard deep and the same in breadth and upwards of seven feet in length. The lid was supported in the middle and at both ends by firm stone pillars of rude form, the walls were compact and well defined and the pavement was composed of a dense mass of coarse sandstone, much stained with a sooty greasy substance mixed with portions of human hair and small fragments of bone. The labourers continued to search for some time longer but still nothing except a very great heap of stones, many of them of a deep red, as if they had been exposed to the action of fire, presented themselves".

When they opened the second tumulus they found another great mass of burnt stones, charcoal and pieces of bone and in the middle a round earthernware urn with incized zig-zag decoration full of bones. On examination these were found to be from many different bodies and all had been calcined. It was evident that these people cremated their dead!

The Victorians opened all the tumuli and what happened to all the relics they found in them? The answer is - almost nothing! One or two of these urns full of calcined bones are now in the Dorman Museum in Middlesbrough. It was said that Sir John Lowther had an out-building at Wilton Castle full of the relics he had found on his land on Eston Hills. There they lay neglected for years until at last thrown away and lost!

The great earthworks of the round Iron Age fort on the top of Eston Nab have been of considerable interest to local historians and several arrow heads have been found nearby. Originally the Celtic fort was circular in shape and it was where the women, children and cattle were taken in times of danger while the men put up their defence. During the three thousand or more years of its history a large part of the circle has fallen over the cliff edge but sufficient remains for us to imagine its great size. The wide views which open up in every direction make Eston Nab a superb look-out station which has been so used down the centuries. Mr Maurice Wilson in his "Story of Eston" sums this up very well when he writes "The British fortress with its ditch and ramparts on Eston Nab could have been originally a tribal redoubt, later a strong regional outpost against seaborne raiders from across the North Sea and a very possibly in turn, used by those same sea robbers as a base for their own foraging and eventual colonisation. It was a natural strong point, a perfect observation post and a handy base in immediate and close contact with their boats in the River. Eston Nab - a fort:; Eston Nab - a base:; Eston Nab - Eston Beacon, a link in the chain of fire giving warning of the approach of the Spanish Armada; Eston Beacon, topped with a solid sandstone tower, four square to the wind and the weather, built by the patriotic Thomas Jackson of Lackenby during the Napoleonic Wars once again to send the spark of warning on its way. The "Lighthouse". always so called when I was a boy, survived bravely the storms, winds, weather and ravages of unrelenting time for more than one hundred and fifty years but could not, after ceasing to be occupied, withstand the vandals of the 1950's. Even so, its penultimate chapter recorded once again its proud purpose, as in the Second World War it served as an observation post for the Home Guard deployed to guard against another threat of invasion - this time from the air".

The Beacon tower became so dangerous that it had to be demolished but I.C.I. who own the site (being within the Wilton Estates) erected a monument using the beacon stones, on which is a plaque briefly recording the history of the site.

Whether it was St. Cuthbert or one of the lesser-known Celtic teachers who roamed over this part of the country during the sixth century the villagers of Great Ayton together with those of its neighbouring villages were converted to Christianity. First a cross would be set up on the village green around which the people of the area would gather to hear the Good Word. Then a small daub and wattle church would be built and in time, beside it a priest's house. He would probably have been trained in one of the monastery schools, perhaps at Hartlepool or Whitby. He would be able to read and write, an almost magical accomplishment in the eyes of the parishioners. During these seventh and eighth centuries the weather too seems to have been particularly good, that is to say warmer than now. For example it is known that the sea-ice around Greenland would have prevented the Vikings landing there and establishing their colonies had it been as it is now in the twentieth century.

The Church had a very strong influence both at the court of the Northumbrian Kings and in the countryside. The Venerable Bede paints a picture of a land of peace and contentment. Of course there were the "earls and churls", that is the ruling class and the peasants and also a number of serfs, like slaves bound to the land. But the church actively discouraged slavery and urged the Saxon Lords to save their souls by freeing the slaves. That they did so is evidenced by the name of "Carlton" the village of freed slaves, near Stokesley.

Although these simple peasants of the villages could not have known it, they were living in what was almost a Golden Age for this part of the world. The Celtic Church with its monasteries, schools and high degree of culture and learning had spread from Ireland via the island of Iona and St. Columba to the kingdom of Northumbria which at that time spread from Edwin's capital (Edinburgh) and the Forth, south to the Humber. In time the province of Deira which stretched south of the Tees could boast of monasteries which were seats of learning at Whitby, Lastingham as well as York. Some believe that the monastatic chapel and small cell, the site upon which Middlesbrough now stands, may have originated as a Chapel-of-Ease for Celtic monks as they travelled down the coast from Lindisfarne, Jarrow and Hartlepool on their journeys to the monasteries of Yorkshire.

Based on Lindisfarne monastery and Holy Island, backed by friendly Kings, such saintly men as Aidan and Cuthbert spread Christianity and learning throughout the kingdom. Later Chad and Cedd, the saintly brothers of Lastingham spread the good work to the Midlands and the south and trained others to spread the Gospel, together with the learning and culture which followed in its wake. Europe at this time was in the throes of the complete chaos of warring tribes in the Dark Ages. With a zeal almost amounting to seeming madness, the Celtic monks went overseas walking the highways of Europe fearlessly carrying their message. It was almost entirely due to their efforts that Christianity, together with its civilising influence, was rekindled on the continent during the seventh and eighth centuries.

The names of two men, both from Northumbria, stand out in the annals of the European cultural revival during the eighth and ninth centuries. The Venerable Bede was the greatest scholar, writer and teacher of his time. From the Monkwearmouth monastery near Jarrow where he was brought up from childhood, he taught daily, wrote commentaries on the Gospels and theological books but for us, above all, the first history of this country. He was a real scholar meticulous in gathering his facts by means of a correspondence with all the prominent churchmen and scholars in the country. The monks in the scriptorium of his monastery and many others were for many years kept busy copying his works and illustrating them with their intricate designs. These leather bound, parchment paged books are treasured, not only by the famous libraries and cathedrals of this land, but also abroad. Being written in Latin they were taken by the Celtic missionaries and preserved in the monasteries they founded all over the continent. Books were so precious that they were the greatest possessions, even of kings, while Latin was the tongue spoken by all cultured people.

The other great man of continental fame at this time was Alcuin of York. Charlemagne at the end of the eighth century, had subdued the warring tribes of Europe and by his firm control restored peace. At Christmas 800 A.D. The Pope crowned him Emperor in Rome. Being illiterate and unhappy about it, he now sought for a man who would teach him and his court to read and write. There was only one country where such a teacher could be found and in York, the Emperor wisely chose a scholar named Alcuin. He gained great honour and esteem at Charlemagne's court and became known as "the schoolmaster of Europe". In the troubles of the Dark Ages most of the books had been destroyed but with the coming of peace, Emperor and scholar did their best to establish libraries, where any remaining books could be cared for and others written and copied. One interesting sidelight of this is the way in which it has influenced our writing to this day. The monks like Bede wrote their Latin books in the beautiful rounded Celtic script but throughout Europe at this time there existed the old Roman script and numerals. Alcuin was largely responsible for the combination of these two scripts which we use today, - for example, on the typewriters capital letters are in the Roman script e.g. A.M. and small letters are in the Celtic script e.g. a.m.

In the ninth century all this was to change for with great ferocity, the dreaded Norseman began to raid the coasts of Northern Britain and sail up the rivers. They too beached their beautiful wooden ships whose high prows were topped by carved beaked heads, on the shelving shores stretching from Coatham to Marske. Up and down the coast they sailed destroying the rich monasteries they found there - Lindisfarne, Jarrow, Hartlepool, Whitby. In them they sought and found what they coveted most - gold! With it their skilful craftsmen could fashion rich ornaments to display on their fine sturdy, flaxen-haired bodies, and they were ruthless in their pursuit of the precious metal.

After the first terrible onslaughts had abated, their intelligent minds realised what a very beautiful, fertile countryside they had found here in Deira - soon to be named Yorkshire. The stolen wheat produced good flour, so much better than the coarse rye flour which was all their homeland could produce. The barley and oat crops this land produced made good ale and fine food for cattle. Their chiefs, like those of the Angles before them, decided to colonise the land and make their homes in villages among the woods beside the running streams. So they too marched along the old trackways and founded villages as they went along. They added the endings "by" and "thorpe" to the names of the villages they founded and among them the village of Nunthorpe.

At first sight it may seem strange to establish a settlement here when the first requirement was a suitable stream of fresh water. Surprisingly Graves, writing in his "History of Cleveland" (1808) states that Nunthorpe is situated on the River Tame. On his map (1805) is shown the river rising on Barnaby Moor, flowing through flat fields, to the east of Nunthorpe village, under Tree Brig (marked Tree Bridge) and so on till it joins the River Leven just beyond Stokesley. This was the stream which powered the water-mills which went on grinding corn from the village's foundation till the coming of the Industrial Revolution.

What has happened to this once useful small River Tame, a tributary of the River Leven, joining it at Tamebridge, outside Stokesley? A study of a modern map reveals that its flow is unimpeded until it reaches a certain point in the fields lying between Morton Carr Farm and Nunthorpe Village. There the stream divides into the Main Stell and the Nunthorpe Stell, (a stell is a canalised stream). The Nunthorpe Stell continues near the village where it is joined by a small tributary running through the grounds of Nunthorpe Hall and on to Tree Bridge. The Main Stell runs in a wide sweep round the flat fields draining as it goes, till it joins up with the Nunthorpe Stell at Tree Bridge and becomes the Tame.

These Stells are not shown on Ord's map in his "History of Cleveland" (1843), but appear on the first O.S. map, surveying 1853-58. Geologically speaking the area they are flowing through (and draining) is known as Morton Carr. A carr is a peaty area which was once a natural lake or swamp during the Mesolithic Period, following the melting of the glaciers about 11,000BC, as has been reckoned by a pollen count at Seamer Carr, which was too marshy to be used for farming, was reclaimed in 1815. Morton Carr, however, has been farmed for centuries. Then in the 19th century when railway engineers wished to build a line across it, the land was considered unstable and they devised this plan to stabilise the land and improve the farming by digging these stells for the little River Tame.

There were two massive invasions of Norsemen into Yorkshire. The first were the Danes, the enemies of Saxon King Alfred of Wessex. Yorkshire was the first target of their main attack as this record of their settlement shows:
"*In 876 Healfane portioned out the land of the Northumbrians and made a livelihood of it*".
The Danes captured York in 867 but not long afterwards when Guthram, the Danish leader, signed a peace treaty with Alfred, Yorkshire then became officially part of the Danelaw, the large slice of England to be ruled by and colonised by the Danes. Ever since then the Scandinavian influence has never been in question in North East England.

About the year 915 another great wave of Norsemen flooded over Northern England. Some came in ships pouring out from the east coast and rivers while others marched over the Pennines from the west down the valleys of the Dales. On the whole these latter Vikings preferred to settle on the high Dales land, giving places there the Norse names they bear today. These new invaders captured York and turned it into a great trading centre.

However the ending THORPE in NUNTHORPE suggests that the founders of this village were Danish rather than Viking. It was known as T(H)ORP until 1210. The ending "thorpe" usually suggests a small village attached in some way to a larger one - in this case Great Ayton. It remained in the parish of Ayton for about a thousand years until the present parish church was built in 1926.

After the treaty of Wedmore (878) where King Alfred insisted that Guthram, the Danish leader, be baptised a Christian, the Danes everywhere accepted Christianity and the Vikings too soon settled down and did likewise.

The Church became a vital social centre for the village but in the halls the people listened as the minstrels sang sagas of their pagan past. No doubt too the combined experiences and mutual help needed in hard winters, draughty summers and times of plague cemented the different tribes together in a short time. Within a few generations the mixture of Roman-British, Angle and Norseman blood produced the English! - though in Yorkshire the most potent ingredient in that mixture is Scandinavian - both Danish and Viking! The real Yorkshire dialect, so seldom heard nowadays, is so strongly laced with Scandinavian words that Dr. Raistrick, the dialect expert, found that using the Yorkshire dialect as spoken in Staithes, he was able to make himself understood in the valleys and fiords of Norway!

These newcomers, the Vikings, were indeed a remarkable people, especially those originating from the fiords of Norway. At this time they had produced a race of people, possibly the finest specimens of the white Europeans ever seen on earth. In a country where the land suitable for farming was minimal and food from the sea difficult to obtain in winter they restricted the population by allowing only the strongest babies to live and not too many females! It is not surprising therefore that after many generations of specialised selection the men and women were of splendid physique and amazing energy. Many of their fighting men were over seven feet tall and in battle wielded heavy double-headed axes!

They were excellent farmers and superb craftsmen in wood and metals. Rowing in their high prowed, square rigged ships they made astonishing voyages in the trading missions. One route they opened up was across Russia where, starting from the Baltic near where Leningrad now stands, they sailed up the rivers, carried their ships over land and then down other rivers till they reached the Black Sea. They traded and set up settlements and trading posts from Iceland to the Mediterranean. They brought back the goods to such a centre as that which has now been excavated at York. Goods from all quarters of their known world have been found there. In the tenth century York was second only to London as a trading centre in England.

Yet their most permanent contribution to the welfare of the whole country was the administrating skill of their Anglo-Saxon and Danish Kings especially Athelstan and Canute. During the tenth and eleventh centuries the Danish Kings ruled over an Empire comprising of the whole of Scandinavia and England. It was they who were largely responsible for dividing our country into shires. The process had begun tentively in the eighth century when the Saxon earls fixed boundaries to their lands, but by and large with certain exceptions to be noted later, the newcomers fixed the boundaries of the shires which lasted till the boundary changes of 1974 in our own time. The word "shire" means to divide like share and shear. When the extent of a district was agreed it gradually became united under one overlord - an earl or alderman who delegated his authority to a sheriff. The shire was usually centred round an important village which gradually developed a market for trading. At the shire mote, held twice a year, the earl or sheriff had equal jurisdiction with the bishop who had the power to fix the shire boundaries where they were indefinite.

The word "county" comes from France where it denoted the district ruled over by a count. From there it passed over with the Normans in 1066. With the firm administration of Henry II the four Northern counties, Cumberland, Westmorland, Northumberland and Durham, were brought under the jurisdiction of the Crown. With Lancashire and Cheshire, Durham was declared a County Palatinate which meant their rulers were given exceptional powers because they occupied positions of exceptional danger. This was especially so in the case of the Bishop of Durham who at one time had a private army to repel the invasions of the Scots.

York being naturally a great trading and administration centre was the obvious capital of this shire and so became named Yorkshire. Being so large it was divided into three (TH) RIDINGS - hence the former name of this area - the North Riding. Each shire or "riding" was divided into twelve wapentakes. When a new Saxon earl was installed each man serving him and holding his land, was required to touch the earl's spear with his own spear as an oath of allegiance. Under his leadership they were responsible for the defence of their countryside - their wapentake - and had to follow him into battle should he require them to do so. A council of responsible men formed a court of law, known as a THING, to settle disputes and was presided over by a BAILIFF. A Shire-reeve or SHERIFF, as we have seen was responsible for law and order in the whole shire and attended the wapentake court meetings twice a year to see that their organisation was in order.

The meeting place for the council of this wapentake was on the low ridge of land near Nunthorpe Village, which runs almost parallel to the Ayton road as it goes from Tree Bridge Farm to the foot of Roseberry Topping. They named it Langbaurgh, meaning long hill, a name lasting to this day. The Langbaurgh Wapentake extended in the south as far as Egton, Danby and Whitby, that is, the boundary ran along the north bank of the

River Esk. In the west it extended as far as Ingleby Arncliffe and Yarm, while the whole of the Cleveland Hills were included. The south bank of the River Tees formed the northern boundary. It was a very large area of moorland, woodland and fertile valleys and Langbaurgh, an outstanding feature in a fairly central position. They may have also recognised that it is of an almost unique geological structure being an outcrop of a band of hard whinstone rock, known as the Whinstone Dyke, which runs across North Yorkshire reaching the sea near Robin Hood's Bay.

Writing in his "History of Cleveland" (1808) Graves gives this description:

"A rocky ridge runs east and west called Langbaurgh Ridge at the end of which there is a singular quarry of hard blue whinstone or granite which has been found of infinite value to the public in the making and repairing of turnpike roads in this part of Cleveland".

A late Victorian writer had this to say:

"The quarries at each side of the ridge were so deep and full of fossils that it was nicknamed Fossil Valley. When the railway made transport possible (1864) the hard stone was carried to Leeds and other West Riding towns to pave the streets. Not far away on the side of Roseberry is a small eminence known as Whetstone Nab where the stone is so hard that whetstones were made from it to sharpen tools".

The quarries were worked out and finally closed in the 1920's. Nowadays a walk along the ridge can be quite dangerous as the chain of very steep-sided quarries form a low valley half filled with water.

By the end of the tenth century the little village of Thorp could be officially classified as being in the North Riding of Yorkshire, in the Wapentake of Langbaurgh and part of the parish of Ayton, for the ecclesiastical parishes and bishops' sees had also come into being. The meeting place for the twelve wapentakes of the North Riding was said to be under the great oak at Thirsk.

The Norsemen must have been very impressed with the most outstanding feature of the area for they called it ODINSBURG or OUNESBERRY (various spellings) the mountain of Odin, their supreme god, and this is the name on old maps. Somehow it came to be known as Roseberry Topping, the topping referring to its beautiful perfect conical shape which was ruined by the great rock fall at the top in 1912.

In the eleventh century yet another invader came to add another ingredient to the stream of Yorkshire ancestral blood - the Normans. Their ancestors too were Norsemen so this but reinforced the strong mixture of Viking blood already flowing in the veins of our Yorkshire ancestors. They were a strong, intelligent and resourceful people leaving behind a goodly heritage.

Photograph – Arnold Kidson

Great Ayton
With River Leven and Roseberry Topping and Easby Hill Behind.

CHAPTER 2

The Coming Of The Normans And Monks

By the beginning of the eleventh century the small village of Thorp in the parish of Ayton, Marton and Ormesby were well established, the mixture of races had intermingled so as to become the English though usually referred to at this time as the Anglo-Saxons, (this was to distinguish them from the invading Normans), and they paid their taxes to church and state. The village had taken the simple form of a large house in its own demesne and a row of cottages on each side of the through track or round a green just before the Norman conquest. The cottages would have seemed to us like mean hovels, one roomed structures of daub and wattle with a hearth of some kind and a shelter, perhaps a lean-to against an outside wall where fowls and a pig might be kept. The manor-house would be made of stone. Around the village were the demesne lands of the Lord and the three large open fields which supplied the food upon which the villagers depended. The whole village would support the craftsmen - the blacksmith working in his forge to produce the simple tools and weapons needed for the villagers and their Lord, the woodworker making trestle tables and stools, the simple wooden frames for the houses and more elaborate doors and benches for his Lord, and the miller living beside the stream, turning the home grown wheat and barley into flour for a fee. Each villager held strips in each of the common fields. Custom decreed which crop was being grown in each, usually according to the "three field system" which was a threefold rotation of crops. The first field would be wheat, the second barley, oats or beans and the third fallow. The fallow field being rested, the cattle were allowed to graze on the weeds it produced and fertilised it sufficiently to produce good crops the following two years. Each villager was obliged to work for so many days on his Lord's land in return for the Lord's protection and patronage. However if a man had an unusual amount of energy and initiative or the pressure of a large family, he might clear a further small patch of the large waste land of woodland and moor which surrounded the village, and grow more food for his family. Moreover each cottage had some land attached on which vegetables and herbs might be grown and a pig kept. In the oak woods for which North Yorkshire was noted, the young swineherds of the village would look after the pigs. Some of the girls may have looked after geese on the green. Sheep too would be kept, perhaps on Marton Moor with the village shepherd responsible for their care. The wool, so provided, would be spun by the women as they went about with their distaff under their arm and woven into home-spun cloth and dyed using lichens and berries. Thus the village would be practically self-sufficient. On Sundays all the villagers of Nunthorpe would walk over the open fields and woods to the ancient church at Great Ayton. After the morning service the families around would gossip and exchange news or on festive occasions dance and play games while the men would exercise their skill at archery. At Christmas and other Christian festivals there would be feasting in the manor house. Such was the Saxon way of life.

But in the early autumn of 1066 this quiet way of life was shattered when news reached them of the landing on the Yorkshire coast of Tostig, the exiled Earl of Northumbria, half brother to their new king, Harold, accompanied by his ally Harold Hardrada the fierce old king of Norway, bringing with him a vast fleet of Viking ships full of Norwegian warriors. Tostig had come to reclaim his lost possessions and seek revenge on his half brother. Such an army would ravage the countryside and strike terror far and wide. With what relief the people of the parish must have heard the news that King Harold had marched up with his army from the south and not only defeated the invaders but the fierce old Norweigan King had been killed at the Battle of Stamford Bridge near York. Their relief however was short lived for soon a messenger from the south brought the terrible news that the Normans had landed at Hastings. In the battle which followed the Saxons had been defeated and Harold killed. Little could the people have guessed at the dire consequences that would bring.

King William of Normandy was crowned on Christmas Day in the new Westminster Abbey in London. The people of the south might accept William and his Normans but the northern earls and their people would have none of it. When the new king sent armed messengers to take over the northern lands in his name they were murdered and all his threats were defied. At last in the autumn of 1068 he marched north himself at the head of his troops and wreaked a terrible vengeance. In Yorkshire and Durham he destroyed every village and every living thing in it irrespective of rank, sex or age, and burnt the homes, the crops and the storehouses. Only once did he stop and that was to celebrate Christmas in the great Minster at York. On leaving after it was over, he commanded his men to set fire to the city.

There is a fascinating legend told about William at this time which is of local interest. William and some of his men were riding through Bilsdale on their way to York when they were overtaken by a great snow blizzard. In the confusion William became separated from his party and was lost. For three days they searched for him in the snowy wastes and at last found him sheltering in a lonely peasants hut. Had he perished in that snowstorm how different the history of England would have been!

Symeon of Durham gives a contemporary account of the effect of William's "Harrying of the North" and it makes a harrowing reading.

"In consequence of the Normans having plundered England - in the preceding year (AD1068) Northumbria and the adjacent provinces - so great a famine prevailed that men, compelled by hunger, devoured human flesh, that of horses, dogs and cats and whatever custom abhors; others sold themselves to perpetual slavery, so that they might in any way preserve their wretched existence; others, while about to go into exile from their country, fell down in the middle of their journey and gave up the ghost. It was horrific to behold the human corpses decaying in the houses, the streets and the roads, swarming with worms; for no one was left to bury them in the earth, all being cut off either by the sword or by famine or having left the country on

account of the famine. Meanwhile the land being thus deprived of anyone to cultivate it for nine months, an extensive solitude prevailed all around. There was no village inhabited between York and Durham; they became lurking places to wild beasts and robbers and were a great dread to travellers".

With travellers bringing back accounts like this no wonder the whole of, not only this country, but Europe was appalled!

Twenty years later in 1086 William's Commissioners came to compile an inventory of the whole land for tax purposes, giving details of who owned the land, its value, the extent of the village, its buildings and its people - the famous Domesday Book, so called because the details entered in it were regarded as the absolute legal authority.

Unhappily in practically every village in this locality, after giving details of who owns the land the account ends with the words WASTUM EST - is waste. Nunthorpe, that is Thorpe is recorded and gives the Saxon names of Aluret and Magbanet as having paid tax on nine carucates of land. It is not quite clear whether these were the previous landowners who had paid tax in the previous reign or survivors from the disaster who managed to make good their claim to the land. If such were the case it would be a sign that the life of the village had begun to return. Six carucates were given by the King to Robert de Brus of Skelton Castle and he retained three carucates for himself. A carucate is believed to have been the amount of land which could be cultivated by a plough and team of eight oxen in a year and estimated at about one hundred and twenty acres.

In his book "Great Ayton" (1983) Dan O'Sullivan gives a full account of the entries in the Domesday Book of the five manors which comprised Ayton. Only one named "other Ayton" (that is now Little Ayton) was declared waste. The land, seventeen years after its devastation was beginning to recover but the small number of ploughs in relation to the number of carucates reveals that the village was "undercultivated and sparsely populated". Unusually there is mention of a church recorded and there is little doubt that this was on the site of the old All Saints Church in Ayton. In the end the four manors were amalgamated into one manor when the owners mentioned in the Domesday Book fell into royal disfavour and they reverted to the King. In any event Ayton was by the early twelfth century in the hands of the Stutevills family who confirmed the grant of the church of Ayton to Whitby Abbey in the reign of Henry II.

Inter alia, there are three points of interest about the Domesday book which are not generally known but which are relevant here.

1) The records in the original Domesday Book of 1086 do not go northwards beyond the River Tees. The land over this boundary seems to have been regarded as too barbarous for the Commissioners to travel safely. The new owners of the manors were Norman-French in culture and regarded the whole of Northern England as barbarous, so that they seldom, if ever, visited their northern manors unless the estates were so extensive to warrant building a strong fortified Castle but appointed deputies to collect their dues. No record of the county of Durham was made until Bishop Pudsey had a survey made under the orders of the grandson of William the Conqueror, Henry II the Law-giver in 1180. It is known as the Bolden Book and will be quoted from later. By this time the Bishop was in his strong Norman Castle beside the new Durham Cathedral enshrining the relics of St. Cuthbert. He had been installed as the Prince Palatinate, a unique position, with a private

27

army appointed to protect the northern frontier of this country. To this day the Bishop of Durham stands at the right hand of the monarch at the Coronation Ceremony.

2) The Norman officials whom William sent to gather the information were foreigners and unused to the country and its language. When the facts were being collected each district was responsible for its own enquiries through a group of people called a "jury". Each jury was composed half of Normans and half of Englishmen and all members took an oath to discover the truth. Their information was passed to the King's officials at the county court and then to the actual writers of the Domesday Book. This system of enquiry or fact-finding, by officials of the King and a jury sworn to tell the truth, later became the method used to try cases in a court of law.

3) It is evident that in the South and Midlands of England at this time, the shires were divided into "hundreds" and not "wapentakes" as in the North. Smaller measures of land were in "hides" in the South and "carucates" in the North, thus showing again the extent of Scandinavian influence here in everyday life.

Although in Ayton and Stokesley the Domesday Book reveals some evidence of the revival of the villages it took a hundred years or more before the villages of Yorkshire and Durham became viable communities once more. Nearly all the pre-Conquest owners of the land had been either killed or exiled, so the wasted, depopulated land was granted in the form of manors, to the knights and soldiers of King William. Under his feudal system most of the land in Cleveland was granted to Robert de Brus I, a knight who had fought at Hastings. He built a fine strong castle at Skelton and under oath of feudal loyalty appointed tenants for his manors. His family were to dominate the area for three centuries and their beautiful memorial tomb can be seen in Guisborough Church.

Like all other villages in England, Nunthorpe came under the manorial system. Under the strict laws imposed by the officers of the manorial court, life was hard for the villagers or villeins as they were known, who were like serfs bound to the land. However it is thought that because of the scarcity of the labour available they were treated on better terms than their fellow sufferers in the South. After the harshness of their treatment by the Normans, it is understandable that their hatred of their Norman overlords was intense. Even Bishop Walcher who, as Bishop of Durham, was responsible for establishing monasteries to help restore the villages, was killed when a mob set fire to the church he was in.

The tenant to whom the manor of Thorp was granted was Walter-de-Thorp. He was granted fourteen bovates of land (approx. two hundred and ten acres) for which he gave his services to his Lord in time of conflict. He was also obliged to pay one pound of cinnamon and one pound of pepper as well as one silver penny every Christmas Day! Spices at that time were so precious that archers were placed on board the ships to guard the cargo!

Robert de Brus was not the only Norman Lord to own land in Nunthorpe and it is not quite clear whether Walter was a tenant of the De Brus family or whether he was connected with the great Norman de Meinill family, the remains of whose Whorlton Castle still lie near Swainby and can be seen from the road. After Walter built his manor house, either he or his heirs built a domestic chapel in the grounds next to it for at the beginning of the twelfth century, Baron Robert de Meinill and his wife Gertrude granted the chapel to Whitby Abbey. The Tithes were paid to Whitby Abbey, but the patronage was in the hands of the Lord of the

Manor. This granting of the chapel and manor away from the de Brus family was to have a great effect in the fourteenth century.

In the survey of Durham by Bishop Pudsey in 1180, known as the Boldon Book, a full account of the services, rights and duties of a village community under the manorial system. As a small village almost recovered from the devastation of the previous century, Nunthorpe would have been about the same size as Boldon, so described:

"In Boldon there are twenty two villeins, every one of whom holds two bovates of land of thirty acres and renders two shillings and six pence of scotmoney and half a scot-chalder of oats and sixteen pence of averpenny and five wagonloads of wood and two hens and ten eggs; and works throughout the whole year three days in the week except Easter and Whitsun-week and thirteen days at Christmas-time; and in his works he does in the autumn four boondays at reaping with his entire household, except the housewife, and they reap moreover three roods of the standing crop of oats and he ploughs three roods of oat-stubble and harrows it. (A rood = 1/4 of an acre). Every plough of the villeins also ploughs two acres and harrows them and then they have once a dole from the bishop and for that week quit of work, but when they make the great boon days they have a dole. And in their works they harrow when it is necessary and they carry loads and when they have carried them every man has a loaf of bread; and they mow one day at Houghton in their work until the evening and then they have a dole. And every two villeins build one booth for the fair of St. Cuthbert. And when they are building lodges and carrying loads of wood they are quit of all other works. There are twelve cottars there, every one of whom holds twelve acres and they work through the whole year two days in the week except at the three feasts aforementioned and they render twelve hens and sixty eggs".

(N.B. villein = Peasant cultivator entirely subject to a Lord or attached to a manor. - Oxford dictionary)
(cottar = Villein who occupied cottage with attached land, usually five acres, in return for labour service. - Oxford dictionary).

Like a serf these villeins were bound to the land and could not leave the village without the Lord's permission. However in time many of the villeins were able to become free either by somehow buying their freedom or as the church actively encouraged the Lords to free their serfs, on the death of a Lord or at some other occasion, as a sign of penitence. Many obtained their freedom at the time of the Crusades when the Lords needed money for armour and horses etc. for their journey.

No doubt the greatest factor in the restoration of the land was due to the influence of the monasteries. Both church and state welcomed the monks to the barren land. William appointed Walsher as Bishop of Durham (d.1080) and Symeon of Durham gives this contemporary account of how he welcomed these Benedictine monks:

"Not long after this, certain meek spirited monks belonging to the southern parts of England, having been admonished from heaven that they should go upon a pilgrimage for God's service into the province of Northumbria, came to Bishop Walsher and entreated him that he would assign them a place within his bishopric, in which they might reside and that he would permit them to associate with their number such persons - if there were any such - who might be able to serve God along with themselves. The Bishop rejoiced at this request, embraced them with affection, as if they had been sent to him by God; he thanked heaven for their arrival and welcomed them kindly, and dispatching

them to Jarrow and Wearmouth, two places within his bishopric which had formerly been the habitations of holy men..... They did as he had directed; and having rebuilt the ancient dwellings of the saints, several persons profited so far by their life and example that renouncing the world, they attached themselves to the originators of the design".

These were but the first of the many Benedictine monasteries which were founded throughout the North East in the twelfth century notably Durham, Lindisfarne and Whitby. Next came the Cistercians from the continent. These were especially welcome for they were the agricultural experts of their time. At the end of the eleventh century the order had been founded by French monks who thought the Benedictines should be stricter. In the twelfth century the Abbot of Citeaux, their headquarters, sent a chapter (that is an abbot and twelve monks) with a letter to the King asking permission to found a monastery in England. He sent them to Yorkshire where they founded Rievaulx Abbey. They preferred sites near rivers or running water and were very skilful in draining the land using the running water for sanitary as well as other purposes - hence Rievaulx (valley of the Rye) Jervaulx (valley of the Yore) and Fountains Abbey. They worked on the land and were herdsmen. Their influence in reviving the ravaged land in the twelfth century was tremendous.

However the monks who came to this area were Augustinian Canons. They occupied the Priory which Robert de Brus II founded at Guisborough in 1119 with his brother as its first prior. Wearing black habits they were all ordained priests and responsible for the services and pastoral care of the people in surrounding parishes and taught in the monastery school. The task of farming the great stretch of manorial lands was left to numerous lay brothers and labourers. Having to walk or ride on horse-back across the Yorkshire moors, it was probably they who were first responsible for the "Monks Trod", and other paved paths, carefully laid out and bridging skilfully tiny streams. They are to be found in many places across the moors but their especial one crosses from about half way up Birkbrow Hill a few miles from Guisborough and crosses to Castleton in the Esk Valley. Of course time is eroding them but in recent years restoration has begun.

There were never many Canons in an Augustinian Priory but they were good administrators and gradually the land and the villages under their care became productive and so relatively prosperous. Unlike the other villages in the Guisborough valley the Priory never seems to have owned land in Nunthorpe.

In the twelfth century it was the nuns who came to Nunthorpe - then Thorp. The details of the nunnery buildings are non-existent and the nuns themselves seem to have been somewhat disreputable! About 1162 Adam de Brus gave permission for Ralph de Neville to found a Cistercian nunnery at Hutton Lowcross, then a secluded valley under an overhanging cliff, a site suitable for quiet meditation. It consisted of a Prioress and eight or nine nuns who seem to have been drawn from noble families according to the few names of the prioresses which are known. But it was not long before they left Hutton in disgrace or after a dispute with their neighbours. Whether by accident or intention their buildings were totally destroyed, only pieces of stone have been dug up. They were granted lands in Nunthorpe where they built a Priory and a mill. The site of their nunnery is thought to have been either in the grounds of Nunthorpe Hall or possibly on the site of the former Grange Farm which until recently stood near to the present churchyard. Recently remains of an old wall have been found in the grounds of Nunthorpe Hall and an archeological 'dig' is being considered. No foundations or even identifiable stones of this nunnery have ever been found but their presence added the name NUN to THORPE and the road through the village until this century is shown on maps as Nunhouse Lane. Again they did not stay long. Evidently their behaviour was so bad that the authorities moved them to that loneliest of moorland dales - Basedale. Under the benefaction of Guido de Baringcourt in the latter part of the reign of Henry III (1216-1272) they were given grants of lands in many places and retained their lands in Nunthorpe till the Dissolution.

What happened to them when they had settled in Basedale in the parish of Stokesley? Not surprisingly they were very unhappy and in "Stokesley Selection" there is the sequel to their story. From the point of view of the ecclesiastical authorities their behaviour went from bad to worse. In the fourteenth century "They were very unhappy, poor, isolated and disobedient". Among other unhappy details it tells how one prioress, Joan de Percy stole a horse, was reprimanded for her "excesses and perpetual misdeeds". She was so desperate she ran away with some of her nuns but was caught. She was deprived of her position as head of the Priory - but still disobeyed and finally had to be sent in disgrace to another nunnery for punishment. She was removed in 1338 and who could have been her successor, Katherine de Mowbray was removed and replaced by another prioress in 1343. In 1349 came the Black Death to devastate the land and records everywhere are very scanty but their unhappiness is very evident.

"Think of Basedale - its solitude, its isolation, its scanty fare, its discipline. How many were there who could resolve to endure it?"

Confirmed Prioresses with dates of Handale Priory after leaving Nunthorpe as far as can be gleaned from the scanty evidence available.

Only eight nuns were living at Basedale at the time of the Dissolution and they received pensions.

In 1535 the Priory was dissolved by Henry VIII and the lands at Nunthorpe came into the possession of Sir Ralph Bulmer of Wilton Castle.

Before seeing how Nunthorpe was looking in the Middle Ages let us take note of an event which was to have national significance. Richard I was a popular king but his Crusades were very costly and by the time he died the National purse was completely empty. His brother

NAMES	DATES IN WHICH LIVING
Joanna de Percy	1301...1317, 1338.
Katharine de Mowbray	Removed and replaced by another prioress in 1343.
Alice Page	1377, Confirmation noted in Archbishop Neville's Register.
Elizabeth Cotham	1461, died while still Prioress.
Elizabeth Darel	1481, Resigned.
Agnes Tomlinson	1497.
Margaret Buckton	1523, was one of the Sisterhood.
Joan Fletch	1524, was a nun from Basedale.
Elizabeth Raighton or Rowton	1527, a nun from Keldholm who had been pensioned from Basedale at the Dissolution.

John who succeeded him, went to war unsuccessfully with France which caused complete financial ruin for the country. At this point, John decided to sell off the land which technically belonged to him. In 1207 Peter de Brus of Skelton Castle, the descendant of the Norman Knight, bought the whole of the Langbaurgh Wapentake for 400 marks and the promise of an annual rent of £20. He seems to have been an enlightened landowner with a gift for statesmanship. In 1208 he drew up the Langbaurgh Charter for his tenants. In it he promised among other undertakings that no freeman of the wapentake would be subject to imprisonment without trial. When the Barons rebelled against King John and forced him to sign Magna Carta in 1215, Peter de Brus took a leading part. When scholars compare the two documents it is evident that he used his influence to base the great Magna Carta on his own Langbaurgh Charter.

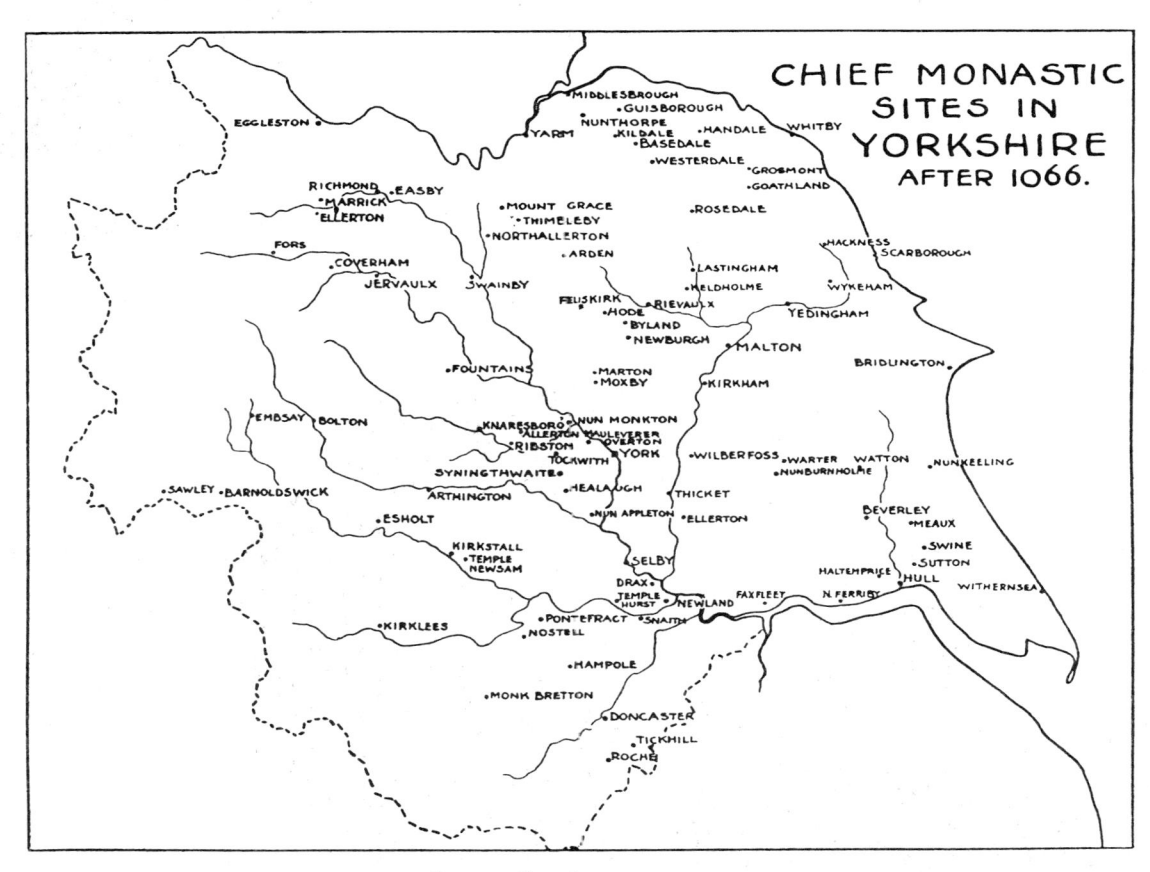

Map of Monastic Sites

Skelton Castle in 1950

Whorlton Castle

Was built by Robert de Meynell in the late 11th century.

View from the door of Guisborough Parish Church showing the ruins of the doorway which led into the old Priory.

Guisborough Priory

Photograph – Arnold Kidson

CHAPTER 3

The Middle Ages

During the thirteenth century Nunthorpe was a medieval country manor with its small manorial hall and rows of cottages along the central track leading from Ayton to the village green and beyond through the woodland at Marton Moor. It was a small community within the parish of Ayton and the centre of all social activity was the Parish Church of All Saints there which all attended for mass each Sunday. During the week under the direction of the Bailiff and Reeve, the manorial officers, the villeins and bordars did their allotted share of work on the Lord's demesne lands, probably the priory lands and their own strips in the common fields. The village would probably include two or three freemen with their own holdings who might employ landless labourers. These free farmers, later known as yeomen, were to become the backbone of village society when the manorial system collapsed in the next century. As always there would be the village craftsmen with the miller and the brewer to serve its needs so that the parish of Ayton was very largely self supporting.

To discover what the cottages looked like at this time and what they contained, one needs to go no further than Ryedale Folk Museum at Hutton-le-Hole. There, a one roomed medieval cottage has been built according to all the archaeological and historical evidence available, though in the brochure it warns that the original dwellings would not have been built with such skill nor, of course, been so clean.

Here is the description of the Crofter's Cottage given in the brochure:

"It is a simple tent-like structure with no internal walls, providing one room accommodation for the family, and also hens and possibly pig. Notable features include a hip ended thatch (said to be more resistant to heavy winds than the straight edged thatch), the lattice protection covering the window openings, the simple but effective door pivots, the earth floor, the crucks allied to the wall timbers with their infillings of wattle and daub, the opposing doors, the unprotected fire burning on the floor, the absence of any chimney or opening for the smoke and the curved crucks. The roof of the cottage is quite high. This would allow the reek from the fire to rise above the occupants before it escaped through the thatch. Sometimes height was gained by digging out the floor to below ground level, hence the step down in many entrances. The nuisance of the reek

was not as bad as we imagine it, perhaps because, unlike coal, dry wood burns with very little or no smoke".

Although crucks are mentioned here, this is not a "cruck house" but the usual medieval peasants cottage found in most parts of the country at this time (crucks = pairs of large curved blocks of wood cut from great oak trees which formed the gable ends of the wooden structure and to which the ridge roof pole was attached). The "cruck houses" which were a feature of North Yorkshire were generally built in the seventeenth and eighteenth centuries and will be described later. If to our modern ears this peasant's cottage sounds like an insanitary hovel, it must be remembered that except in the worst weather, these people spent most of their lives working out of doors.

Usually the floor in the crofter's cottage would be covered with rushes which were changed from time to time. The furniture would consist of a wooden trestle table and wooden stools or benches. The cooking pots of iron would be very precious and consist of a large "witches cauldron" which hung by a strong chain from a large hook on the strong oak beam overhead. There may have been also iron pots to put among the hot ashes as billy-cans are now put on camp fires, and a flat griddle pan with a handle for baking bread cakes a la King Alfred! As they grew more prosperous, especially in a yeoman household, there might be a spinning wheel and a coffer or large wooden chest for keeping spare clothes. As the village was largely self-supporting with its craftsmen and its own corn mill worked by that stream known as the River Tame, articles bought from outside would be regarded as luxuries with the exception of pins and needles which were very precious indeed to the housewife, especially needles. These would be supplied by travelling pedlars who were made welcome everywhere for they brought news of faraway places. Later the needles may have been obtainable at the local fairs held at Stokesley and Guisborough. Here they might be bought by barter for the farmwife's butter or cheese, or the money she obtained for her produce. All women would be expected to spin wool using a distaff and this would be made into homespun cloth either by themselves or by a weaver in the village.

The highlights of the year would be the various fairs held on feast days. May Day would be celebrated with traditional dancing, bow and arrows contests and games on the village green. At Yuletide the Yule log would be dragged into the Manor Hall before a day of feasting and merry making.

What about the health of the people? To whom did they turn for help in case of illness or accident? By modern standards we would have been appalled by the high mortality rate among children even in the well-to-do families. With little or no means of combating such common aliments as tooth decay and rheumatism, men and women looked old by the time they were forty. Death was a frequent visitor in every home. If strong enough to survive the ailments of infancy, childhood was short but relatively happy for the peasant children among the animals and with the freedom of fields and woods. In the families of the nobility such as the de Brus family at Skelton Castle and the Meinhill family at Whorlton Castle near Swainby, the boys especially were often brought up in another knightly household as squires. Their natural exuberance would be checked by the enforced courtly manners expected of them and their miniature adult clothes. The children of the manor house would have a tutor for the boys and the girls would be educated in the art of housewifery by their mother or a nursery governess. If the boys showed a scholarly bent they would go to the monks school at Guisborough Priory. Rarely a young man might find his way to Oxford where learned scholars were gathering to form a university of international standing. Among other matters he might study the use of plants in medical science which was just beginning to be systematised.

In the Middle Ages every monastery had its special herb garden and caring for the sick was part of their spiritual duties. One or more monks would be deputed to grow the medicinal herbs and distil them for use in the Infirmary. The monk in charge of the Infirmary and his assistants would not only be wise in the use of herbal medicines but in the skills required for mending broken bones and healing wounds whether caused by accidents or fighting. The Lords and their families would be taken to the monastery if very ill to be cared for by the monks or in the case of women to be cared for by nuns at a nunnery. Many valuable pieces of land were given in gratitude by a lordly patient or as a fee for prayers to be offered to ease a soul in purgatory!

To be taken to a monastery or a nunnery to be nursed would mean that the patient was regarded as being very ill. Even a young lady brought up in a castle and being trained to be a Lord's lady, the chatelaine of a castle, would have to be very knowledgeable about the use of herbal medicines. Up to the nineteenth century under varying social conditions it was regarded as part of a woman's role in life to care for the health of her family, by knowing how to nurse the sick and what medicines to prescribe for simple ailments. Up to Georgian times each large house had its herb garden and still room from which necessary medicines were made, drying and distilling with great care the various parts of the plants needed. Every cottage too would have its patch of herbs for use in the kitchen or sick-room.

This would seem to place a heavy burden on a young wife and mother, but in every village there would be one wise woman to whom all could turn in an emergency. She it would be who could assist the mother at the time of childbirth or when the children were ill. She would be there when death made an unwelcome visit to the home and there was a body to be "laid out".

Sometimes and especially in later years when the monastery herb gardens had gone, one woman would devote her life to growing herbs in her garden and picking carefully those growing wild in the woods and fields. From these she would brew her medicines and dispense them to the villagers and all in need of them. Elizabeth Gourge in her book "The White Witch" gives the story of one such woman living in the mid-seventeenth century.

She was of gentle birth being related to the family living in the Manor House and lived in a comfortable cottage in the village with her white cat, Pen who followed her everywhere. She loved her garden with its herbs and flowers. It was a fragrant and musical place, alive with the humming of the bees as they gathered honey for her among the flowering herbs. Fronga, for that was her name, loved all her plants as she walked along the grass paths which separated the knots and parterres filled with the colours of the flowers. Best of all she loved the great rosemary bush, her lavender hedge, and beds of mint, germander and marjorie. She had a hundred herbs and knew not only their names but their uses, their healing qualities. The people of the neighbourhood knew and loved her, for she gave freely of her herbs and advised them of their use.

Animals too came under the wise woman's care and here her skill was not so sure. It might happen that when a poor man's cow died in spite of her care, he might turn in resentment and anger against her, charging her with witchcraft, a very serious offence in those days of superstition and ignorance.

Undoubtedly knowledge of herbs did have its sinister side and when combined with the dark forces of nature, produced black witchcraft which gave rise to superstitious fear among the people. Witches are mentioned in the Bible and Shakespeare as well as in legendary tales such as those told of Mother Shipton in Knaresborough. Built into the old cruck houses of the 17th and 18th centuries were witch-posts, as posts in the partition near the fire-place. They were made of rowan or wickerwood, a wood feared by witches and carved with mystic signs to protect the household from evil spells.

This fear of witches persisted until well into the 19th century among the country folk and it is a surprise to find that there was a reputed Nunthorpe witch in the 19th century who was both male and one-eyed. (A witch can be male or female - a wizard being a magician and enchanter like Merlin).

Richard Blakeborough gathered the rapidly vanishing folk-lore of the North Riding of Yorkshire at the end of the last century. This is the story he tells:

"A man who lived at Broughton had a spell cast on him, by whom he did not know, at least he was divided in his doubts. He suspected first Nancy Newgill, a Broughton witch and also a man with an evil eye at Nunthorpe. But he could not really say which of them had cast the spell on him so he went to the wise man of Stokesley but in this he got little comfort. The wise man told him, before he could do anything he must be quite sure who had cast the spell, because if he worked a countercharm on anyone and they were innocent, what he did would fall on the complainant, in addition to what he was already suffering. He advised him to plump (accuse openly) both Nancy and the Nunthorpe man with it. On accusing Nancy, she was so indignant and looked him so straight in the face and swore such a fearful oath that he felt certain she, for once, was innocent; in such contrast was the evil-eyed one of Nunthorpe that he was equally satisfied he was the man. So sure was he, that he told the wise man he would chance it, so they set to work. A fire of wickenwood (rowan) having been lighted close on midnight, a ball of clay was beaten flat with the back of an old Bible; on this a rude figure was scooped out in the shape of a man. In this rough mould was poured a mixture of pitch, beeswax, hog's lard, bullock's blood and a small portion of fat from a bullock's heart. The whole having been melted and well stirred on the wickenwood fire, what remained of the mixture after filling the mould was divided; one half was thrown into water, worked into a ball and thrown away; the remaining portion was poured on to the fire causing a most tremendous blaze; when this died out, the ashes were buried in the church-yard. The figure, having been removed from the mould and two small holes made to represent the eyes, a pin was thrust into one of these eyes, an incantation pronounced and the spell was concluded. The pain left the man as he was returning home and that very night the evil Nunthorpean was seized with a fearful pain and before morning was blind of an eye - the eye corresponding to the one which the pin had been thrust in the wax figure. I had the above from one who well knew the trio".

In her book "Witches in North Yorkshire" Mary Williams wrote of a good deal of witch activity in this area. Not only are there the memories of old folk but in an old diary appears evidence of witch activity in Stokesley.

"6th July 1699 Susan Ambler was whipped and put on the ducking stool for causing an evil spell on Adam Clark's sheep. He only got two score lambs and nine were black ones".

Evidently the Stokesley authorities had to keep a ducking stool beside the River Leven to keep the witches in order!

This was probably some poor old woman who was beginning to go senile and the villagers in their superstitious fear were punishing her instead of caring for her.

In the 18th century Great Ayton had a very unpleasant witch named Nancy Garbutt who lived in a tumbledown cottage in a far corner of Low Green near the mill. She was easily offended and haunted people with her "familiars" - of owlets, bats, goblin dogs, and great big frogs. People were afraid of her and reckoned she murdered a young woman named Martha whose body was found on the moor "She spelled the soul out of her" they said.

A Broughton witch named Hannah Waugh rightly identified the Squire of Anngrove Hall as a murderer. Anngrove Hall is shown on Grave's map in his "History of Cleveland" (1808) on the Ayton to Stokesley road. Her curse in front of everyone was most effective;

> "*You'll have your day*
> *But lambs will play*
> *And skip where Anngrove stands*
> *No lime shall hod (hold)*
> *Its stones, no sod*
> *Shall wrap up the deed of thy hands*"

This is an unusual tale because the witch is not feared by the villagers but helps them to obtain restitution against a hated Squire.

Though not recorded in official records, for obvious reasons - the Squire would be a Justice of the Peace, the events are believed to have happened mid 18th century. The Squire of Anngrove Hall had a daughter who fell in love with the coachman, Henry Edwards. When the Squire found out he gave the young man his notice to quit but as a last errand sent him to Stokesley with a box of valuable jewellery and orders to deliver it to a gentleman catching the London coach. Henry never returned home or was seen alive again.

Of course it was assumed that he had run off with the jewels. The Squire instituted a search and offered a reward for the return of the jewels but nothing was found of the jewels or the man.

Henry Edwards had a sister named Polly who was a maid at the Grange which was half a mile from Anngrove Hall and she refused to believe that her brother was dishonest. Something must have happened to him. Then one night she returned to the Grange, white and shaken saying she had seen her brother's ghost with his head battered in. Her brother had been murdered but who had done it? She went to consult Hannah Waugh. Hannah told her to get hold of a horse-shoe, one of those worn by a horse which her brother had tended and that had pulled the Squire's carriage when he set out in pursuit of the thief.

Hannah took the horse-shoe to the blacksmith and between them did certain things with it to "inject" magic. Polly was then told to hang it up in some conspicuous place. Polly, no doubt with the help of other servants, managed to do this without attracting unwelcome attention. Then one day the people at the Grange gave a party to which the Squire came. As he passed the place where the horse-shoe hung, he staggered and became suddenly ill. That was enough for Polly and her friends but they did not dare to say anything for the Squire was an influential man. But it was then that Hannah took action. She met him at Stokesley and in front of all the people attending the market in the Square, she delivered her curse. It had its effect and public opinion turned against him. Eventually he had to leave his hall which fell into ruins and soon nothing was left of it. But - years later the body of Henry was found, with his head battered in!

It must be remembered that this was the Age of Faith when the church was the centre of village activity and its teachings of paramount importance in mens' lives. As an act of faith and comfort it always helped to pray at the shrine of a favourite saint. Those who were free to do so would go on pilgrimage to a shrine at least once in their lives. Like Chaucer's pilgrims they would regard it not only as a pious duty but as a kind of holiday, a welcome break from the hard round of everyday life. This was the time when the great Gothic cathedrals began to take shape, joyously fashioned to the Glory of God. The shrine probably most favoured by Ayton parishioners, and others nearby would be the famous shrine of St. Cuthbert in Durham Cathedral. What tales the pilgrim would have to tell his family and neighbours when he returned!

If poor, the pilgrim would go on foot joining a party of others like Chaucer's pilgrims as they rode or walked along the dusty highway. He would meet others who perhaps had been on pilgrimage to Canterbury or Walsingham. He might even meet a "palmer" who was almost a "professional" pilgrim having been to the Holy Land bringing back a piece of palm and wearing a cockle-shell in his wide hat. What tales the simple country pilgrim would hear from him! Though most would wish to go on a pilgrimage, the average villager in Nunthorpe or Ayton would never in their lives go beyond Stokesley or Guisborough. But all would hear and enjoy the tales which the pilgrims brought back and marvel at the miracle cures of the favoured saint. No doubt cases of faith-healing did take place and much would be made of them in order to enhance the reputation of the saint. But, like the majority of people who go as pilgrims to Lourdes today, the greatest benefit derived by those going in a truly Christian spirit would be spiritual upliftment and refreshment.

The twelfth and thirteenth centuries also saw those great expeditions of knights and their followers known as the Crusades. They began these journeys to the Holy Land with high ideals of knightly religious duty but in the end became little more than raiding parties sacking cities and taking off the booty. However, they did have some surprising effects on the life of the people at home when the Crusaders returned. The Lord of the Manor of Nunthorpe would be obliged to go if his Liege Lord required him to do so, providing his own weapons, horses and servants. This required urgent money and many a villein was able to buy freedom for himself and his family at this time. Many a lady found herself left in charge of the castle estates or manor. One wonders whether she enjoyed the chance to exercise authority or just longed for her Lord's safe return years later. When the knights and their followers did return they were changed men. They had seen so much and learned so much that their whole horizons were widened. They had seen the luxury of Venice with its goods from China and perhaps brought back a piece of precious silk for my lady. They had seen beautiful gardens and tasted new spiced dishes. They brought back new damascene roses from Damascus and new herbs with healing properties. They had come in contact with the Arabs who were the most civilised people living round the Mediterranean at this time, whose especial fields of learning were in mathematics and including astronomy and medicine. New orders of knights had been formed and among them was the Order of St. John of Jerusalem or the Hospitallers. Their especial religious duty was the care of the sick and wounded whether the pilgrims or the Crusaders wounded in battle. They learned a great deal from their enemies, the Saracens, in nursing skill and the use of medicines and this perculated throughout Europe benefiting all. This great institution still functions today in the form of the St. John's Ambulance Brigade.

Besides the roses, herbal medicines and spices which the Crusaders brought back with them, they introduced

Witch Post in the Ryedale Folk Museum

The post was made of rowan wood and carved with mystic signs which the witches feared.

Original Drawing – Barry Wright

Pack Horse Bridge

The pack horse bridge at Stokesley over the River Leven. In the 18th century water mills beside the River Leven produced sailcloth and linen which was exported far and wide. Mules carried the cloth in panniers on their backs in the charge of a pannierman, going over these narrow bridges. The finest linen was made at Hutton Rudby where there was stabling for 50 mules. They would go over this bridge on their way to distant markets.

a new form of accountancy using Arabic numerals instead of the Roman ones which had been used up to this time. When making up their account books the merchants found that instead of writing for example the clumsy Roman numeral VIII; to write the Arabic 8 was much simpler.

Another innovation affecting the lives of all the people also took place in the thirteenth century - the introduction of surnames. In his book "Great Ayton A History of the Village" Dan O'Sullivan quotes a Tax List for Ayton - the 1300-01 Yorkshire Lay Subsidy of Edward I. It shows the transition stage by which surnames were developed. It also shows the transition from Roman to Arabic numbers for both are used. This is the full list:

Aton

De domina de Wake	1Xs Xld.
(widow of Baldwin Wake, late owner)	
De Walters filio Thurstani	4/9
Waltero Greyneman	5/2
Willelmo Preposito	2/4
Willelmo filio Hugonis	2/7
Wyot Forestario	3/4
Ada de Thorpe	2/7
Hugone le Mercer	2/10
Thusstani	3/1
Henrico le Harper	2/2
Rogero Marchande	2/4
Willelmo del Byre	5/-
Ricardo in le Wra	2/7
Johanne de Semer	2/1
Johanne filio Ede	3/8
Thoma filio Ede	2/2
Johanne de Thorpe	3/2
Roberto filio Thurstani	2/10
Hugone Daivel	2/5
Mariota le Walker	3/1
Johanne Malbys	3/1
Johanne Furhode	3/-
Johanne Brin	3/1
Waltero de Thorpe	2/9
Henrico le Forester	3/1
Ricardo de Marton	17/8
Summa	v.li O
	(£5)

On examining this list of names it reveals the principal ways in which surnames were derived. For example the family names. The Thurstan family at this time was evidently a well-to-do one in the village - a father with two sons who would become Walter and Robert Thurstanson; likewise John and Thomas Edison and William Hugoson. Another common distinction was the name of their trade, William Prosito was a steward, Hugo Mercer and Roger Marchand were merchants, Marie Walker a presser of cloth, Henry a Forester, while the other Henry, the Harper, a musician. Others are distinguished by either their place of origin or the place where they are now living. There is John from Semer and Richard from Marton, while there are no less than three in Nunthorpe sufficiently prosperous in that hamlet to pay tax, Ada, John and Walter. Richard evidently lives in Ayton near the corner of a hill (in le Wra) while William paying double the tax lives in or near a cowshed (del Byre). The other common origin of surnames was to be named after some peculiar feature or characteristic. For example did Walter Greyneman always wear green? The three Johns had to be distinguished by adding "Malbys" "Furhode" and "Brin" but the Norman French makes it difficult to know what their distinguishing characteristics were.

The amounts of money paid in a tax at this time reveals that for the parish of Ayton this was indeed a prosperous time. Its larger neighbour Stokesley had fifty eight

43

inhabitants paying tax but the total only amounted to 75s.11d. as compared to Ayton's £5. This tax was a fifteenth of property. The commissioners came to the village and made an inventory of all the property they could find including personal ornaments and jewellery.

This prosperity however was not to last for much longer for the end of the thirteenth century saw the dawn of a desperately unhappy period for the whole district which continued for almost the whole of the fourteenth century. In the first place the weather was consistantly wet and cold throughout Europe resulting in poor harvests and consequent semi-starvation. In the North East of England however, the greatest distress was caused by the Scottish Raids which began in 1312.

It is generally assumed that the Scottish Raids were confined to the Border Country where the English and Scottish Lords had raided each others territory for centuries. In fact, particularly in this fourteenth century hordes of Scotsmen came marching through Northumbria, Durham and even as far as South Yorkshire many times. The scale and ferocity of these raids can be gauged from the following contemporary account from "The Chronicles of Froissart". Froissart was a French chronicler dealing with the affairs of France and England from 1325 to 1400.

"These Scottish men are right hardy and sore travailling in harness and in wars; for they will enter into England, within a day and a night they will drive their whole host twenty four miles, for they are all on horseback, without it be the followers and laggers of the host, who follow after afoot. The Knights and Squires are well horsed and the common people and others ride on little hackneys and geldings; for they carry with them no carts or carriages. They take with them no purveyance of food nor wine for their usage and their soberness is such that in time of war they will pass in the journey a long time with flesh half-sodden, without bread and drink of the river water without wine, and they neither care for pots and pans, for they seethe beasts in their own skins. They are ever sure to find plenty of beasts in the country they will pass through. Therefore they carry with them none other purveyance but on their horse; between the saddle and the panel they truss a broad plate of metal, and behind the saddle they will have a little sack full of oatmeal, to the intent that when they have eaten of the sodden flesh, then they lay this plate on the fire and temper a little of the oatmeal and when the plate is hot they cast of the thin paste thereon and so make a little cake in the manner of a cracknel or biscuit and that they eat to comfort withal their stomachs. Wherefore it is no great marvel that they make greater journeys than other people do. And in this manner were the Scots entered into the said country and wasted and burnt all about as they went and took great numbers of beasts. They were to the number of four thousand men of arms, Knights and Squires mounted on good horses; and other ten thousand men of war were armed after their manner, right hardy and fierce, mounted on little hackneys, the which were never tied nor kept at hard meat but let go to pasture in the fields and bushes".

There were several occasions when even the most powerful Lord Bishop of Durham had to flee to his strong castle by the River Tees at Stockton for protection. In 1318 the people of Hartlepool built walls round their town to protect it and the harbour, the King Edward II granting them one hundred marks to do so. He had used the harbour when carrying his troops to Scotland but it was his defeat at Bannockburn which led to the worst trouble for the people of the North East. Under Robert Bruce the Scottish King who had defeated him, things for them became desperate.

His English title was Robert de Brus VIII, a member of the de Brus family at Skelton Castle and he spent much of his boyhood in this district. He was Lord of Allandale in Scotland and through his Scottish descent claimed the throne of Scotland but he also owned the estates of Hartness and Carrick in South Durham which included the town of Hartlepool. On the 10th February 1306 he met John Comyn in a church in Dumfries and in an angry quarrel killed him. Because of this crime he was excommunicated and outlawed in England, was disowned by his English relatives and his English lands were confiscated by the Crown. He never forgot or forgave and when he had the power of the Scottish throne behind him he wreaked a savage revenge.

Minnie Horton in her book "The Story of Cleveland" describes its effect:

"The sufferings of the people here in the North reached a culminating point of horror after the defeat of the English at Bannockburn in 1314. Robert Bruce set up his headquarters at Chester-le-Street and sent his troops to Hartlepool which was plundered and its men and women taken back over the Border into Scotland as slaves. Indeed the people of Hartlepool were so terrified that they put their women and children into boats with their most precious possessions and took them to sea whenever they heard the Scottish maurauders were in the district...."

The troops of Robert Bruce came over the Border five times between the years 1312-1322. They plundered the towns and villages, setting fire to the crops and killing all who stood in their path. Because the crops were destroyed so often and the cattle stolen, famine stalked the land. Moreover the people were not even "able to gather the grain from the fields which escaped the ravages of the Scots for there was a period of torrential rain when the corn had been ready for harvesting". The people were exhausted, hungry and terrified. The Prior of Durham sent to the south of England for food which came in ships to Hartlepool harbour. Unfortunately the good Bishop Kelloe of Durham died exhausted by the extreme efforts he had made on behalf of the people so stricken.

The Archbishop of York instructed the Prior of Yarm to excommunicate Robert Bruce because he was destroying both churches and manors alike. The raids became more and more violent until the Bishop of Durham was glad to purchase a truce for £2000 and submit to the humiliation of allowing the Scots to pass unmolested through the Palatinate in order to raid Yorkshire.

It was now that this district of North Yorkshire took the full brunt of the Scottish King's ruthless power. He "even pillaged the Priory of Guisborough where his ancestors were buried and also the Abbey of Holme Cultram where his own father had been interred". As if the de Brus connection were not enough to inspire his revenge, the ancestral home and estates of his rival for the Scottish throne, John Baliol were situated at Stokesley. (His grandfather John de Baliol had founded Baliol College, Oxford.)

Having endured the horrors of the first raids and seen the destruction further north, the practical Yorkshiremen devised an effective way of defending themselves and their family's property. They planned to rebuild their township in such a way that it has become a recognised form of defensive townscape almost unique to this part of the country. The most typical town quoted in books on the subject is Stokesley, although features of this plan can be seen in Yarm, Thirsk and Northallerton. Their plan was to build the houses round a large square having narrow entrances to the through road on opposite sides of the square which could be defended by strong gates. Behind each house was a walled garth which thus formed an extra line of defence and cattle could be driven into it in times of danger or even bitter weather. When the inhabitants received warning that the Scots were on the march, they and their cattle sought safety within the town and it, no doubt provided shelter for neighbours such as those living in Nunthorpe and Ayton. Seeing the people so prepared the Scottish invaders would turn aside to seek easier prey. Though their crops might be burned the lives of the people and their precious food stocks were saved.

Towards the end of his life Robert Bruce was haunted and filled with remorse because of his murder of John Comyn and the great slaughter of the innocent people he had caused. He planned to go to the Holy Land to do penance but this was denied him for he was dying a horrible lingering death from leprosy. This damage which he and his army inflicted upon the North of England and this countryside took a long time to repair. In fact some villages such as that of Levington near Yarm, never did recover.

It may be a folk memory of this time that is responsible for the tradition of Carling Sunday, the Sunday in Lent before Palm Sunday. It is said that at a time when the people were starving a ship came aground at Hartlepool filled with small brown peas called Carlings. The people boiled and fried them, so saving themselves from starvation. In commemoration of what the people regarded as a miracle they set aside this Sunday for thanksgiving and ate the Carlings boiled and then fried for supper. It was the custom until recently for them to be served in public houses on this day.

Scarcely had Robert Bruce died and the land began to recover from the raids than in 1348-49 came the Black Death. Bubonic plagues had swept Europe from Asia periodically for centuries but this time as it swept from one country to another the mortality was devastating. One reason may have been that the poor food resulting from the bad harvests had weakened the resistance of the people. This area was especially vulnerable on two counts. Firstly they said it came on the east wind - that is it spread from the south via eastern ports. Secondly the people at this time were in such a weakened state after the years of famine, for the Scottish raids did not cease till 1342. The Guisborough valley was particularly hard hit by illness and though documentary evidence is scarce the effects which the Black Death had upon the countryside speaks for itself. There was just not enough people left in the villages to cultivate the fields and tend the livestock. It is after this time that the villages in the valley disappear completely or only remain as small hamlets consisting of a farmhouse and a few labourers cottages.

Guisborough Priory owned most of the land and seeing it was impossible for the land to be worked as it had been, the monks, in common with several other monastic landowners, decided upon a drastic policy. They turned the valley into what was virtually a great sheep run. English wool and in particular Yorkshire wool was considered at that time to be the best available and fetched a good price, not only in England but when exported to the Continent, especially Flanders. Among the Priory documents is evidence that in the case of the village of Tocketts the monks brought the remaining people into Guisborough and on the site of the village built a grange. A grange was a large medieval farm run by lay brothers of the monastery who lived there, assisted by peasant labourers. Granges were built at Upsall, Barnaby and Morton but what happened to the medieval village of Middleton nobody knows, for even its site is unknown.

According to previous tax returns the largest village was Pinchinthorpe with its church and village green. The Priory only owned one plot there, but its fate was the same.
In his classic book on the subject "The Lost Villages of

England" Professor H.W. Beresford states that nationally 1200-1300 villages disappeared between 1450 and 1520 due to the change from corn-growing to sheep-rearing. Although the Lords of the Manors accounted for a great many of the losses, it was the ruthlessness of the monasteries, particularly the Cistercians who were responsible for most evictions. The Guisborough monks, who owned most of the land around Guisborough were Augustinian Priors, noted for their pride and enjoyment of good living. In the first half of the 14th century they were in financial difficulties, no doubt due to the ravages of the Scots raids. In the area covered by the parishes of Guisborough, Ormesby, Marton and Ayton, the following medieval villages are listed as lost, with their grid references - Barnaby (580/159), Upsall (564/160), Morton (555/144), Pinchinthorpe (578/142), Tocketts (619/175); all within the Guisborough valley; Coulby (536/138) and Tollesby (510/160) near Marton; Dromanby (534/157) near Kirby; Tunstall (531/126) near Nunthorpe. Due to its sheep-rearing enterprise the monks of Guisborough had not only become wealthy but were engaged on a large building project by the end of the century.

The extent of the devastation caused by the plague and its after effects can be gauged from the will of John de Fauconberg who died in 1349. He lived in Skelton, a descendent of the de Brus family and his property is desribed in these terms:

"In demesne 24 bovates of weak and moorish land worth 4/- before the mortality of men in these parts this year" and at Marske "a capital messuage (manor house with outbuildings) in ruins and worth nothing".

Even sixty years later Skelton is described as "a waste burgage, 4 waste messuages, a ruinous granary and a bovate of land now in decay".
Nunthorpe too must have suffered from the ravages of the Black Death but though small, it survived as a village. The parish church of All Saints at Ayton and its own small chapel were under the patronage of Whitby and its grange belonged to the nuns of Basedale so that Guisborough Priory had no jurisdiction here. Its near neighbour, Morton, however was until this century in the parish of Ormesby which did come under the patronage of Guisborough Priory. Morton is named in the list of properties which the monks owned at the Dissolution as their most westerly holding. Undoubtedly it suffered the same fate as the other villages in the valley. A grange was built on the site of the present Morton Grange Farm which still flourishes today as does its neighbour Morton Carr Farm. There is a waste swampy area of scrub land just over the railway line which runs near the farm house. Could it be that this is the remains of the village pond? It is impossible to say. Morton remained on the tax lists as a small hamlet till 1801 when the first census of the country was taken. It is recorded as having three houses and disappears as a separate unit thereafter.

No accurate figures are available but it has been estimated that two thirds of the population in this area died in the Black Death. However the results were patchy and more people survived in some places than others. It is interesting to compare the fates of Guisborough and Stokesley in this connection. The tax list for 1300-01, previously mentioned reveals the comparative size and prosperity of the places. Previously it was seen that Ayton though smaller than Stokesley was more prosperous. Comparing Stokesley's 58 men paying £3-15-11d tax, in Guisborough there were 85 men who paid £7-15-1d showing it to be the larger and more prosperous town apart from the Priory. By the end of the century however the position is reversed, for Guisborough is worth only £12 as compared with £53-6-8d for Stokesley. Indeed Guisborough was so badly affected that the law courts, market and great fair were transferred to

Stokesley thus making it the capital of Cleveland for a time. In fact before the end of the century it was prosperous enough in money and man-power to build a large new church in a revival of religious faith.

Slowly a period of prosperity dawned for the whole district in which the common people shared. It saw the end of the feudal system and its serfdom. The fifteenth century saw the Wars of the Roses when the ruling classes squandered their resources in fighting and killing each other. On the whole this benefited the ordinary citizen whether living in town or country. It led to the rise in power and influence of the yeoman in the country and the guilds in the town. Now England was becoming prosperous and ready to be put on the map of Europe as a force to be reckoned with, under the firm rule of the Tudors.

CHAPTER 4

In Tudor And Stuart Times

When that economically minded monarch Henry VII came to the throne in 1485 he ushered in a period of autocratic but stable government in England, at a time of great trade expansion in Europe. The use of the mariner's compass and the discovery of America by Christopher Columbus in 1492 gave sailors the confidence to explore the oceans of the world. New trade routes to Russia as well as the New World and the Far East were opened up.

The adventurous spirit of the sailors was backed by the gold of the merchants and England came to the fore as a maritime nation. The reflected glory and optimism, with the prosperity it promoted, helped the whole country including this corner of Cleveland. Better trade meant a higher standard of living and better prices for the produce of the farmers and craftsmen. On the whole, the sixteenth and seventeenth centuries were good times for the common folk who lived in the Yorkshire villages depending on agriculture but proved uncertain and very difficult for the gentry caught up in the politics of the period. Though for the most part the villagers lived their contented lives unaffected by events outside their small world, there were times when such events did intrude. It was easier for small humble places like Nunthorpe and Marton for they had no noble family to demand their loyalty or monastic house upon which it depended. The people however must have felt concern for their neighbours.

At the time when Henry VIII dissolved all the monastic houses, Nunthorpe was little affected when Sir Ralph Bulmer bought the land formerly belonging to the nuns. But in Guisborough, so dependent on its Priory, the effect of its closure was devastating. "Guisborough has become a widow" was one contemporary comment. In 1536 most of the local nobility and their followers, together with ecclesiastics such as James Cotterill, ex prior of Guisborough, marched to York with other similar groups from all over Yorkshire to form "The Pilgrimage of Grace". The smaller monasteries had been closed but the common people hoped to persuade their popular King to halt the process of destruction. All was in vain. The leaders were punished and among those executed and their lands seized by the Crown were George Lumley of Kilton Castle, Sir William Bulmer of Wilton Castle and Sir Francis Bigod of Mulgrave, while Prior James Cotterill of Guisborough was burned at Tyburn.

The last Prior of Guisborough was Robert Pursglove and his name has had associations with the town for four centuries yet he was in fact a native of Tideswell in

Derbyshire and only lived in Guisborough for a very troubled four years (1536-40). Guisborough Priory, the third largest and wealthiest of all the Yorkshire Abbeys was a very valuable prize in the eyes of Henry's appointed commissioners. Doctors Layton and Leigh called there one winter's morning in 1536 and on the pretext of corruption, the Prior James Cotterill was deprived of his post. There may have been some justification for their accusations for *"it is quoted that by the fifteenth century the Augustinians were the least fervent and most decayed of all the religious houses"*.

On the 7th February 1536 Dr. Richard Layton reporting to Thomas Cromwell, Henry's Chancellor in charge of the Dissolution, stated *"If you make no promise of that house (Guisborough) to no one till we come up to London, we shall by the way spy out for it one meet and apt, both for the King's honour and the discharge of your conscience and also profitable"*.

In the meantime the management of the Priory passed temporarily into the hands of the cellarer and bursar, assisted by the Master Treasurer, but none of these were suitable for the vacant post. The choice which the Commissioners made, highlights one of the weaknesses of the great religious houses in deciding who should rule. The monastery owned vast tracks of land and after the Black Death established granges and sheep runs as well as producing iron-ore from their workings on the moors. The abbeys became rich and prosperous but in order to manage such great enterprises a man with a good head for business and versed in practical matters was needed at the helm rather than one of saintly character. It was these ambitious men who were responsible for building the great monastery churches of such abbeys as Fountains and Rievaulx as well as Guisborough which we so admire today.

The man the Commissioners chose was Robert Pursglove, a Fellow of Christ's College, Oxford. Understandably he was very unpopular but fortunately for Guisborough he had a good business head and keen sense of responsibility. When the deed of surrender of the monastery on Christmas Eve 1539 was signed, it was seen that he had managed to obtain from the Crown a good pension of £166-13-4d a year for himself and pensions for the twenty five persons living as monks there. Unlike most of the monks and nuns turned out of their religious houses, they could become village priests or in any case, live in reasonable comfort. Before he died, to compensate in some degree the people of Guisborough, he endowed a school for twelve boys which functioned as Guisbouough Grammar School until recently. He also endowed a hospital to care for twelve old people, which functioned till the 19th century.

About twenty years later in the days of Good Queen Bess there was further excitement with the threat of a Spanish Invasion and the organising of the local militia - the "Dads Army" of its day! How very well organised they were at that time is revealed in a contemporary paper published in "Stokesley Selection". How excited the inhabitants of Ayton and Nunthorpe must have been when they saw the beacon blazing on Eston Nab (cost 6/8d)! But it was a mistake. The gentry of the North East were not happy with the Protestant Tudors and plotted to restore the "Old Faith" by putting Mary, Queen of Scots on the throne. "The Rising of the North" in 1569 was ill-conceived and abortive so that it did not take Cecil's agents long to round up the plotters. As a result Robert Pennyman, a gentleman of Stokesley was executed at York. The Earl of Westmorland was also implicated and his land confiscated by the Crown. The land he owned at Great Ayton was sold, and the tenant farmers were allowed to buy it on favourable terms so that the number of independent yeoman farmers in the area increased.

The political events of the age did not affect the lives of the common people in the area greatly, but a side effect of the Civil War in the middle of the seventeenth century certainly did. The noble landowners were loyal to their King Charles I and his Catholic queen. The result was that for long periods the King's troops were billeted in the Cleveland and South Durham towns and villages. In the "Stokesly Selection" two letters are given which date from this period and speak for themselves. Extract from a letter addressed to T. Chaloner Esq.,J.P. and dated May 20th 1646.

"Cleveland has long lain a-bleeding you know - but alas, now it has received its death wound - there are now no less than five regiments of horse in it... There is no safety for any man that has been in parliamentary employment, either military or civil, to come amongst them, for they unhorse all such and rot them too. I, that with so much scorn, that they tell them that it is not fit for a base roundhead, should either ride or have money in his purse. They begin to drive cattle towards Newcastle. Our condition of fortune is very miserable".

Extract from a letter addressed to Luke Robinson, M.P. for Scarborough by Thomas Smallwood of Egton and dated May 25th 1646:

Sir,
"After long silence I am constrained to salute you with uncomfortable news from the distressed County of Cleveland...never were people oppressed as we are. The Commander-in-Chief is one General-Major 'Vandruski, a civil gentleman. His regiments consist of many papists, French, Dutch, Irish, Scotch and those that are Englishmen are four parts of them the King's reduced officers who are now conquerors and tyrants. They are most of them very rude in their carriage for they every day ride abroad and rob all men and women they meet with; none can with safety pass to and fro from a fair or town or market; they have left us with no horses that are able to carry a man and profess whensoever they go away to leave us no other goods".

Here we have a picture of an unruly mob of marauding mercenaries, no match for the ruthless but well disciplined Model Army of Cromwell. How different from the usual impression of Prince Rupert and his Cavaliers!

Finally we have the short account of what happened in Stokesley itself:
In 1646 Colonel Weldon's Regiment was quartered in Stokesley and much mischief done.

"They glory in stealing horses and think it small fault to kill both men and women. They commit every crime up to murder".

Presumably as the King moved south that year and was finally defeated, the people of Cleveland were able to resume their normal lives. At least they were spared the troubles which the victorious Cromwell visited upon their neighbours over the river at Hartlepool! During the Middle Ages Hartlepool had been an important port, and fortified town, supported by the Bishops of Durham and the King, but during Tudor Times its importance had begun to decline. In the Civil Was as early as 1640 Cromwell had his Scottish allies billeted in County Durham. Hartlepool being part of the estate of Lord Lumley became a Royalist garrison town. However in 1644 the Royalists were defeated and the town occupied by the Scots under the governorship of Lt. Col. Dowglass.
"Because the Scottish troops were irregularly paid, they raided the countryside, robbing the farms for food. The fishermen too received no money for the troops billeted on them"

But worse was to come:

The walls were demolished and the sea defences largely destroyed. Moreover the hated Scots stayed until the Restoration of Charles II in 1660. The inhabitants were too poor to build up the walls and maintain the sea defences so the importance of Hartlepool as a port was gone forever.

Now what of the appearance of the village and the life of the villagers with the ending of the Middle Ages? Throughout the countryside there were two periods in particular when a great deal of rebuilding was done. One was towards the end of the fourteenth century and beginning of the fifteenth century when the towns and villages were recovering from the effects of the Scottish Raids and Black Death and enjoyed the prosperity of the wool trade. It is thought that the "Cruck" houses so typical of North Yorkshire began to be built at this time. One of these "cruck" houses in which the yeoman farmer and his family lived then, has been constructed at the Folk Museum at Hutton-le-Hole and gives us a vivid idea of how these people lived. Another dating from the eighteenth century shows how these houses developed.

The cruck houses were definitely higher and roomier than the previous medieval houses and had at first just one pair of tall curving oak timbers standing on the ground or stone foundations, meeting at the apex of the roof. They were secured together with a piece of timber in the shape of the letter A and cross beams which braced them together in two places, the lower being about six feet from the ground. These houses had a ridge pole and rafters all pegged together with wooden pegs. Only strong seasoned oak was used in their construction. The walls between the oak beams were daub and wattle covered with plaster, but later they were made of stone, often whitewashed on the outside and plastered within. They had a large stone chimney and fireplace and several windows. These windows were criss-crossed with thin wooden laths but unglazed. In Elizabethan times in the wealthier homes glazed windows were put in and their familiar diamond panes may have been suggested by the criss-crossing laths. To enlarge the house, further pairs of crucks were added and the ridge pole and walls extended.

The interior consisted of one large room open to the rafters and divided near the middle by an inner wall on which was constructed a large stone chimney and fire place. The stone fireplace had a hood over the chimney breast. At first a large iron cauldron would stand on the hearth stone among the burning embers of wood or turf. But later there would be an iron crane and reckons on which to hang the iron cooking pots. Behind the chimney breast would be a chamber for use as a storeroom and a dairy. Beyond that could be a lean-to or separate shed or barn for animals in cold weather. For sleeping the family had box-beds round the walls of the living room but as time went on and more room and privacy became necessary the lower rafters were boarded over to form a floor for an upper chamber like a loft. It was reached by a ladder fixed near a corner of the room, up which some of the family climbed at bed time. A dormer window or skylight might be added and so the first bedrooms came into use for the farming families. Quite a number of these houses were so strongly built that, though modified, their rubble-filled walls and stone-slated roofs have lasted in the remoter parts of the moorland until this century - one preserved in the Folk Museum being five hundred years old. In Bilsdale there is a typical Yorkshire "long house" restored in situ. It is the old "Spout House" which stands beside the Sun Inn about half way along the dale.

Between the large room and the smaller one, running behind the chimney stack was a paved passage between

Ryedale Folk Museum

The cruck-framed Harome Manor House originally built about 1600.

A Drawing showing a bedroom among the crucks and rafters of a thatched longhouse.

A diagram showing the lay-out of the restored Spout House in Bilsdale. Note the Cross-passage, so characteristic of the longhouses. On a farm the portion here marked "upper parlour" would have been extended by many more crucks to form the Dairy and barns for farm animals.

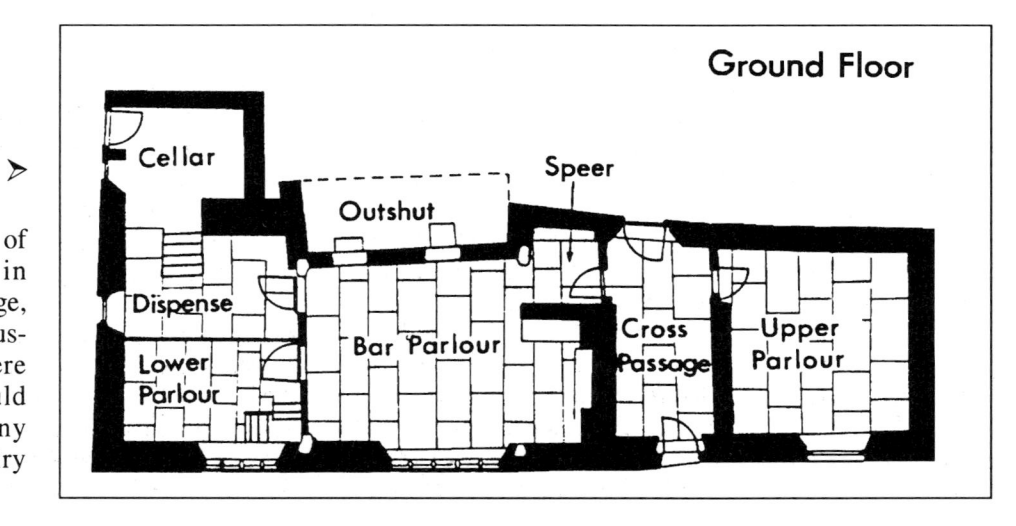

Ground Floor

Cellar · Speer · Outshut · Dispense · Lower Parlour · Bar Parlour · Cross Passage · Upper Parlour

two doors on opposite sides of the house. It was often called a threshold because in early times the threshing was carried out here. The corn was beaten with a flail as it lay on the hard floor, (A flail consisted of a special tool with a wooden handle to which was attached an iron bar about 10" long and bound with leather). The winnowing, that is the separating of the grain from the chaff was carried out on a windy day in this passage, controlling the blast by opening and shutting the doors at each end.

The living room was later called a parlour and in order to enter it from the passage was a door with a sneck. Once inside there was a wooden partition, five or six feet long which sheltered the fire from the draught coming from the door and provided the back for an ingle-nook or settle and warm seat by the fire. Built into the fireplace would be a niche for the salt box, salt being a most valuable commodity. As previously mentioned there might be a witch-post at the end of the partition and there are many examples to be found in the Museum. Apart from the simple cooking pots and vessels needed in the dairy (for nearly every household kept a cow) there would be very little furniture, especially before Elizabethan times which ushered in a period of comparative prosperity for country folk. The beds were the most precious items. In the more well-to-do houses such as manor houses and stately homes, the bed was a four-poster hung with thick curtains. Though unsprung with only cords forming a net to join the four sides together underneath, the mattresses filled with goose and duck feathers were deep and many so that it formed, as it were, a soft warm nest to hold several children or their parents on cold winter nights. How long, cold and dark those nights were, might be judged from the fact that some of the first Jacobean furniture made for wealthy homes were bedroom cabinets with airy, that is wooden fretted cupboards, where food and drink could be kept for a midnight snack! So precious were these four-poster beds that they became family heirlooms to be handed down in wills from mother to daughter. In the living room or parlour, there would be trestle tables, forms and "jointed" stools with a chair for the master of the house (hence the term chairman). If the family could afford it, in Elizabethan and Stuart times they would have a strong heavy oak refectory table. This would have thick stretchers between the legs so that the family could put their feet on them as they sat down to eat. It was better to keep them out of the draughts and above the rushes which were strewn on the often dirty floor.

All these pieces of furniture would be made by the village joiner as would the wooden bowls and platters upon which the food was served. At first the spoons, and platters also would be wooden, but these were all replaced by pewter in Stuart times. In the seventeenth century each person would carry not only his own knife but also his own spoon. Was this the origin of giving christening spoons to babies? Even in aristocratic circles forks were not used till late in the seventeenth century and not in general use till late in the eighteenth century.

Clothes were kept in wooden chests and other things in wooden boxes. Gradually the chests developed into dressers with cupboards and eventually chests of drawers were developed. In the wealthy homes where the skill of English craftsmen were appreciated and encouraged these became the beautiful valuable antiques we prize so much today.

In the countryside as time went on prosperity brought larger homes and more extensive farms. More crucks were added at each end of the house, chambers built over the rafters and dormer-windows rose from the thatch. In this way the "long houses", the typical farmsteads of the North Yorkshire Moors came into being during the eighteenth century and in the remoter areas well into the nineteenth century. They always had a passage across the middle, while the animals were kept at one end of the building and the farmer with his family and workers the other.

It was in the second great building period at the end of the reign of Queen Elizabeth I and the early Stuarts, that the first Nunthorpe Hall was built about 1630, for the changes extended to all sections of society in both town and country.

The story of Ormesby, a farming community centred round a manor house, was virtually the same as that of Nunthorpe and Marton until the advent of the Pennyman family in the time of Good Queen Bess. It's church dedicated to St. Cuthbert is of Saxon origin but was extensively altered in Victorian times.

The name ORMESBY would seem to indicate that its Viking founder was named ORM. In the Domesday Book, written approximately two hundred years later, one of the owners of the manor was named ORME, and he may have been responsible for a famous Saxon sundial. It is over the door of an ancient Saxon church called St. Gregory's Minster at Kirkdale, situated on a by-road between Helmsley and Kirbymoorside. Translated into modern English from the Anglo-Saxon the inscription round its face reads as follows:

"Orm, son of Gamal bought St. Gregory's Minster when it was all broken down and fallen and he had it built anew from the ground; to Christ and Gregory in the time of Edward, the King and in the days of Tostig the Earl". The date is about 1055.

In 1600 James Pennyman purchased the Manor of Ormesby from Ralph Rokeby and built the Jacobean Hall which is now the kitchen wing of the Georgian Hall. Over the fine sculptored door of the house is the coat of arms of this first James Pennyman. At the time of the Civil War the Pennymans were ardent Royalists as were their neighbours, the Hustlers of Acklam Hall. There is a legend that Prince Charles took refuge at both houses when fleeing from Cromwell's troops. James Pennyman's grandson was at the court of Charles I and during the Civil War was knighted on the field for his bravery. He fled to France with Prince Charles and part of their estate also being confiscated. At the Restoration James Pennyman was rewarded with a baronetcy and their lands restored. His son eventually became Lord Privy Seal to William III and High Sheriff of Yorkshire in 1702.

The present hall was built by Dorothy Pennyman, daughter of William Wake, Archbishop of Canterbury, for the family had become very prosperous. It had been completed and furnished at the time of her death in 1754. Evidently the remaining family did not like it for they stayed at their family home at Thornton Hall near Stainton. In 1770 the sixth baronet, Sir James Pennyman came back to Ormesby, an extravagant flamboyant figure. In eight years he almost bankrupt the estate but he engaged the finest workmen to decorate the hall. These Italian artists painted and decorated the fine plaster ceilings and gave it its elegance which we so admire today. He engaged Carr of York, the finest architect of his day to build the fine stable block in the style of Castle Howard. One can wonder whether the police horses housed there now, appreciate the elegance of their home.

At the present time research is being made into this important county family which in pre-Tudor times served the Court of Chancery in London as lawyers and thus made their fortune before buying an estate in the Stokesley area. In Elizabethan times, when implicated in the Conspiracy of the North, one of the Pennyman's saved himself from being hung, drawn and quartered like so many of his friends, by being chosen to marry one of the daughters of a judge. Another, when in disgrace fled to America where he is honoured today as the founding father of the State of Nebraska.

There are two fine halls in the heart of Captain Cook country which were built in Stuart times, that is, have Jacobean interiors. Ayton Hall was probably built in mid 17th century, and Acklam Hall which had a superb Jacobean staircase and one of the finest Jacobean interiors in the North. The Hustler family had lived in the Acklam area since 1612, but the present hall was built in 1673. It too is noted for its superb plaster-work. Acklam Hall was the ancestral home of the Hustlers till it was sold to Middlesbrough Council in 1929 to be established as a Grammar School.

Indeed the building of new halls was but a feature of the even greater changes taking place over great tracts of the English countryside, but before considering the transformation brought about by enclosures let us look at what was happening to gardens.

The English are said to be a nation of gardeners. Not including the army of those who begrudgingly cut the lawn at week-ends, and plant a few bedding plants outside the front door, it is reckoned that nowadays gardening is second only to angling as the foremost hobby of the nation, and millions of pounds are spent on it annually. The magnificent gardens of the stately homes, mostly laid out in the eighteenth century attract thousands of visitors each year and there are the allotments of the practical gardeners outside every town, but what is the essentially English feature of the countryside is the cottage gardens of the villages and they came into being about this time.

Beginning the year with the first snowdrops and aconites in January until the last dahlias are cut down by frost and the chrysanthemums fade in November, cottage gardens are filled with a wide variety of shape and colour. There is nothing to compare with them on the continent where our European neighbours love their formal beds, window boxes and rows of pot plants. Our climate with its succession of sunshine and shower, never too hot to scorch severely and seldom too cold to kill plant life, is largely responsible for producing the beauty of our gardens. But, there also seems to be an inbred love of flowers in the hearts of most, which infects us all from the Queen Mother to the toddlers picking buttercups and daisies in the park!

The poor villein of the Middle Ages each had a plot of land round his cottage on which he grew peas, beans and the more primitive herbs for the cooking pot and sometimes kept a pig or a cow. No doubt the housewife being truly a woman, would sometimes bring from the fields and woods surrounding the village, the roots of a wild flower or two to find a place outside the door or in a shady corner. It is thought that the first flower to find its place in the cottage garden was the lily-of-the-valley. This will not surprise the gardeners for they probably know that these flowers hate being cosseted and thrive on "healthy neglect". If left in a shady corner and neglected they will spread happily, even between the stones!

During the prosperous Elizabethan Period and early Stuart Period before the Civil War, many country houses were built throughout the country and their proud owners constructed formal gardens with "knots" and small plots edged round with dwarf hedges of box and lavender. In these they planted a great variety of herbs, bulbs and plants, not only from our own country but from our European neighbours and increasingly from the Far East. To maintain these gardens a great many gardeners had to be employed. These workers lived in the village on the estate and so some of the hardier flowers from the big-house found their way into the cottage gardens.

In the Middle Ages and the early Tudor times a small "pleasaunce" for the ladies to walk in, had been maintained in the Castles apart from the useful vegetable and herb gardens. Legend has it that Henry VIII courted Anne Boleyn in the garden of Hever Castle in Kent but the great reservoirs of medicinal herbs and certain flowers had been in the monastery and nunnery gardens. After the Dissolution of the Monasteries the housewives could no longer depend upon the monks and their herbal remedies in time of sickness. So from the monastery gardens they took roots to the healing herbs and planted them in their own. No doubt some of the displaced monks, wise in their medical use, taught others how to grow and prepare them. The country names of many of these lovely plants still suggest their use. So we have lungwort (pulmonaria) with its lovely blue and pink bell flowers in early spring and speckly silver leaves in summer, fever-few with daisy like flowers and pungent smell, eye-bright (speedwell) its shiny blue flowers so aptly named, to name but a few. Onions and garlic were the disinfectants, and digitalis is still a specific for heart disease. Madonna lilies, always associated with nunneries now appeared as a regular feature outside the cottage and the "sweet eglantine" of Shakespeare, the climbing roses competed with the honeysuckle up the cottage walls. The housewives loved the sweet-scented flowers such as pinks, violets and wallflowers while they made hedges of lavender in front of their homes. It was so useful to them for dried flowers were put in the family chests of bedclothes and gowns, while sprigs of it strewn on the floor among the rushes, gave a fragrance to the whole cottage. Rosemary bushes were grown to give an alternative flavour to mutton instead of the mint which grew so lushly. Parsley too was grown for the sauce eaten with fish. As the bees from the skep in the corner buzzed among the scented wallflowers, stocks and mignonette, an air of contentment pervaded over all in the mellow light - completing a scene so typically English!

To this heritage of woodland, manorhouse and monastery in the eighteenth century were added the flowers of the plant collectors from far away - the dahlias from Mexico and the chrysanthemums and peonies from China and Japan. Hollyhocks too appeared among the michaelmas daisies and columbines. Their very names sound like poetry and there is every reason to believe that the cottage gardens of Nunthorpe and all the others in this area were like this.

Here to end this survey is the Cottage Garden Calendar taken from the "Book of British Villages"

"Snowdrops decorate churches in February.
Primroses illuminate the winter-seared grass.
Daffodils - brave trumpets proclaiming spring.
Lily of the Valley - perhaps the first cottage flower.
Columbine - grown to stave off the plague.
Double Peony - a favourite since the sixteenth century.
Pansy - a relative newcomer to British Gardens.
Madonna Lily - a survivor from monastery gardens.
Moss Roses - a perfect companion for old cottages.
Honeysuckle - provided food for goats and hens.
Everlasting Sweet Pea - rare but lingers on.
Stocks - for sweet-scented summer evenings.
Foxgloves - made mittens for fairies.
Canterbury Bells ring all summer long.
Marigolds - a delicate flavouring for broths.
White Jasmine's fragrance lasts till October.
Lavender sprigs - for protection against clothes moths.
Hollyhocks were an invaluable source for indigo dye.
Golden Rod was thought to indicate buried treasure.
Christmas Rose clumps may last for one hundred years.

CHAPTER 5

The Landscape Changes

During the Middle Ages all the villages and small country towns were self-supporting in food using the three field system dating from Norman times whereby the three large fields divided into strips surrounded the houses and village centre. England was a land of villages and around each village, being slowly eroded with the passing centuries, were great areas of woodland and waste, mostly moorland through which tracks of varying widths linked the towns and villages to each other. During the sixteenth century was begun a movement, and greatly developed in the seventeenth century and onwards, known as the Agrarian Revolution which was to change the whole countryside. New ideas were being developed in agriculture chiefly in East Anglia, which were to affect the whole of rural England. Yorkshiremen have always shown initiative whether in working on the land or in industry and so it was as early as 1658 that in the parish of Ayton and the surrounding district the enclosure of the land and the subsequent planting of hedgerows round the new fields was begun. The new ideas which these progressive landowners and yeomen farmers determined to put into practice were radically different from the old traditional way of farming and could not be carried out unless the land was enclosed and the fields fenced in.

By the authority of a manorial court (as in the case of Ayton) or in later times an Act of Parliament, the land belonging collectively to a village was enclosed and divided amongst all those who could prove a claim to it. Each portion allotted had to be enclosed, that is fenced in. If the portion were large, fences usually in the form of hedges, divided it into fields. The usual form of enclosure took the form of a quickset hedge of hawthorn, as it was the quickest to grow and the familiar pattern of the "patchwork" English contryside came into being. In hilly districts and on the moors where this was impractical, stone walls were used to mark the boundaries. The stones were picked up from the ground and piled in heaps, usually by the women, while the men built the rubble-filled walls with such skill.

Another peculiarly English feature of the countryside also came into being at this time - the country lanes. A typical one runs between two fields bounded by hedgerows and below the hedges on either side are drainage ditches. These lanes gave access to the new farms, built in the midst of the fields owned by large landowners where their tenant farmers lived. The lanes with their hedgerows and ditches gave a new mini-environment which was eagerly filled by wild flowers, wild birds and small animals, all of which had been disturbed by the revolutionary changes. Nowadays though tractors and estate cars, instead of the traditional farmers horses and traps, often hurtle along them, these leafy lanes still add beauty and charm to the countryside. Even today the perennial spirit of joy in a country springtime lane is still mirrored as when John Clare in 1820 wrote these lines:

*"A little lane - the brook runs close beside
And spangles in the sunshine, while the fish glide swiftly by
And hedges leafing with green springtide.
Here a beetle runs and there a fly
Rests on the arum-leaf in bottle green
And all the spring in this sweet lane is seen"*

With fields enclosed, it was now possible for the landowners and yeoman farmers to adopt the new agricultural methods. In past centuries the three common fields had yielded wheat, oats, barley and beans and were kept fallow in rotation. Most of the scrawny cattle, half the size of those seen today, were slaughtered in the autumn and the meat salted down for food because the farmers could not feed them during winter. Now new deeper ploughs furrowed the fields bringing richer soil to the surface especially valuable on the heavy clay land of this area. They needed the full strength of the oxen to pull them. Oxen were also used as drought animals. Indeed the only means of transporting heavy loads was by means of strong carts with thick iron bound wheels pulled by oxen yoked together in pairs along deeply rutted dusty roads. Lighter loads were carried long distances along roads and across tracks over moor and mountains by trains of mules tied together and led by a muleteer. It was not until the eighteenth century when proper roads were built and the tar-macadam surface used, that horses took the place of oxen as the means of transport, for the harder surface hurt the cloven hoofs of the oxen.

In the fields too, horses began to replace the oxen as the large strong shire horses were bred, for farm use. These beautiful, gentle giants are now familiar to us as pullers of brewery dray carts. Instead of the corn being scattered by hand over the tilled ground, gradually it was sown in rows as Jethro Tull's new sowing drill came into use. But, the most revolutionary idea was the new rotation of crops, over four years alternating wheat, roots especially turnips and mangols, oats and barley, grass and clover. By planting clover and turnips the fallow year could be avoided. The cattle could be fed during the winter and soil deterioration avoided for the clover brought new fertility to the land.

With the land enclosed, movement of the cattle could be controlled which avoided the spread of disease and haphazard breeding of inferior animals. The scientific breeding of animals now began in earnest. Up to now the medieval cattle, small by our standards, large-boned and scrawny with large curving horns had roamed over the fallow open fields and wastelands. Now they were kept in fields. Barns were built to house them and their precious winter feed. To improve the local stock a landowner would buy a prize bull, perhaps at one of the cattle shows which were beginning to be held, and let it serve the cows on the farms on his estate. The pedigrees of such cattle would be kept to enable the farmers to build up a good herd. The Yorkshire farmers were particularly successful in raising good cattle for beef production. Indeed it is said that the ancestors of all the short-horn cattle in the world (that is the brown and white ones familiar in children's books) were raised on a farm not far away. Thomas Bates of Kirklevington living at this time is given the credit for their introduction. Indeed where would the reputation of Yorkshire be without its roast beef and Yorkshire pudding!

Breeding of Pigs in the 18th Century

In the 18th century the native pigs were crossed with Chinese pigs to produce the fat animals we know today.

Native English Pig

Imported Chinese Pig

Black Berkshire Pig

Picture Source – "Farmers Weekly"

Oxen

Oxen were used as draught animals and for ploughing fields in Yorkshire up to the end of the last century, but their cloven hooves were not suitable for the hard roads.

Courtesy of Rural History Centre, Reading University

A Meeting of the Cleveland Hunt at Nunthorpe circa 1935

Nor was it only roast beef and Yorkshire pudding that the stage-coach travellers of the eighteenth century enjoyed at the inns of Yorkshire on the Great North Road. They sampled the egg and bacon breakfast and tasted the excellence of York hams; for the breeding methods applying to cattle had also been applied to pigs.

If the new methods of the Agrarian Revolution brought prosperity to the Yorkshire countryside, it was in the breeding of horses that the squires and yeoman farmers of the seventeenth and eighteenth centuries brought their greatest love and enthusiasm. The horses kept by the squires for their own use were held in such esteem that their horses' portraits were painted and hung in the gallery of the hall beside those of their ancestors. Stud books, some to be seen to this day, were assiduously kept and pedigrees carefully worked out. Most greatly prized, as now, were the thoroughbred racehorses, said to be bred from six Arabian stallions imported from the Middle East about this time. Race-courses were coming into existence which provided tracks where the lively young sons of the gentry could race against each other. The first race-track in this area was opened at Stokesley in 1752.

Of greater interest to the older men were the breeding of the hunters and other personal mounts both for men and women on and off the hunting field. All but the poor farm labourers had their personal mounts and except on the farms, grooms were kept to look after them. Each household of any standing had its "carriage and pair" much as people today have cars. Hence in a farming community the breeding of horses was of primary importance. The breeding of racehorses was the speciality of the farmers of Malton and Middleham, further south in Yorkshire, but the farmers and breeders in this area were noted for their hunters and evolved a special breed, the famous Cleveland Bays. Strong and yet agile enough to carry a heavy man on the hunting field, they achieved a reputation for drawing heavy carriages. Even to this day they draw the heavy royal coach on ceremonial occasions. The chief farm still specialising in them and from which they are bought for the Royal Mews was kept by Joe Sunley at Grange Farm, Girrick. It is an isolated moorland farm at the end of a farm road off the Guisborough-Whitby road. Others breed them but he was judged the champion and regularly supplied horses to such unlikely people and places as the Emperor of Japan and the Government of Pakistan!

Until the middle of the nineteenth century when the Railway Age began, all the coaching inns kept relays of horses for pulling the stage coaches and fast mail coaches but the real pride of the farmers were their useful and so beautifully feathered great Shire Horses and Clydesdales.

As early as 1722 the Cleveland Hunt was formed and twice, or three times a week "Tally-ho" would ring out as the colourful company of horses and hounds would chase their fox over field and moor - as indeed they do to this day. All would make a special effort to attend the Horse Fair, held every Palm Saturday at Stokesley until 1926.

It was during this period that the typical small English village or hamlet took its final form. The common wastelands disappeared. The village itself consisted of a manor house with church and a cluster of houses, mostly cottages where the farm labourers and craftsmen lived, including the blacksmith's forge and the inn where the innkeeper brewed his own beer. Around the village were the farm houses surrounded by their fields. Nunthorpe, Marton and Ormesby were no exception to this rule. In the early years of the reign of Charles I the first Nunthorpe Hall was built - that is a large Jaobean house instead of the medieval manor. A tenant farmer ran the surrounding farm, with the fields which had farmed the demesne lands, and the nearby Grange Farm, probably the former lands which had belonged to the nuns owned by the successor of Sir Ralph Bulmer, was farmed by his tenant. Morton Grange Farm would have its own land for fields. There was a similar pattern at Ormesby.

Until the building of the housing estates in the late 1950's the parish of Nunthorpe consisted of farmland except for two small areas of building - Nunthorpe Village and the houses built for commuters round Nunthorpe Station. Some of the outlying farms with their fields still remain, but the most notable farm, Marton Moor Farm and its adjoining farm, High Farm, are completely swallowed up, the fields being covered with housing estates. Marton Moor Farm stood on the main Guisborough road, facing the Stokesley road at its junction with it. Up Gypsy Lane, which like Marton Moor Lane was truly a country lane with hedgerows and ditches at each side, were several smallholdings with their hen houses, goats and two or three cows.

Before leaving the subject of agriculture and going on to consider the living conditions on the Nunthorpe farms at the end of the seventeenth century, mention must be made of a worry that creases the brow of every stockman to this day whether he be a farmer breeding a prize winning herd or a smallholder with his lone cow. The "Stokesley Selection" gives an account of an outbreak of cattle disease in mid eighteenth century which they called "distemper" possibly a form of todays dreaded "foot and mouth". As cattle rearing was such an important feature of rural life in Yorkshire the authorities took it very seriously and imposed stern methods to contain it. Without the aid of modern disinfectants or antibiotics and the skill of the vets of today, they were able to protect their precious stock effectively in this area as this account shows:

"The tragic cattle plague rampant in the North Riding of Yorkshire in the mid eighteenth century devastated the bovine population throughout the area for almost six years. The Fairs and Cattle markets were closed and private sales could not be made without strict control. Many a small farmer was ruined, for although compensation, usually half the current value of the beast was awarded by the Government, it in no way compensated for the lost labour and prospects of the farmer. All infected cattle had to be shot and buried within twenty four hours of the ailment".

It was first detected in other parts of the country in the spring of 1747 and every J.P. in the country was ordered to have notices printed and the constables of each parish had to inform all farmers, tanners and all people associated with cattle in any way. In the spring of 1748 the disease was raging in the East Riding and the Malton district where a watch was kept on the bridges to prevent any infected cattle crossing over. Certificates had to be produced for the movement of any cattle, In the winter of 1748 all bridges over the Rye and Derwent were watched but in spite of this, the disease reached the Bedale area and all trade in leather stopped. The disease was rampant in Wensleydale where all bridges from Ripon to Boroughbridge were watched.

In Cleveland there was an odd outbreak at Cold Kirby where the certificate of immunity had been ignored and two oxen slaughtered, and another at Thornton, near Stainton. The nearest to the Ayton and Stokesley area was an outbreak at a farm at Kirby-in-Cleveland where the cow was duly killed and buried at more than four feet in depth before the Constable and witnesses. No further cases followed. In the Quarter Session Reports there is no reference to the disease after February 1750 so that it would seem that these strong measures had been successful in containing the outbreak. How relieved the farmers of the area must have felt that their

Marton Moor Farm, & High Farm.

Were demolished and new houses built on the site (1960), although a preservation order was obtained for the Lime trees.

precious breeding stock was safe!

At this time Nunthorpe farmers were prosperous, for inventories of three of them are available and it would be interesting to know exactly which farms they worked. Inventories are extremely interesting documents revealing so much of the daily life of our forebears. We are about to consider those of the farmers but in the "Stokesley Selection" are given those of the shopkeepers of Stokesley at this time, so we are able to know something of the kind of shops the farmers wives visited when they went to Stokesley market to sell their butter and eggs.

In his book "The Common Stream" Roland Parker gives this explanation of what inventories are and their history:

"Inventories were an idea given legal status by a statute of Henry VIII whereby the probate of wills in ecclesiastical courts were authorised subject to the presentation of the deceased's possessions made by two disinterested persons, reputable neighbours. It does not appear to have been compiled with the first hundred years or so and very few early ones exist. However, there are many to be found in the latter part of the seventeenth century and the beginning of the eighteenth century. The reason why there are so few is that it was impossible to find two respectable people in the village who could write.

These lists written on tattered sheets of rather flimsy paper, all bear at least one signature as often as not, the other signature is "So and so" - his mark. The first thing that strikes one on seeing an inventory is the appalling writing. In order to decipher it you have to unravel the spelling at the same time, though one cannot help but chuckle at some of the efforts these worthy yeomen made grappling with untractable words, much as they would grapple with untractable animals. But, because these men obviously spelled as they spoke, one is thereby enabled to recapture something of the actual speech of the times... Estimates of the value of the crops, wheat, barley etc. and animals were fairly consistent and correct but the value of household goods varied widely".

Here is the inventory of the first Nunthorpe farmer:

William Jackson of Nunthorpe June 1st 1696

Purse and apparrell £4
14 milk kine and 1 bull £60;
4 steers and 1 why 3 years old £10;
5 two year old steers and 3 heifers £9-5-0;
8 year old stirkes £9-5-0;
(steers = mixed beasts, probably oxen; why = a dry cow;
stirks = young beasts under a year; heifers = young cows)
3 draught horses;
5 other horses £18-10-0;
11 ewes and 8 lambs £6;
8 calves, weanlings £2-10-0;
1 swine 15/-;
13 acres of winter corn growing in the field £16-13-9;
10 acres of oats growing in the field £10;
Corn in the barn and chamber £6;
A little stamp of hay £1.
(Stamp of hay = A small stack of hay under cover, possibly a helm-shed such as in the Folk Museum. Transitionally this was a small farm building consisting of a series of timber posts upon which was placed a flat base of rough wood to hold a stack of corn or beans or hay out of the way of vermin).
One waine, one waine body, 2 carts and 1 cart body with other things £5.
(Wain(e) = a large ox cart with open slatted sides to

carry corn and hay. A cart was flat).
5 butter furkins and 7 in the house and 11 own (owing) to the party deceased £21.
(furkin = a small cask for carrying butter to market, when full containing 56lbs).
Own 60 bushels of oats £4-5-0
In the FOREHOUSE - 1 table, 1 frame, 1 long sickle, 2 chairs, 2 forms, 1 cupboard, 1 rang and tongs, 1 sealing with other implements £2;
Puder (pewter), brass and iron pots and pans £2;
Milk vessles as skieles and bowls and churns and other things £1-5-0;
In the PARLOUR - 1 table and frame. press with chests and other implements £1-10-0;
3 bedsteads with all bedding thereto belonging £4;
1 baking tub, 1 spinning wheel with other implement, 10/-;
Table linen and other linen £1; Hens 2/6

Total £206-10-10.

(Forehouse = the chief ground floor apartment or living room which later became the typical farm kitchen.
Rang and tongs = possibly reckon an iron bar with hook upon which a pan or iron pot could be hung over the fire and fire tongs.
Sealing (seeling) = unable so far to ascertain exactly what it was.
Skiel (skeel) = large milking pail with two handles.
Press with chests = forerunner of the chest of drawers).

Here is the inventory of the second Nunthorpe farmer who died only three years later, which does not give such detail of his stock. He has not left so much as William Jackson, the first farmer, but has obviously spent money on improving his farmhouse.

George Ward of Nunthorpe April 20th 1699
Purse and apparrell £2

GREAT PARLOUR 1 bedstead and bedding, 2 chests with table linen and 2 pieces of cloth £3-5-0
LOW PARLOUR Coales and a baking table with other things £1-10-0
LITTLE PARLOUR 1 bedstead with bedding, 1 chair £2-10-0
FOREHOUSE 1 table and 2 forms with 2 chairs and seeling and one cupboard with pewter and other things £2-1-0
MILKHOUSE bowles and shelves and other things £3-10-0
ENTRY 3 sythes and one hoper and other things, 2 carts and cartgear; 2 ploughs, 2 harrows with other husbandry gears £4-2-6
IN THE BARNE 1 windercloth, yoakes and peck and padds and saddle and garthes, sises and ridles 15/-
3 stand hecks and 1 sledd with 2 ladders 5/-
The beasts, horse and sheep and 1 pig £65-15-0
The corn on the ground as oats and wheat and corn in the barne £30
The geese and other pullen 7/6 a piece of cloth 13/6

Total £121-11-0.

(Windercloth - a strong cloth used for winnowing the corn. The cloth was held at the corners and the corn was put in and shaken in the wind - possibly as it blew through the open doors of the "cruck" house across the threshold)
(Peck and padds - a cheap saddle made of cloth for a horse.
Stand hecks - hayracks
Sled - sledge for agricultural use to be pulled by a horse over grass, especially in steep fields.
Sises and ridles - possibly riddles for use with corn).

There is the inventory of the third farmer who lived at Tunstall - still only a small hamlet not far from Nunthorpe village and who died only a few years earlier.

Chris Samson of Tunstall 20th January 1688

Purse and apparell £22
FOREHOUSE 1 table and cupboard with other implements £2-10-0
DARIE HOUSE 20 bowles with other implements £1-10-0
CHAMBER OVER DARIE HOUSE 1 bedstead and bedding with other implements £5
13 kine and 1 bull £21; 3 sheep and 3 calves £1-16-0; Hay £3
Corne in the barne £4-5-0; 4 acres of hard corn growing £5-6-8;
1 cart with other husbandry £2
Money in Sir Thomas Pennyman's hand £2-10-0
1 sow and a pigg £1 Poultree 8/-
More owing for oats £2-16-0
Debts owing to deceased £100

Total £192-15-2

Debts owing by deceased £28-10-0
Funeral Expenses £2-13-0

Undoubtedly these were well managed prosperous farms. They were mixed farms, that is both stock rearing and arable, with pigs and sheep as well as cattle and the farmer's wife had her poultry. The sheep would provide her with the wool she needed for her spinning wheel, itemed in one farm but undoubtedly among the "other implements" in the others. This is at the end of the seventeenth century and the Agrarian Revolution in the country as a whole is just beginning but these farmers are forward-looking and the great changes which took place in the eighteenth century would be carried out by their sons and grandsons. The first farmer William Jackson is obviously building up a fine pedigree herd of cattle. One hopes that he has left behind a fine son who would bring his father's hopes to maturity. We can compare the value of £60 for his herd of "14 milk kine and 1 bull" with that of 13 kine and 1 bull £21" of Chris Samson who was not so interested in cattle. On the arable side all the farms have fields of corn which means they were enclosed. It is interesting to note that they had adopted the then new idea of sowing winter corn, but the idea of growing crops of turnips for cattle feed would have to wait till the next century.

Just how prosperous these farmers were at this time, can be judged when compared with a set of statistics given in an historical agricultural review for 1689 entitled "17th Century Farming in Yorkshire". For Cleveland, the AVERAGE value per farm was £67. Average livestock per farm was 15.9 cattle, 29.2 sheep and 3.5 horses.

As Nunthorpe was a farming community it is at this period that the landscape underwent such a radical change. Putting these farms in a wider context it is evident that even at this comparatively early date enclosures had taken place here as well as in Ayton. This must have been done by private treaty among the landowners, farmers and villagers which was usual at this time. It presupposes a very progressive outlook, for the Board of Agriculture that is, the beginning of the new measures at national level, was not founded till 1695. That was the body responsible for the Parliamentary Enclosure Acts by which most of the land in England was transformed. An extract from the book by W.G. Hoskins "The Making of the English Language (1955)" gives a general picture and puts this progress in perspective.

"At the beginning of the eighteenth century the rural landscape of England was still far from assuming its present likeness. Over large tracks of land, especially in the north and west, the pattern of field and hedgerow,

hamlet and farm had established itself pretty much as we know it. But over millions of acres between Yorkshire and the Dorset coasts, the country scene was still largely medieval. Farming was carried on in open fields that had not changed basically since the thirteenth century, and beyond the arable fields and their meadows lay great tracks of common pasture, much of it covered with gorse, rising in places to moorland and mountains...."

"The enclosure of open fields into the smaller fields that form our familiar world today and the reclamation of the wild lands, had been going on intermittently and at a varying pace in every century. But after the Restoration the government ceased to interfere with the enclosure of open fields by private landlords and the pace of change quickened sharply".

The surprise comes when examining the map of the changes brought about by enclosures in the eighteenth and nineteenth centuries, that is, almost a hundred years later. It is only in the East Riding that a large part of the land was enclosed by Parliamentary Acts in Yorkshire. It would seem that after the troubles caused by the Royalist troops billeted here during the Civil War and the repression of the Commonwealth regime, the landlords living in this area lost no time in enclosing the land and using the new progressive methods to improve their land. The "Squire" living in Nunthorpe Hall at this period was called Constable Bradshaw and seems to have been a worthy and responsible man. Unfortunately when he died in 1702, he left no male heir to succeed him. His only child Anne married William Pierson of Stokesley Manor and for almost a century Nunthorpe was without any gentry at the Hall to give a lead. However, the pattern had been wisely established and the farms, worked by progressive farmers, prospered.

This raises the question of how independent were these farmers of their landlord. Were these Nunthorpe farmers independent yeomen or tenant farmers? No mention is made of the value of the farm buildings but this would be beyond the scope of the inventories. In the case of Chris Samson of Tunstall, where the writer of the inventory seems to have been very money conscious, is the item "money in hands of Sir Thomas Pennyman". The Pennyman family owned estates at Tanton nearby so that this money could have been rent paid in advance. Whether they were completely independent of the landowners or not, it is interesting to think that these inventories probably belonged to fine, sturdy practical men who were the first to work out the great agricultural changes which transformed the landscape.

Before leaving the subject of these farmers and their farming let us note what can be gleaned of the farmhouse itself. The farmhouse of William Jackson has only two rooms - the forehouse (living room or farm kitchen), and the parlour where they slept and the women worked at the spinning wheel. Perhaps this room was a room where the women were able to work quietly, tend their children and gossip, away from the rough farm workers. There is also a barn with a chamber (loft) for storing corn and presumably sheds, whether attached to the house or not, for the cattle. The next generation living here during the prosperous eighteenth century would probably add further crucks, (for it seems to have been a cruck house), and form it into a typical long house. Eventually, however, it would form a typical Yorkshire farm, such as we see today - a two storey farmhouse, adjoining a flagged or cobbled quadrangle around which were set the cow byres, pig styes and barns. By the end of the 19th century very few longhouses were left. The Ward farm at this time seems to have been a typical longhouse having three bays, (parlours), but it also had a barn for storing corn. In the Tunstall farm they evidently went upstairs to bed and to have bed-chambers in farms was a new idea in their day. But eventually all would evolve into the set pattern.

What of the women living at this time? Inventories of two women who would have known these farmers have survived. There could not be a greater contrast in their style of living. Almost unconsciously a picture of the personality of the person who has left behind these possessions recorded in the inventory builds up in one's mind. For example, William Jackson, the first farmer was a practical progressive farmer whose chief concern was his valuable breeding herd of cattle and paid little attention to the comfort of his home, so long as it was serving his needs. George Ward, the second farmer, had spent his money modernising his farmhouse and even had "coales" for his fires, a great luxury. Nevertheless his farm was well run and prospered. The third man had a poorer farm, but seems to have been very money conscious, perhaps even a business man, lending money for new enterprises, as was necessary before the advent of banks.

The women with their personal possessions, offer to the writer, at least in imagination, a vivid picture of themselves. The first is one of the villagers:

4th April 1691 Alice Maisterman of Nunthorpe

Purse and apparrell £1-1-0
An old press and cot in the forehouse 10/-
A glass case with other impliments in it 1/6
Tongs and fire shovell with some impliments 2/-
2 bedsteads and some bedding £1; 1 old chest; 1 desk,
2 chairs and some impliments 5/-
1 pair of harden cloth 5/6
Debts owing to her £7-9-0

Total £10-4-0

Poor Alice! Somehow she gives me the impression that she was an old lady who had seen better days and was held in high esteem in the village - hence the inventory. Perhaps she had been a housekeeper or governess at a large house. There is a desk which might indicate perhaps that she was able to write, having had some education and yet she had been living in a one roomed cottage. Were the "pair of harden cloath" a pair of coarse linen sheets and what were the precious things, perhaps momentos she kept in her "glass case"? Above all, how did it come about that of an inventory at £10-4-0, £7-9-0 were debts owed to her? One feels that somehow there is a tragedy here!

Mistress Elizabeth Turner of Tunstall 1709

Purse and apparell £100; Plate £100;
Kitchen £18-3-4; Milkhouse £6; Garden House £4;
Stable Chamber £4-5-0; Parlour £30; Green Chamber £3-15-0;
Middle Chamber £9; Chamber over Kitchen £85-6-0;
Little Chamber £6; Chamber over Milkhouse £4;
2 mares, charrit and harness £48;
Sheep £5-10-0; Cattle £28-15-0;
Corn £14-10-0; Hay £6-10-0; Carts and ploughs £4;
In the Brewhouse - 1 copper masfatt (mash-vat) and anckers (casks), and other brewing vessels, baking-tub, pair of rax, 1 limbeck £5.

Total £490-14-4.

Elizabeth was indeed a wealthy women and the title "Mistress" suggests a gentlewoman. At this time there was a well-to-do family named Turner owning estates in the Stokesley area to which she probably belonged. In fact one of the witnesses to the will of a neighbour, William Pennyman of Tanton, who died in 1659 is named Elizabeth Turner. It is possible it could have been her had she been a very old lady when she died. It is evident that Elizabeth kept a fine house surrounded by a beautiful garden, kept in order by many servants, who probably slept in the little chamber, and the chamber over the Milkhouse. One regrets that details of its furnishings are not given for the "Chamber over the Kitchen" and "Parlour" must have been luxuriously appointed to have justified a valuation of £85 and £30 respectively. If the first was a grand salon or drawing room and the other a dining room one can imagine how they looked when Elizabeth entertained her guests. In the dining room crystal chandeliers would be throwing light mellow candlelight on a late Jacobean style, polished table, loaded with rich dishes and set with glinting silver and glass. On the heavy chairs, possibly with cabriole legs and broad seated enough to accommodate the wide fashionable dresses of the ladies, would sit the guests wearing their great wigs and rich colourful satin clothes. They would not be drinking the home brewed ale from the brewhouse but wines and brandy from France and Portugal, possibly obtained from the smugglers working along the Cleveland coast! Leaving the gentlemen to finish their port and brandy, the ladies would retire to the "Chamber over the Kitchen", the drawing room. Here the furniture of tables, chairs, sofas and small chests which would normally be set along the walls would have been set out, by the servants, for playing games. On the beautiful specially made game tables of the periods they would most likely play cards, for following the lead of Queen Anne, card playing was very fashionable.

In my imagination Elizabeth appears as a fine upstanding independent lady of lively disposition who in her stately "charrit" drawn along by her beautiful thoroughbred mares in their fine harness and driven by a groom in livery, caused a stir wherever she went. In other words she was a character and I would have loved to have known her!

The Hearth Tax Returns of 1674 reveal that in Nunthorpe there were only seventeen households so these people would all have known each other. In imagination let us leave them as they stand outside All Saints Church at Ayton after attending morning service. Elizabeth is standing chattering to the vicar, giving him the benefit of her advice while her carriage waits. Nearby the farmers and their wives are discussing the latest news and gossiping, while their families play about in the churchyard before either walking home across the fields or going home with their parents in the farmer's gigs. Alice too is there, waiting quietly, for one of the farmers has given her a lift.

Now let us glance at what was happening in the village churches during these Tudor and Stuart times. For it was now that the peculiarly English Anglican form of worship had its origin. Henry VIII had only sought to make himself head of the church and rob it of its wealth. Edward VI, his son, and his Protestant advisers had produced Cranmer's Prayer Book which until recently has been the established form of service in the Church of England ever since. His sister Mary, the ardent Roman Catholic, tried to turn the Protestant tide and cruelly punished those who opposed her, even as the Protestants had punished the Catholics. In these turbulent times of the church no doubt the common people went humbly on their way doing what their priest told them. The priests no doubt did what their Bishops told them and they, except for a few brave souls, kept "their heads down" and out of trouble - most were like the Vicar of Bray! It was to face this situation that Good Queen Bess came to the throne and she was determined that England would avoid the bitter conflicts between Catholics and Protestants raging on the continent at this period and have one church for her people.

"In 1559 Anglicanism had been hardly so much a religion as an ecclesiastical compromise decreed by a

shrewd, learned and moderate young woman, with the consent of Lords and Commons. But at the end of her reign it had become a real religion; its services were dear to many, after more than forty years of use in the ancient churches of the land". (George Trevelyan).

Let us now glance at what it was like to attend a service in the little All Saints Church at Great Ayton at that time. It would still have its medieval stained glass windows and possibly paintings on the stone walls but its roof was probably thatched. No seating was provided so you either stood or sat on a wooden stool which you had brought. The service itself would be familiar but instead of the altar at the east end on which to celebrate mass, there would be a long wooden table in the middle of the nave of the church. There was no intoning either of prayers or psalms but the congregation greatly enjoyed the singing, not of the hymns in a modern sense, but of the psalms in the rhymed, metrical version of Sternhold and Hopkins. This old psalter is now forgotten but the "Old Hundredth" psalm from it, beginning "All people that on earth do dwell" is still a great favourite hymn. The old Elizabethan psalters supplied the music in four parts so that each could with a little practice sing the part suited to his voice. The parts were Cantus, Altus, Tenor and Bassus. The singing was accompanied by the music of viols and wind instruments such as trumpets if the occasion required. When the church of All Saints was restored in the eighteenth century a musician's gallery was built to accommodate them. It had a little curtain to hide their activities lest they should disturb the people's worship.

When King James' English Bible was published in 1615, a lecturn was installed and a chained Bible put upon it in every church. Most of the rural population were unable to read it but most learn of its contents from the parson's sermon. Here was his opportunity to teach his people and it went on for at least an hour or even two. All were compelled by law to go to church each Sunday but no doubt many would have liked to have done what a Cornish Gentleman called John Trevelyan did at that time. He attended the service to avoid paying the fine, but when the time came for the sermon, he used to walk out calling to the parson in the pulpit "When thou hast said what thou has to say, come and dine with me".

With this glimpse into their lives let us leave these Ayton parishoners and enter the progressive eighteenth century.

CHAPTER 6

The Progressive 18th Century

The turn of the 18th century in this area saw great changes in the ownership of the land. In 1690 the "Manor, Barony and Lordship of Stokesley" was bought by William Pierson, a lawyer, admitted to the Middle Temple in London in 1682 and a Roman Catholic. He married Ann Bradshaw of Nunthorpe Hall. When her father Constable Bradshaw died in 1702 she inherited the Nunthorpe estate there being no male heir. Her son Bradshaw Pierson inherited Nunthorpe Hall and the estate on her death but neither of them lived there. In fact he was very unpopular, being a Roman Catholic and credited with supporting the 1745 Jacobite Rebellion. Ann probably remained a Protestant for her daughter married the local rector of Stokesley, Mr Cooke. Another daughter married Sir Samuel Marwood of Busby Hall whose family was traditionally the improprietors of the Parish of Ayton, which included Nunthorpe and therefore were Anglicans. When Bradshaw Pierson being Ann's only son died childless, the estates descended to a cousin who had no interest in the area and had in fact married an Italian. The result was that in this century the Stokesley and Nunthorpe estates were gradually sold off in lots, to the advantage of the local buyers, often farmers. The last lot sold in 1799 included the land at Nunthorpe which went for £30 an acre which at that time was reckoned to be of great advantage to the local buyers. Thus during this century Nunthorpe Hall itself was let from time to time by an absentee landlord but there is no reason to believe the village did not prosper as well as the rest of the district.

During this period the law of the land required that all should attend the established Church of England services regularly. All dissenters, Roman Catholics, Quakers and non-conformists of all kinds were frowned upon by the authorities. Also by law it was required that all "Papist" Estates should be registered. Thus in 1717 was drawn up the details of the estate of William Pierson which gives us a clear view of life in Stokesley at the beginning of the 18th century, before the great changes which were brought about by the Industrial Revolution.

The whole estate comprised of more than the parish of Stokesley. The report gives details not only of the many properties themselves, but also the names of the tenants and the rent they paid. Surprisingly it begins by giving details of his overlordship of the markets and fairs held in the Market Place at Stokesley and reads as follows:

"A market wert there every Saturday and a fair there every year upon the Saturday next after the feast of St. George the Matyr, and a fortnight fair yearly every second Saturday afterwards until the eve of Holy Trinity with tolls, pickage and stallage".

It was to this weekly market and the fairs that the people of Nunthorpe would come, the farmers' wives bringing their eggs, butter and poultry to sell and their husbands driving any stock there, that they wished to sell in the cattle market. Among the stall-holders would be travelling tradesmen selling the goods which the normally self-sufficient Yorkshire towns and villages could not produce themselves. There would also be stalls with rolls of homespun cloth, made by the local weavers. Becoming more plentiful and popular as the century progressed would be the fairings and cheap cottage pottery beginning to be produced in Staffordshire and in the North East at Sunderland. These were the first ornaments to brighten poor homes. However the most essential purchase the housewife would make would be pins and needles! - necessary for her sewing and knitting (though thick wooden knitting needles could be made locally). The men too might have to buy iron nails for their joinery efforts as these were now beginning to replace wooden pegs. These small metal articles were only manufactured in the Midlands, needles being the speciality of Redditch. On the whole the market scene of rows of stalls with their awnings would resemble that of any large market town like Stockton Market of today.

The Nunthorpe villagers would do most of their weekly shopping at the market stalls, but there were fine shops in the square at Stokesley too. These, of course were the ones which the well-to-do like Mistress Elizabeth Turner and Mistress Ann Pierson would patronise and many of them in 1717 belonged to the Squire William Pierson. In the registration document it states:

"4 shops in the Tollbooth, one let to Mr Ralph Ware, another to Thos. Browne, another to Richard Browne, another to Fra. Marsey at 30/- apiece, the room above the said shops is in my possession and the Sessions of the Peace and my own Court (Court Lect - a court dealing with disputes between the Lord of the Manor and his tenants) are held therein and the market measures kept there".

The Tollbooth was the office where the stallholders and others would pay their fees - a kind of estate office. Although he owned the Courthouse where the Justices would sit, he would not be allowed to take part in the proceedings as he was a Roman Catholic. The "Stokesley Selection" gives this note on the Tollbooth:

"The Tollbooth occupied the site of what is now Westbrook's Garage at the west of the present town hall. On the ground floor were four shops and above was the Court house where the Sessions were held and the market measures stored. An old drawing shows these displayed outside the Tollbooth".

These were probably small lock-up shops and we do not know what they sold but in the "Stokesley Selection" are given the inventories of several shopkeepers who lived in Stokesley at this time. By far the richest and the most interesting inventory giving details of the goods was that of George Jackson "Mercer (draper) and Grocer". He had "ye little shop" and "ye great shop" but each sold a great variety of goods, unlike the usual shops with one category only, such as for example, leather goods made on the premises, as another obviously did. The little shop sold - stuffs, canvas, buttons, silk, paper books, liquors, tobacco, soap, whalebone etc. and among the things sold in "ye great shop" are listed, as well as those above, more luxurious articles such as stockings, books, paper and pins, ribbon, silver thread and silver buttons etc. Like most householders he also kept two horses and two cows.

The register document is very long and detailed, but in places it reveals the close personal relationship between the Lord of the Manor and his tenants. Even at this late date some rent was paid in kind. The following extracts give some idea of Stokesley as a typical small country town before it emerged into the Industrial Revolution.

1) "Four closes of 20 acres called Longacres; of these, the present Rector of Stokesley mows about 2 acres every year which they call tythe acres and takes away the hay, and also takes tythe hay in kind of the rest (but I take it to be wrong to me that he should take both)".

2) "A little paddock let to Wm Morley at 12/- and he also holds for me a little house built in TOWN STREET on the waste with a little cowhouse and a little garden, which being ready to fall down, he repaired or rebuilt at his own charge, he pays only a couple of hens yearly".

3) "A dwelling house and garth let to Richard Browne now in possession of Fr Harnby, his under tenant at 12/- per annum, and a couple of rabbits payable to me".

4) "A little dwelling house and the COMMON BAKE-HOUSE and 2 acres let to Robert Harparley at £5-15-0".

5) "Two dwelling houses with outhouses, garths, gardens and a croft, let to James Bartram at 40/- and 2 fat geese and hens at Christmas".

6) "Anthony Watson, dyer holds a small parcel of ground adjoining his own tenter-garth, for which Thos. Metcalfe used to pay me 6d per annum when he was the owner of this house and garth. Mr Watson has not paid me any rent, nor agreed with me for it, it is worth about 5/- per annum".

7) "Michael Easby does by my consent fence in part of a lane at Easby Friers for which he paid me 6d per annum, but is to buy it open when I please".

In the following extracts it will be seen that most of the tradespeople had land with their houses, often a walled garth, where vegetables could be grown and a pig or a cow kept. The larger buildings also had out-buildings for horses and carriages:

8) "A messuage, barn, beast-house, garth curtilage (area attached to a dwelling house and forming an enclosure with it) and farm let to John Hebdon, bricklayer and his mother at £10".

9) "Part of a messuage and a garth let to Charles Stewart for £2, but I repair the said house with all but glazing; another part of the said house is let to John Hansell at 20/-, and another part thereof, to the Overseers of the Poor for Jane Twedale at 10/-".

10) "One part of a messuage, lately erected but not yet inhabited and part of the garth and old houses thereto belonging let to Mr Addison, Supervisor of the Excise, and the other part of the said new house, old houses and garths let to John Kay, curryer (dresser of tanned leather) at the several yearly rents of £3-10-0 a piece, and they are to enter upon their said parts at Mayday next".

It was usual for the craftsmen and/or shopkeeper to have his workshop behind the shop and for him and his family to live over the shop. This can be clearly seen from the inventories. But besides the shops under the Courthouse at the Tollbooth, Squire Pierson had other "lock-up" shops, some rented by butchers living in other places.

11) "Two shops at the west of the Shambles, for one

whereof and for having the liberty of setting out stalls in the market, as my stallage, John Parkins pays me 4/- per annum and holds the said shop and office from year to year; the other of the said shops is let to Thomas Pierson at 30/-, 3 shops at the east end of the Shambles are let to one Lyonell Slater and another to John Carter, barber at £1-6-8 and the other to John Snowdon at £1".

12) "I have 24 butchers' shops or covered stalls in the Shambles whereof 17 are left".

Details of these are given and some of these butchers come from some distance, e.g. a butcher of Acklam, John Preston who paid 20/-, and William Trenham of Barwick-upon-Tees who also paid 20/-, and the item ends "the rest are all untenanted and when any butchers make use of them they usually pay 6d apiece every market day then so to use them".

It is evident that these shops or covered stalls in the Shambles were the meeting place for the local farmers and butchers to agree on prices for the animals for sale. It would be here that the Nunthorpe farmers would go each week.

The Nunthorpe estates had come to Squire Pierson through his wife, Ann, where he had a farm rented for £53 a year, also let off rooms in it. Mary Rowntree, widow, paid 6/- a year and Henry Denton paid 5/- for a room.

"The main portion of the said messuage was let with 2 mills, stables etc. at £20".

Could this have been the farm attached to the hall or possibly the house itself? "Stokesley Selection" notes that the terms messuage, tenement, house or cottage seemed to have been used indiscriminately in the deeds.

The Nunthorpe and Faceby estates had to pay a minister for performing Divine Service in a Chapel of ease at Nunthorpe.

Before leaving the "Registration of the Papist Estate" of Squire Pierson further consideration might be given to the Courthouse over the Tollbooth. Although as a Roman Catholic he would not be allowed to sit as a Magistrate he would be expected to preside over the ancient Courts Lect where petty private, though not criminal disputes were settled and the Courts Baron which settled land disputes. In practice this was where boundary lines were fixed and rents agreed upon. However this was the situation in 1717 but in 1725 the whole system was changed. The Justices of the Peace were for the most part the local landowners and they were all powerful. These changes are well explained in the "Stokesley Selection" from which these notes are taken:

"The administration of the law of the land was largely under local control until the 19th century. Official officers were few and remote; the local Justices of the Peace were all important, they delegating their authority to lesser individuals the local constables, drawn from the ordinary villager who had to accept, however unwilling, the office of constable for at least one year. Church Wardens too, had an official standing beyond their ecclesiastical office.

The Justices, composed of the district gentry, met four times a year as established in the reign of Henry V to dispense justice, hearing the presentment of the local constable...

Quarterly sessions were held at Thirsk, Helmsley, Northallerton, Stokesley, Richmond and Malton until 1725 when the Stokesley and Helmsley meetings were transferred to Guisborough, and Easingwold. Emergency meetings were held at the home of the nearest J.P. or some convenient centre.

The offences dealt with at the Sessions clearly fell into separate classes which comprise of Crime and Morality, the Poor Law, the Upkeep of the Highways and Bridges, Market Regulations and economic controls.... All offences tending towards breaches of the peace were tried at the Sessions. More serious crimes such as murder were rare and went to the Assizes... Punishments often prescribed whipping in the local market town or a fine, for there was not sufficient accommodation at York Castle, the County Gaol, or at the Houses of Correction at Thirsk and Richmond''.

At parish level the constable had the power to apprehend anyone causing a disturbance such as a drunken man and put him in the local tiny jail or stocks. In Ayton there was a Roundhouse at Bridge End and the stocks were nearby. That the stocks were used is shown by an item in the Constable's Account Book when a new lock was needed in 1783.

In the papers relating to law enforcement at this time, the name of Nunthorpe is only mentioned twice. In 1620 a poor servant girl called Jane Phillip was accused of stealing articles from her mistress at Nunthorpe Hall and was publicly whipped in Stokesley Market when found guilty. The only other occasion was when the people were fined in 1606 for not keeping the road in repair. As will be shown later this was a common offence when each parish was responsible for the upkeep of the roads within its boundaries and Nunthorpe being in Ayton parish had to bear its fair share. A government inspector found that "a layne being the King's Highway between Nunthorpe Lane and one layne being likewise the King's Majesty's Street called Nunhouse Lane leading from Marton to Stokesley are in great decay''.

No doubt matters improved when Bradshaw Constable became the Squire in Nunthorpe during most of the 17th century for he was a J.P.

Around the square at Stokesley were not only the shops but the Inns which do not appear as such in the 1717 survey. Especially on market days these were always centres of activity but never more so than in the bustling 18th century. Here the farmers on market day would all meet after doing their business and refresh themselves. Travellers would be accommodated and any news they could give would be eagerly sought and commented upon. At the beginning of the 18th century with Queen Anne on the throne in far away London, this news might concern the Duke of Marlborough and his victories as well as the doings of his Duchess at the Court. However Queen Anne died and the German speaking George came to rule over the land. Fears were expressed that the Scotsmen might once more cross the Border in support of the Stuarts. Their fears were almost realised with the 1715 Jacobite Rebellion. The gentry living in the manor houses and the stately halls in the area would have a more reliable source of news for with the introduction of mail-coaches the first newspapers could be sent through the post.

Yet as always, it would be the local affairs which would dominate the conversation of this rural community. The topics would, of course, be the current prices of cattle, sheep and pigs and the happenings at the cockpit, the meeting of the fox hounds and later 1752, the horses running on the local race-course. Over cups of tea, if gentile and wealthy enough, or mugs of ale if living in cottage or farm, the women would exchange homely recipes for meals and remedies for common ailments, the latest fashions as well as gossiping about their neighbours.

No schools are mentioned in this document but from the

number of inventories written at this time it is evident that among the villagers more people were literate, even if it meant only the ability to write one's name and keep simple accounts. The translation of The Bible into English gave a great impetus for the general public to be able to read it for themselves. Anybody able to read would feel a moral obligation to teach others to do so especially within the family. Schoolmasters, unregistered and unlicensed set up small schools for boys, and later small "dame schools" catered for small girls as well as boys. As time went on, throughout the country literacy spread throughout the middle classes who could pay the school fees but the poor farm labourers and mill workers for the most part had to wait till the second half of the 19th century for free schooling.

Apart from the Guisborough Grammer School, set up by Robert Pursglove in Tudor Times, the first mention of a school in the area was the Postgate School at Ayton. To quote from a contemporary account:

"In the year 1704 did Michael Postgate build a single room for a school house and chambered it, with a salary of £4 a year to the master for teaching eight poor boys".

Little is known of the founder and although later in life he ceased to pay the £4 a year to the school master, he gave the land and building to the village and the authorities maintained it. The inspiration for it and many other such small schools was "The Society for the Propagation of Christian Knowledge" started in 1689. Its aim was to inculcate the poor with sound religious principles. The Postgate School flourished and soon was charging a small fee, so that the Rev. Ralph Jackson was able to report in 1743 that instead of the "eight poor boys" it had "between twenty and thirty children taught in it".

Its most famous pupil, of course, was Captain James Cook who was brought to Ayton at the age of eight. Although his father was only a farm labourer, he already knew how to read, for he had most fortunately been taught by "Dame Walker" who lived at the Grange, Marton, where his father was employed. Ord says "during the evenings she taught him his alphabet and reading. When eight years of age, his father moved to Ayton where he was put to school at Mr Scottowe's, (his father's employer) expense and instructed in writing and arithmetic in which he made considerable progress". He stayed at the school till he was thirteen when he was thought to be sufficiently educated to become a shop-keeper. Unfortunately the present room housing the museum, is not the actual schoolroom he was taught in. Although the Postgate School continued, the building was pulled down in 1785 when an enlarged school was built together with a Poor House. The money for the School and Poor House was raised by public subscription and the salary for the headmaster was increased to £10-10-0 a year. This school functioned till 1851 when it was superseded by the Marwood School. In spite of this school where attendance rose to its peak in 1833 with 48 boys and 6 girls, this was a very small proportion out of a population of about a thousand.

A government report of 1818 states that some four hundred to five hundred children in the Ayton district were without education of any kind. It is most probable that the children of the prosperous Nunthorpe farmers attended this school but there would be none for the farm labourers. James Cook was a notable exception and most fortunate that his outstanding intelligence was recognised at an early age.

The chance for poor children to learn the rudimentary knowledge of the three R's, was not altogether neglected by the community for in the Churchwarden's

The Postgate School in 1704

It was the first school in Great Ayton and was rebuilt in 1785.

Captain Cook's Schoolroom (Museum), Great Ayton

Another View of Postgate School.

In 1743 between twenty and thirty children were being taught. Instruction was given in reading, writing, arithmatic and Church Catechism. James Cook attended this school for three or four years from 1736.

Originals – Ruth Gaudie

Accounts for 1791-2 is the item:

"To Ann Fordy for Sunday School Salary £2-12-0".

This suggests a Sunday School for poor children, (many of whom would be working), where they were taught reading, writing and arithmetic as well as Christian Knowledge.

At Guisborough a most remarkable lady with a most remarkable family founded a charity school at the beginning of the 18th century. She was Mary, the mother if Ralph Ward, a most eminent business man and public servant living in Guisborough at this time and grandmother of Ralph Ward Jackson, the diarist. Mary Ward's will, or at least a long extract from it, is given in the "Stokesley Selection" and reveals her indomitable character. In it she decrees that money should be set aside yearly by her heirs to support and maintain the charity school which she had founded. She specifies that they are to pay £13 a year "for teaching and instructing poor peoples children and appoint a proper discreet woman of the persuasion of the Church of England to teach and instruct such children in reading, spinning, sowing and knitting and that a house be provided for such a woman to live and inhabit". She died in 1721. The idea behind the education this provided, was that the poor children, especially orphans should be able to earn a good living. She had no less than eleven children, and one very interesting feature of her will is her anxiety concerning the disposal of her valuable collection of silver plate, coins and medals. Valued at £1200 even in those days, it was truly worth a fortune then and one can hardly imagine what an astronomical sum such a collection of early Georgian silver would fetch in today's auction rooms! For example:

"I give and bequeath unto my said son John Ward (her eldest son) the large silver dish which was given to my late dear husband by his Allum partners of Guisborough's Allum Works and also two silver plates and two large silver candlesticks and silver snuffers and snuff pann belonging them which said several pieces of plate I allow my son John to let one of his own brothers have the refusal of buying them".

There is also the coins and medals and "other curiosities, kept in One Oak Cabinet now in my possession" all at the disposal of her eldest son John. It is obvious that she would have wished these prized possessions to have been handed down the family as heirlooms but, alas for her hopes, John went off to London and died a bankrupt! She would have been far wiser to have left them in the care of her third son Ralph. Of her six sons, Edward, the fourth, died in 1721 before his mother but all the others, except Ralph, went to London where they lived out their lives in various ways. Ralph stayed at Guisborough in the family home as a bachelor with his unmarried sister Ester, keeping house for him. He was an outstanding man of business, shrewd and enterprising but of unquestioned integrity. He and his family were landowners but also managed and financed alum mines, linen factories and were concerned in most industries in the surrounding Guisborough area as far as Boulby and Sandsend. In those days Ralph Ward, whose judgement was sound and who was wholly trustworthy, was a man to whom one would apply if money were needed to start a new enterprise, for there were no banks to grant loans. It was obvious to him, long before the acts concerning Turnpike roads, that trade and industry needed good transport. Becoming road surveyor in a voluntary capacity, he built good roads, giving work to the poor. These roads were free of tolls thus encouraging their use by the mule-trains. In many ways he served the community well and assumed the role of a wise and caring head of the family until his death in 1759. The inventory of the goods and

Marton Grange Farm

Where Capt. Cook's father was employed and Dame Walker taught him to read. It was demolished in 1968.

Old Marton

A contemporary drawing of labourer's cottage where Captain James Cook was born in October 1728. It was demolished when Bartholomew Rudd built his mansion, Marton Lodge in 1786. A granite Vase now marks the site.

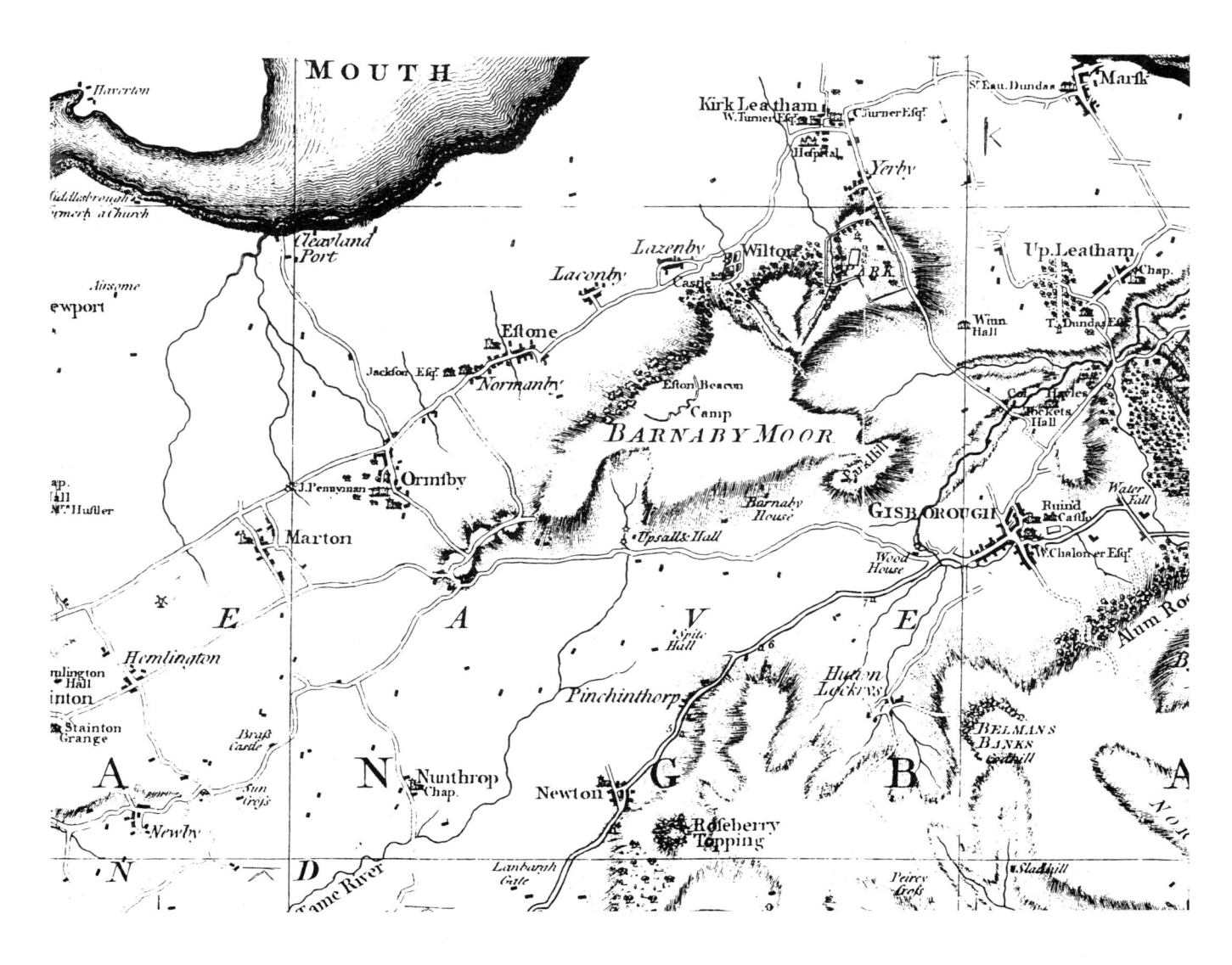

Jeffrey's Map 1771

money he left is given in the "Stokesley Selection". They amount to an astonishing £21,449. When this is compared with other inventories given, it will be seen what great wealth this represents. The most prosperous trader in Stokesley, George Jackson, "a grocer and mercer" (dealer in fabrics with two shops) left £660, George Ward, a prosperous Nunthorpe farmer left £121 and Elizabeth Turner, a gentlewoman with a fine house left £490. It is characteristic of Ralph Ward that he should educate and train his nephew Ralph Ward Jackson to inherit the family business after having provided in his will for those members of his large extended family he thought to be in need. In 1756 Ralph Jackson came to live with his uncle, now seventy six, in Guisborough so that there would be a smooth changeover of authority.

We know a great deal about this family because both uncle and nephew kept diaries which can be seen to this day in Middlesbrough Public Library. Ralph Ward Jackson kept a diary almost daily from being a schoolboy of thirteen in 1749 till his death in 1790. This gives local historians a fascinating account of the daily life of a prominent citizen and his friends during almost the whole of the second half of the 18th century. The friends and relations of the Ward family were indeed very noteworthy especially those with a naval connection. George, Ralph Ward Jackson's brother went to London where he became an administrator in the Admiralty and Captain Cook's patron. His sister Rachel married Commodore Wilson, a very famous sea captain of the East India Company who had discovered a new route to China. When he retired only forty seven years old he bought the manor and estate of Great Busby from the Turner family of Kirkleatham for £2,500, and lived at Ayton House in Easby Lane. He was a friend and colleague of Captain Cook who used to visit him. Ralph Jackson wrote of one such visit in his diary:

"*26th December 1771. Spent all day in Ayton; this afternoon came Capt. Jas. Cook (and his wife) whose father lives in that town, this gentleman lately commanded the King's Bark, the Endeavour, on her voyage round the World and made many discoveries in the south seas and in high Southern Latitudes; Mr Pickersgill (John Lee's nephew) went in the same vessel as Master's Mate; he and his wife lodged at Brother Wilsons*".

This extract is quoted in the chapter which Dan O'Sullivan devotes to Ralph Jackson in his book on the history of Great Ayton called "Great Ayton".

Ralph Ward Jackson moved to Normanby Hall in 1770 where he took a prominent part in business and public affairs until his death in 1790. His descendants continued the family tradition by playing a distinguished part in the development of industrial Teesside throughout the 19th century.

During early Georgian Times trade and travel were increasing rapidly but the means of transport by trains of pack-mules, cumbersome wagons drawn by oxen, or in boats and barges along undrained rivers were wholly inadequate. Locally until the middle of the 18th century the roads were in a very bad state and the River Tees, shallow and winding with its tidal estuary choked with sand-banks could only take small sailing ships up it. The 18th century saw the dawn of the Canal Age but this passed the area by, for the canals were not suitable for farm produce. When the coal-mines of Durham were beginning to be opened up a canal along the Tees valley was considered but as the whole world knows the first railway was built instead.

In spite of Ralph Ward's efforts some idea of the state of the roads in mid-18th century can be judged from this extract from "Guisborough before 1900".

"In 1756 at the beginning of the Seven Years War with France, Ralph Ward recorded that Mr Cholmley Turner of Kirkleatham Hall desired some bad places on the way might be repaired so that he could pass in his coach from Kirkleatham to Guisborough where he intended to come on Monday 23rd instant to meet the rest of the Justices in order to settle watches upon the coasts agreeable to the King's Proclamation".

Mr Turner would appeal to Ralph Ward to do something in the matter knowing of his interest in road-building and as a fellow J.P. The journey from Kirkleatham to Guisborough would not be an easy one for a coach in bad weather in any case, for it would include climbing the steep Yearby bank. At this time Ralph Ward largely financed and supervised the building of two bridges at Skelton Ellers, the dip in the road between Skelton and Guisborough. A man had drowned trying to ford the stream there. One bridge was built in 1755 and the other in 1756. They stand to this day.

Ralph Ward Jackson not only succeeded his uncle in being a J.P. and landowner but also took a great interest in road-building and subscribed generously to the building of the turnpike roads as his diary shows. One interesting entry suggests that he was responsible for building the raised pathway or causeway in Ayton which passes Suggitts shop along the pavement from the West end of the village to the High Green.

It was earlier that in 1606 the inhabitants of Nunthorpe had been punished for neglecting to repair the highway through their village between Stokesley and Marton, then an important place. In 1606 this "highway" would not even be a lane, as we know it today. It would be a very winding rutted path perhaps thirty or forty feet wide in places, for at this time the fields had not been enclosed. It was when the land was properly measured and enclosed in the 17th century that hedgerows would be planted after allowing about twenty feet for the width of the road and ditches dug each side for drainage. Nevertheless what a very winding road resulted! Anybody cycling or riding along the road from Nunthorpe Village before the road improvements made after World War II will remember its numerous twists and bends. It used to be said that the roadmakers sent a cow in front of them and made the road where it went! Personally I thought this a joke but later found it to be substantially true for the cattle were able to pick out a firm track over marshy land!

Not until Victorian times was the direct road to Marton and Middlesbrough made, Brass castle Lane was a farm track off the Stokesley to Stockton road leading to a house, probably the farm called Brass Castle. From the old maps it seems to have been about where the Golf Clubhouse is today. In the 18th century the highway through Nunthorpe Village was not used by stage coaches and would not be well maintained. It was known as Nunhouse Lane. From Stokesley it winded its way through the village then turned at Marton Moor Corner to wander on through fields until it joined the main road from Guisborough at Gypsy Lane End. The shortest way to Marton from Nunthorpe would be along Gypsy Lane but this did not go directly to the centre of Marton village. Old maps such as that found in Ord's "History of Cleveland" 1843 show a small lane off Gypsy Lane leading to the centre of Marton which at the time was situated about where the Cook Museum is in Stewart Park today. The small road led off Gypsy Lane about where the Brunton Arms is today.

By the middle of the 18th century the chaotic state of the roads had become a national problem and in 1773 Parliament passed the Highways Act by which paid Surveyors of Highways were to be appointed in each district and made responsible for the repair and maintenance of the roads. They were to organise men with horses and carts to fill up the holes and lay a firm surface with rubble. The act placed a statutory duty upon each man in the township to participate in this work. In this part of Cleveland however a scheme was devised whereby this statutory duty could be commuted by men who could afford to do so and the money used to pay poor men to do the work under proper supervision. Ralph Ward Jackson refers in his diary to gathering this money and it is possible that he and his uncle devised the scheme. The result was that as early as 1770 John Wesley was able to comment in his journal when visiting Stokesley that the road from Thirsk to Stokesley was "better than most turnpikes". In 1794 Webbs "History of the Highway" states:

"*Cleveland had long to boast of what no other district perhaps in England of equal extent, via excellent roads extending in different directions for nearly sixty miles in length without any tolls, being maintained by voluntary subscriptions and the statute duty of the inhabitants*".

Perhaps it should be made clear that at this time the term "Cleveland" still indicated the area covered by the old Langbaurgh Wapentake and Guisborough was locally regarded as the capital of this area. These good roads were not turnpikes for they were public roads and charged no tolls, thus pleasing the business men like Ralph Ward. The turnpike roads were run as a profit making enterprise, but they made good communication possible for trade and personal travel. It is interesting to compare three maps covering the late 18th and early 19th centuries which was the heyday period of stage-coach travel. The stage coach and mail coach stimulated road building much as the motor and lorry does today. One is Jefferies map of Yorkshire 1771 and the other two maps contained in the two classical histories of Cleveland - the first by Rev. John Graves of Yarm (map dated 1803) and the second by John Walker Ord of Guisborough (map dated 1843). When comparing the roads on the Jefferies map with those on the Graves map thirty two years later, it is obvious that the road systems have been taken in hand and improvements made. In the Ord map, printed just before the great industrialisation of the Teesside area, the road systems are beginning to assume a modern framework.

When we trace the routes on the two earlier maps, there are a few surprises. On both is the same very winding road from Stokesley through Nunthorpe Village via Marton Moor Corner (A172) and on to Gypsy Lane Corner. Here is a road junction. The main road continues to Guisborough but a side road branches here to go to Ormesby and Normanby and the main Yarm Road (A174). When the coach reached Gypsy Lane Corner it would turn left, proceed a little way up the Gypsy Lane hill, turn right at a road junction, along a part of what is now Rothsay Grove and straight across what is now the top of a field, reaching the present Ormesby Bank road. (Until about forty years ago a broad farm road with hedges each side went across this field). At this point the coach to Ormesby would turn left again to go first up and then down the hazardous Ormesby Bank. To go to Normanby, after leaving what was the field track, the light horse and carriage or horseman (not coach) would continue its way up what is now the steep path which passes the reservoir and on to the point where a green lane would wend its way down the hill, meeting Flatts Lane near where the Norman Conquest Inn now stands. Older readers may remember this green lane branching off Flatts Lane, for it was a favourite camping ground of Gipsies when Gipsies all lived in caravans and their horses cropped the lush grass of the lane.

This route is given on both of the oldest maps but on Grave's map not only are more roads shown but they are

85

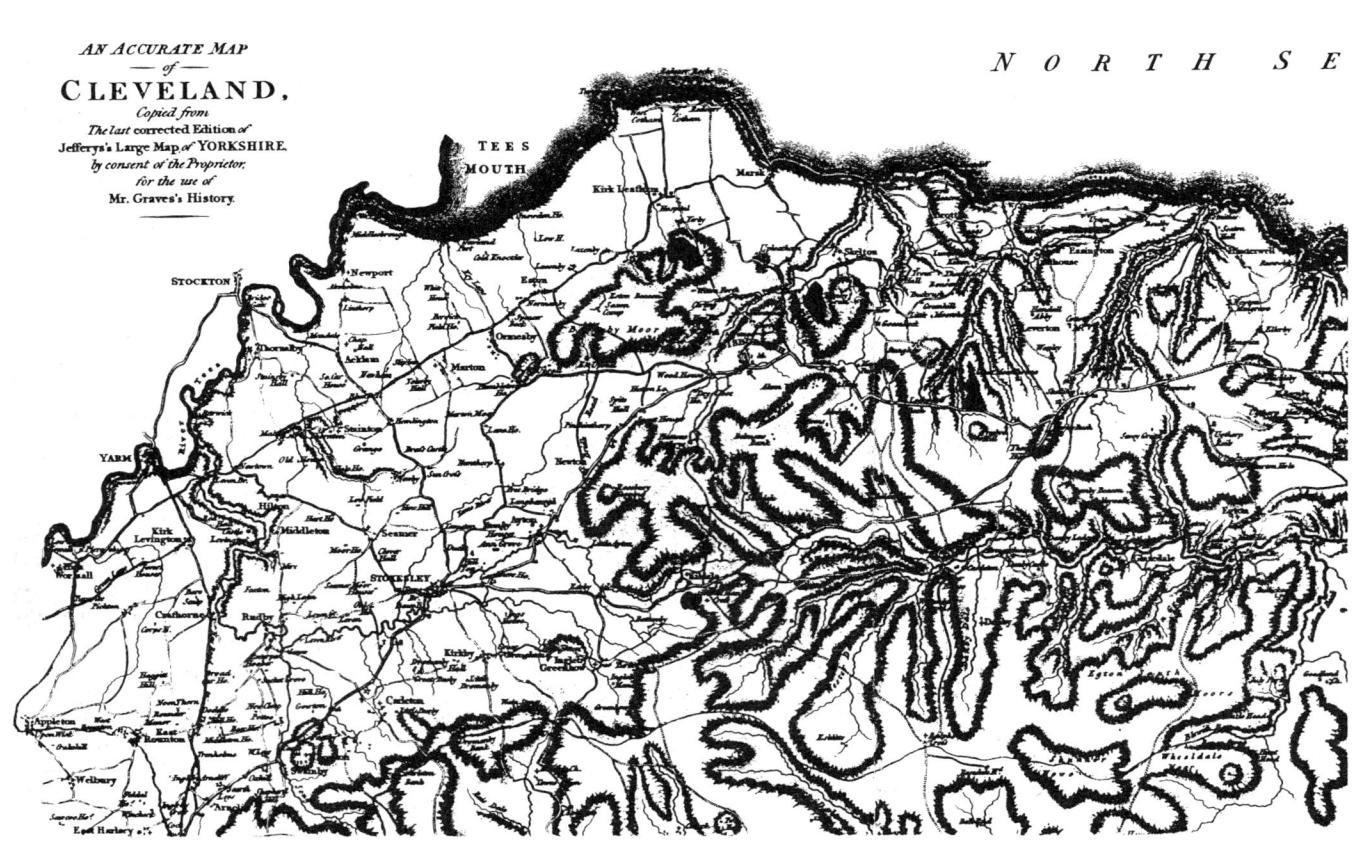

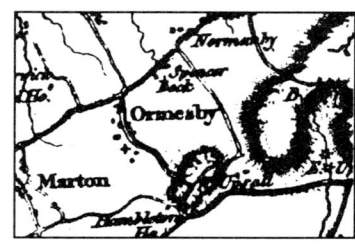

Grave's Map 1803

Enlargement showing Ormesby Bank area.

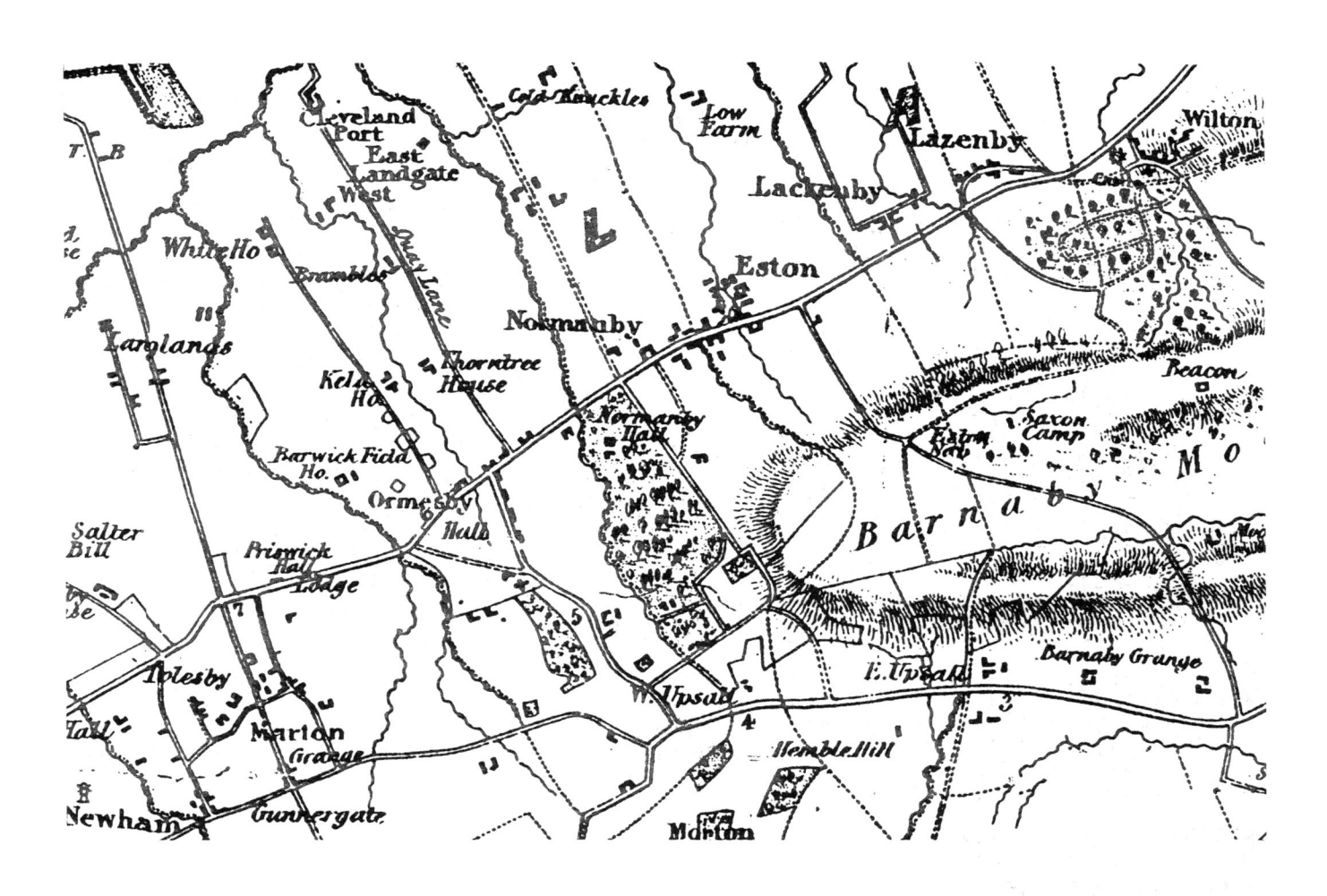

Ord's Map 1843

marked as being of three types. These are:

1) The main roads along which the stage coaches presumably ran.

2) The by-roads suitable for horsemen and light horse carriages, farmer's gigs etc. but which were not so well maintained.

3) Bridle paths for horsemen only. By this time the roads being used by stage coaches were being metalled with a surface of broken stones and tar so would have a more modern aspect.

However even these "Main Roads" would have appeared to us as leafy lanes with ditches and high hedges on each side, while the by-roads would appear to be no more than a good farm track along which farmer's gigs and an occasional horse-drawn light carriage would travel at a leisurely pace.

On the Grave's map (1803) the road just described between Stokesley and Ormesby is shown as a main road suitable for coaches but the road turning off to Normanby is a by-road. Guisborough was a centre for coach travel so the coaches from there travelling north would have to turn at Gypsy Lane as well as those from Stokesley. Later a road was cut at what is now Swan's Corner, making a straight run over Ormesby bank and avoiding this awkward turn at Gypsy Lane. Before the end of the century "direction posts" or sign posts were made compulsory so there would have been a new white post to direct the coaches. Later also Dixon's Bank down to Marton was made which would be easier for the coaches to manage. Both of these changes are shown on Ord's map of 1843.

Ormesby Bank was notorious but if you wished to avoid it, in the 18th century and were travelling on horseback or in a light carriage, there was another route to Stockton via Gypsy Lane. It was a by-road but avoided the steep hills. After turning from the Guisborough road into Gypsy Lane, you would travel along passing the two road ends of the lanes leading to Marton village, through the village of Hemlington and eventually join the turnpike road from Thirsk and Stokesley (B1365). Soon you would come to the junction with the Yarm road at the Blue Bell Inn. Being at the junction of these two busy roads this Inn made a convenient stopping place for passengers and horses. It is marked by name on the Grave's map.

An alternative route for Nunthorpeans would be to walk across the fields to Great Ayton where possibly at the Royal Oak Inn they could catch a coach to Stokesley or if going to Guisborough by the somewhat shorter route via Newton-Under-Roseberry, then a large village and Pinchinthorpe. A bye-road shown on Ord's map (1843) across Barnaby Moor is a real surprise. It runs from the main road along the Guisborough valley (A171) at a point where a farm road leads to Barnaby Grange, goes across Barnaby Moor and Eston Nab and comes down the steep slope to reach the main coast road (A174) to the east of Easton old village. In the 18th century and maybe many years before, light traffic must have passed over it, over the wide buggy moor and down the steep escarpment to the village of old Eston. There are no signs of a broad road down the Eston side but later mining activities could have obliterated them. This short cut across the moors must have been used for the maps to have marked it. It must have been a hazardous journey even in fine weather but our forefathers were intrepid travellers! Graves shows only one bridle path (for horses only) in this area which runs across the fields between Pinchinthorpe and Upsall.

In the 19th century better roads were built to cope with the new industrialisation and rising population. About

1842 the new road up Dixon's Bank from Marton was built and it was often possible to avoid the notorious Ormesby Bank. Nowadays it is hard to imagine what a great hazard to traffic this bank presented. Since the last war it has been straightened, the top removed and flattened so that the I.C.I. lorries coming from the Wilton Chemical Works could use it. In the stage coach era it was very steep and very winding. Let us suppose you were living in the 18th century and returning from Stockton market one Wednesday afternoon to go to Guisborough. When the stage coach arrived at Ormesby, it would stop at the Red Lion Inn, (approximately on the site of the present Fountains Inn). The passengers would alight for refreshment and the horses changed. Then the coach would set off up what is now Church Lane. When the road became very steep the male passengers would get out and walk to ease the strain on the horses by lightening the coach. On a fine day this might be welcomed as a chance to stretch one's legs but on a frosty or snowy day it would be necessary to put stones under the carriage wheels to prevent it slipping backwards in the steepest part of the road. The coachmen would have to hold the straining horses' heads and encourage them if caught in a blizzard. No doubt there were many accidents and the carriage ended up in a ditch. How pleased passengers must have been to turn the corner at Gypsy Lane and ride safely along the straight level road to Guisborough - and no doubt the horses were too!

The Red Lion was a coaching inn, a necessary stopping place for Guisborough passengers but it was not one of the large inns which catered particularly for passengers, staying overnight as was the Blue Bell Inn a few miles further along the Yarm road. However the Red Lion is no more for it jutted out into the road and was regarded as an obstruction to modern traffic. Old cottages which stood on its left side in the centre of the village were also demolished to make way for the supermarket and car park. "The Fountain" commemorating the drinking fountain and horse-trough of the old inn was built in its place.

Writing in 1846 John Walker Ord wrote "Ormesby is a well built and pleasant village situated on the road between Guisborough and Stockton". Nowadays even the old Ormesby Bank road leads to nowhere for modern road improvements have cut it off. Now called Church Lane it is a pleasant by-road leading to St. Cuthbert's Church and the beautiful Georgian Ormesby Hall, owned by the National Trust and open to the public. Its elegant stable-block designed by the famous architect Carr of York, once staged Shakespearian plays. The last mistress of Ormesby Hall, Ruth Pennyman wrote poetry and plays. She accommodated famous actors and actresses from the West End of London in the years before the last war. They gave performances of famous plays to a local audience seated on wooden staging round the stable courtyard. She had a warm heart and strongly held socialist views. Her sympathy not only extended to the needy on Teesside but during the Spanish civil War she cared for Basque children refugees at the hall.

In a book written by Robert Kettlewell concerning Great Ayton and named "Cleveland Village", he quotes a series of entries taken from the Great Ayton Surveyors' Book at the turn of the 18th century and reveals something of the state of the roads by the necessary repairs which had to be carried out. To quote a few examples:

ROAD REPAIRS
1794-5   Thos. Shimmin - 2 days filling ruts, Tanton Lane 3s.0d
1801-02   To 44 loads of stone at 2s per load £4-8-0
To working at roads 15 days @ 1s per day   15-0
To Wm Smalwell - Cowling Road   8-6

Cowling meant removing mud with a toothless instrument or raking the loose stones in ruts made by carriage or cart wheels.

Another feature of the roads made necessary by the increased use of them was the provision of signposts. Up to this time stone milestones such as those still seen on some of our moorland roads were set up at infrequent intervals. Now the authorities were required to provide wooden signposts, hence this entry in the same Surveyor's Book:

1796-97
To 21+1/2 Oake wood for 5 direction posts £1-15-0
For bordes and painting   11-0
To lettering of the same - 165 letters @ 1d each
                                                    13-9

An essential feature of the days of coach travel were the coaching inns where the horses were changed, passengers could snatch a meal, warm themselves in winter or stay the night if necessary. The history of many of these inns goes back to medieval times. The inventories of them at the beginning of the 18th century establish that many were very well founded. In the pre-railway Victorian era they were a very important feature of life as Dickens revealed in the capers of Mr Pickwick and his friends!

In this area the position of Guisborough, situated between the coast and the rural Yorkshire hinterland made it an important centre for coaches. At the time when the Graves map was made in 1803 there were daily departures from ''The Cock'', ''The Buck'' and the ''Seven Stars'', all coaching inns, situated in Guisborough Market Place. Coaches using them went to Stockton and Middlesbrough (after 1840) in one direction, across the moors to Whitby in the other, as well as to Stokesley and Thirsk. There were extensions on these routes to Skelton and Redcar. As can be imagined there must have been a great bustle as passengers changed from one coach to another. Great Ayton was on a coach route from Redcar to Bedale and in 1823 these coaches were passing through the villages on three days a week, Mondays, Wednesdays and Saturdays. The mail coaches travelled along these roads as well, bringing the post from Thirsk which was the local sorting centre, leaving the letters and parcels at Stokesley and Ayton inns as they passed.

The most famous of the coaching inns in this area was the ''Cleveland Tontine'' which is at the junction where the road to Stokesley and Teesside forks off from the main Thirsk to Stockton road (the A172 with the A19), not far from Osmotherly. From the middle of the 19th century it was the main posting house for changing horses and had a large stable block. Now in the 20th century its stable block is a centre for breeding Shetland ponies and it has earned a reputation for its fine cuisine. It was purpose built for stage coaches and behind its name lies the interesting history of its origin. From the Oxford Dictionary we learn the definition of TONTINE:

''*TONTINE - Financial scheme by which subscribers to loan receive each an annuity for life, increasing as their numbers are decreased by death until the last survivor enjoys the whole income. (Lorenzo Tonti, Neopolitan instituted the scheme in France c.1653)*''.

Towards the end of the 18th century a group of wealthy business men decided to build a turnpike road from Stockton to Thirsk with a coaching inn at its junction with the Stokesley and Guisborough Road. They paid £2,500 each for the enterprise and devised a tontine-like scheme. Each would get an annuity from the profits till his death but he also nominated an heir who would inherit the whole enterprise after the death of the last survivor. Brian Cooper-Abbs of Ingleby Hall had two shares because he owned the land upon which the inn and the beginning of the road stood. Eventually it was his heir who inherited the property. Later a member of this family brought back the very fine gates of wrought-iron still there, from Italy where he had been enjoying the Grand Tour.

In the "Stokesley Selection" are given some interesting data concerning coach travel. For example it is obvious that travel by stage coach was not cheap and certainly beyond the means of the average villager. Even the carriage of goods must have been a considerable item on the business man's balance sheet. No wonder Ralph Ward and his nephew Ralph Ward Jackson were so concerned with the state of the roads! In 1736 the magistrates at the Stokesley Sessions decreed that carriers were to charge no more than 4d a stone for goods between York and Stokesley. At a time when a labourer had to keep his family on less than £1 a week, to charge 2s 8d to transport a cwt. of coal approximately forty miles seems excessive! In 1753 the Stokesley solicitor, John Matthews, went to London and Newbury by coach and the journey cost £24-15s-6d - a fortune in those days!

To enquire about a journey by coach at the inn of departure, one needed to know, not only the day and time of departure but also its name. The same named coach kept to the same route, For example, "The Telegraph" ran between Thirsk and Redcar via Stokesley and Guisborough from 1823. "The Emerald" coach ran from Leeds to Redcar in 1840, taking over from "The Hope" which ran through Stokesley in 1829. Market days were very important to a farming community so a coach went from Stokesley every Wednesday to Stockton. Such special coaches went no doubt from Guisborough too. As for goods transport a six-horse wagon went weekly to Thirsk from Stokesley.

To go a long journey by stage coach necessitated many changes and overnight stops. Ralph Ward Jackson went many times to visit his married sister Dorothy who lived in London and recorded them in his diary. Details of one such journey are give in Dan O'Sullivan's book on Great Ayton:

"16th June 1770

I spent the forenoon among my workmen, dined at one, wrote this before two. I hope to be ready within half an hour to set out for London - at three I left my house at Normanby, taking my servant, George Kirtley, with me (to London) and drank tea at Brother Wilson's at Ayton where I layed all night.

17th June 1770

About eight Brother and Sister Wilson took Sister Esther and self into their coach and sent us to Bessie Bells at Ingleby Cross, (this would be the turnpike road). They returned but Esther and I proceeded, dined at Northallerton, drank tea at Mrs Staine's at Ripon. I sat an hour about seven o'clock with Doctor Wanley. Sister Esther laid at Mrs Staines. I laid at the inn.

18th June 1770

I got up early and breakfasted at Borrowbridge where I bought many Household Utensils at the Fair, with some Nails etc. Sister Esther came to me about nine and Mr and Misses Sally and Nanny Mauleverer coming to the town, soon after we all got into the two Chaises, changed at Wetherby and dined at Ferrybridge, changed Chaise at Doncaster and all laid at Bawtry.

19th June 1770

Sister Esther and I with George set out at six from

Bawtry (a very Rainy morning) leaving Mr Mauleverer and his daughters to proceed on their journey to Gainsboro' in Lincolnshire where Mrs Mauleverer now is with her father, Mr Wilberfoss. We breakfasted at Scarthing Moor, dined at Coltsworth, and laid all night at Huntingdon. Cousin Wm Stephenson (late of Darlington) spent the evening with us at the Inn.

20th June 1770

We breakfasted at Cambridge, changed at Chesterfield and Bishop Stortford and Epping Place, and reached Sister Dorothy's at Woodford Bridge about one, having had a most rainy journey, particularly this day. Brother Jeffrey (Dorothy's husband) came from London before we sat down to dinner".

Now let us consider that most important form of communication, the postal service. Before the 19th century the number of people able to write and read a letter was very limited and those able to do so would probably have a servant to deliver any message locally whether written or not. The letter like those carried by the King's messengers travelling on horseback would be in the form of a scroll but private letters were in the form of a "mulberry". This would be sealed by a blob of sealing wax bearing the writer's crest or initials imprinted by his signet ring. A letter called a "mulberry" was a piece of notepaper folded in half, lengthwise, and then into three equal parts widthwise. The open ends were neatly tucked into each other and sealed with red wax. The folded paper thus formed a neat oblong on which the name and address or superscription could be written.

As early as 1635 a government postal service had been inaugurated but it was only limited to towns on main roads and was not very efficient. On eight routes through England post-boys rode on horseback stopping at certain fixed points where letters were delivered and collected at a minimum charge of 2d. With increased trade in the latter half of the 17th century, Parliament appointed a Postmaster General with authority to establish a full postal service for "the United Kingdom and the Colonies" - presumably America. Collecting posts were set up along the main roads, usually at inns where the horses could be changed quickly. Later in the 18th century when the stage coaches were running to strict schedules along the newly surfaced roads and turnpikes, the postal service used specially fast coaches which also carried a few passengers. These were the express trains of those days! How efficient they were can be gauged by the fact that in 1836 the mail was carried from London to York, a distance of 197 miles in twenty hours!

In our area in the early days it would be to an old coaching inn like the Royal Oak at Great Ayton that the Squire in Nunthorpe Hall would send his servant to collect the mail. According to the "Stokesley Selection" the first post-office there, as distinct from the inns, is believed to have been No. 62 High Street, in the late 18th century. But in 1823 there were post-offices in Stokesley and Guisborough managed by post-mistresses who collected the money when the people came to collect them. After 1840 when Sir Roland Hill instituted the Penny Post, stamps were fixed to all letters which were put into envelopes and sealed - a new idea! With the coming of the railway system throughout the country, the mails were carried by rail in mailbags. Where the railway was some distance from the township as at Stokesley and Great Ayton, a local carrier would be responsible for meeting the trains, conveying passengers to and from the local post-office with the mail.

The first post-office in Nunthorpe village was opened

in 1879. Previously the people of Nunthorpe had had to go to Great Ayton to post a letter and buy a stamp, though in practice a friendly postman must often have obliged. This small sub post-office functioned until the mid 1960's.

There was also another road system in use by travellers on horse and foot down the ages and of great commercial value from the 17th to 19th centuries. These were the Drove roads. Along these mostly grassy lanes, crossing moorland and valley, the drovers from Scotland drove thousands of cattle to market in England. They crossed North Yorkshire by two routes and their users did not welcome the new turnpike roads. In great herds of three hundred to one thousand, cattle were driven from Scotland to the markets at Malton and York in Yorkshire but mostly through this countryside to the industrial towns of the Midlands and Smithfield Market in London. One route from Western Scotland crossed the Pennines and ran through Wensleydale on its way southwards. The other ran via Durham, Sedgefield and Yarm and crossed the coach road to Thirsk, near Swainby. From here they went droving up the hill to Scarth Nick and at Sheepwash turned on to the long green lane which stretches for miles right along the top of the Hambleton Hills. Not far from Sheepwash there used to be a drover's inn called Checkers with its old turf fire which had been burning for untold years. Along the green road are the remains of other drover's inns and the pounds where the cattle were kept overnight. Today this road provides a most enjoyable walk for hikers. Though this trade did not affect our area directly, except perhaps in the price of cattle, travellers on the road to Thirsk must have been greatly impressed as they watched the Scottish drovers and their cattle crossing the road as they made their way up the hillside to Scarth Nick where they would join the famous Drovers Road across the Hambleton Hills.

Now let us look at what was happening in the villages of Marton and Nunthorpe during the late 18th century and 19th century. According to the records in Ord's "History of Cleveland" Marton and Nunthorpe had always been small rural communities paying their rents to largely absent landlords, and the church, but fairly prosperous. Marton village with its cross-roads was situated on the top of the elevated land overlooking the Yarm road. In 1786 Sir James Ramsden sold the Marton Estate to Bartholomew Rudd of Marske. He was of humble origin but had unexpectedly come into a fortune so bought the Marton estate and also the Tolesby estate to set up his two sons. He himself never lived in Marton. For his elder son, also named Bartholomew, he built a mansion on the best site on the estate which was in Marton village. In order to do so, he had to demolish some of the cottages, one of which was the one in which Captain Cook had been born. Because the whole village was proud of the famous navigator he marked the site with a quadrangle of flint stones. As can be seen by the map in Ord's book (1843) the village with its crossroads on the top of the hill remained virtually the same. Marton Lodge was built, Bartholomew married twice and had no less than fifteen children. He spent his time farming his estate but not very profitably for he had to sell parts of his estate from time to time. This was also the time of the great depression all over Europe which followed the Napoleonic Wars. He died in 1829 and bequeathed his estate to his eldest son, George, who was a clergyman.

However only three years later in 1832 Marton Lodge burnt down to the ground and it was a total disaster. George sold the estate to the Rev. Parke who eventually sold it to Mr Henry W.F. Bolckow, the ironmaster. Writing in 1846 Ord writes of the ruined mansion like this "it still remains a black and shapeless heap of ruins. The stables and outhouses are rather extensive with excellent gardens and pleasure grounds".

For his younger son, Thomas, Bartholomew Rudd

Marton Parish Church

Tollesby Hall

Tollesby Hall was built in 1808 by Bartholomew Rudd. His grandson, Major John Rudd, lived there for Many years. It was demolished in 1984.

J. H. Cousans

bought the Tollesby Estate in 1786 and built a new house near the old Tollesby hall on the north side of the Yarm road, where the Easterside estate is situated today, the old hall was pulled down and a new one built.

He married and had two children, John Bartholomew born in 1813 and Susan Elizabeth in 1819. Sadly their parents died young and they were orphans brought up by trustees. Susan Elizabeth died in 1830 and in later life her brother erected a memorial window to her in the chancel of the restored Marton Church. John Bartholomew was brought up by one of the trustees who was the Vicar of Guisborough at that time. He went to school and university at Cambridge and later studied to be a barrister, but never practiced law and came back to live once more in Guisborough. As the estate was heavily mortgaged he let his house to a Mr and Mrs Rowe who lived there for many years. It was while he was living in Guisborough that the Marton Captain Cook Memorial School was built from the stones of the burnt-out Marton Lodge. It is largely due to him that it was built for he said by it "a disgrace had been effaced from the inhabitants of having no fitting memorial of the greatest navigator that the world has ever produced in his native place". Funds were not very forthcoming for the project so he made up the deficiency himself. It is said that he drove every morning from his home in Guisborough and often worked with his own hands, dressed in labourer's clothes and existing on labourer's fare. The foundation stone was laid in December 1849. A memorial to Captain Cook which was removed from St. Cuthbert's Church when it was being restored, was built into the main classroom so that it was truly Captain Cook's Memorial School.

At this mid-Victorian period there was a movement throughout the country to restore the neglected village churches. The churches at Ormesby and Ayton were also restored at this period. While still living in Guisborough in 1843, he undertook to restore the neglected Parish Church of St. Cuthbert's in Marton. It was in such need of repair that it had to be largely rebuilt and it is chiefly due to him that the inhabitants of Marton have such a beautiful church today.

A church has stood on that site since early Saxon times. It is not recorded in the Domesday Book but is one of the churches listed as being where the coffin containing the body of St. Cuthbert rested, during its journey through the countryside, before coming to rest in Durham Cathedral. It is therefore very suitable that the church should be of a simple Saxon design with a small bell-tower.

In 1855 John Bartholomew Rudd came back to live in Tollesby Hall and was for many years very active in the local Militia volunteers where he attained the rank of Major. It is by the name of Major Rudd that he was popularly known. Sadly towards the end of his life, he had many financial worries so that he was forced to sell his house and estate.

He was in the process of moving from his home and was staying at the Queen's Hotel, Middlesbrough, when he died suddenly on 10th May 1888. The family vault of the Rudd family was at Marske but the Marton villagers insisted that he should be buried in the church which he had restored. He was given a grand military funeral. The Parish Magazine for June 1888 records *"The body was brought to Marton by his old corps of artillery, accompanied by several detachments from other regiments on a gun carriage, the coffin being covered by a Union Jack, at the close of the service, three volleys were fired over the grave as the last tribute of respect to their beloved comrade"*.

Years later Henry Bolckow built an extension onto the

school and here dances and concerts were held in the evenings. At these concerts, usually in aid of church funds or a charity, the "gentry" and villagers showed off their talents to the enjoyment of all. Not only were social functions held here but adult education was taken seriously. The Parish Magazine reveals this when it congratulates those who have won awards for their efforts. Talks were given sometimes by members of the prominent families in the halls and lively debates took place by the men of the village on such topics as the latest improvements in agriculture or even local politics.

For the women of the parish there were meetings connected with raising money for charity or working for foreign missions abroad or the blind and orphans at home. There would be meetings and classes for such things as embroidery and quilt making.

After the first World War the order changed. The army had erected large wooden huts in Marton Hall grounds. During the war, the hall itself had been a military hospital. One of these huts was purchased by the church authorities for use as a Parish Hall, where meetings of all kinds, and an agricultural or flower show could be held. Boy Scouts and Girl Guides could gather as well as the newly founded Women's Institute. The wooden hut served the village well for many years until the opening of the fine new Parish Centre in 1992, when it was pulled down.

A glance at the 1771 map shows the village of Marton itself at the top of the rise on which the Captain Cook Birthplace Museum now stands. It had a centre where cross-roads met, one road going right through the village from the Yarm road (Ladgate Lane) over to Gypsy Lane coming out near where the Brunton Arms now stands. The map in Ord's book dated 1843 also shows this same format. What brought about the radical change to what it is today?

1853 was the crucial year when the sleepy village of Marton woke up. The greatest of the local ironmasters, Henry W.F. Bolckow, bought the whole Marton Estate and the same year the railway running from Middlesbrough to Guisborough was built, passing near to the village. Henry Bolckow's ambition was to build the finest mansion in the neighbourhood on the excellent site now occupied by Marton village, overlooking the new town of Middlesbrough, of which he was its first Mayor.

Major Rudd had already taken the stones of the ruined Marton Lodge and with them built the fine Captain Cook Memorial School and schoolhouse in the middle of the present village and which is still a school today. Henry Bolckow cleared his site by demolishing the houses and roads of the old Marton village and building new houses for his tenants, as can be seen today in the red-bricked Victorian terrace of houses in the village.

By 1858 the prestigious Marton Hall was ready for the family to move in. The great mansion with its imposing dome stood in all its glory at the top of the hill, set in beautiful grounds with two lakes and a park, eight acres in extent. The great and distinguished guests which he hoped to impress, would arrive at his beautiful flower-decked station by the side of the bridge over the Yarm road. They would go down the steps and into the fine carriages waiting for them below. They would ride up the Grove, the tree lined avenue he had created, to the Lodge Gates and thence be carried through the park to the steps on the terrace in front of the hall - most impressive! The Grove was extended to the Stokesley road so that all could easily walk to the station, for this time was the Age of Railway Mania! Henry Bolckow like the other ironmasters in their country homes, would commute to his office in Middlesbrough each

View of Marton Hall with Lake (now Stewart Park)

day. To mark the birthplace of Captain Cook, he erected a fine granite vase. Today this, together with a modified conservatory is all that remains of the great house but the park with magnificent trees he planted, can now be enjoyed by all - Stewart Park.

Although Nunthorpe had its Manor House, later Hall, it was never dominated for long by an ancestral family. Little of interest is known of the families who lived there in the Middles Ages and Tudor times, for none stayed there long enough to make their mark.

The first Nunthorpe Hall seems to have been built in the reign of Charles I (1625-49). Marmaduke Constable bought the old manor house and its adjoining chapel in a state of disrepair and decay. There had been a manor house on the site since the time of William the Conqueror. In 1623 a dispute arose over the payment of tithes to the Rector of Great Ayton during which Marmaduke was accused of pulling down part of the chapel and terrorising villagers into attendance at it. Fortunately there was plenty of evidence forthcoming to prove that in repairing the damage to the chapel he had improved the fabric from what it was before. This all suggests that at last somebody was prepared to take the house with its chapel in hand.

The chapel referred to was the small chapel, or rather its forerunner of that which still stands in the grounds of Nunthorpe Hall. A chapel had been there as early as the 11th century so probably it was built at the same time as the first Norman Manor. At the beginning of the 12th century it was granted to Whitby Abbey by Baron Robert de Meinell and his wife Gertrude, who lived at Whorlton Castle, so that the village tithes were paid to Whitby. After the dissolution of the monasteries the tithes were paid to the Rector of Great Ayton - hence the above dispute. It was never a Parish Church but a domestic chapel for the use of the Lord of the Manor and his household. At one time it was used as a chantry where a priest said prayers for the dead.

Shortly after the dispute was settled Marmaduke Constable died to be succeeded by his son John Constable, who unfortunately died only four years later childless. The estate then passed into the hands of his sisters, Anne, the wife of James Bradshaw and Elizabeth Constable. The lands were split up and as Anne's portion included the Manor House, it was Anne's son Constable Bradshaw, who took up residence there. Here he stayed for the rest of the century. It was at this period that the Jacobean residence was built though the exact date is not known.

Some idea of what the Jacobean Nunthorpe Manor House looked like can be seen at Ryedale Folk Museum, Hutton-le-Hole, it is one that has been restored and reconstructed to look as it did when it was built in 1600.

As this family too produced no direct male heir the Stokesley estate was sold in lots. This was no bad thing for the tenant farmers for it enabled them, if possible, to buy their own farm where they could make what improvements they thought fit and hand it down to their heirs. The last lot in the sale was the Manor House at Nunthorpe and its adjoining farm. It was bought by Thomas Simpson in 1799. No doubt the house and chapel were in a poor state of repair. Eventually he pulled down the old buildings and in 1821 built the fine Regency style house we see today. On 9th January 1834 his daughter, Elizabeth, married Joseph Ibbotson, friend of John Walker Ord, the historian and Vicar of All Saints, Great Ayton with charge of the Nunthorpe Chapel. It may be due to his influence that the beautiful little chapel stands today in the hall grounds. Nunthorpe Hall is now owned by Middlesbrough Council and run as a Residential Home for the Elderly. The chapel looks

Nunthorpe Hall 1992

forlorn and is sadly in need of repair. The Home now, in this year of 1992, is in danger of being closed and its future is uncertain.

After the death of Thomas Simpson in 1848, the estate was bought by Issac Wilson, the ironmaster and one of the founding fathers of the new town of Middlesbrough. He and his family came to live at the hall in 1856. He was one of the directors of the Stockton and Darlington Railway and like Henry Bolckow commuted every day to his office in Middlesbrough. He had a great influence on the area in Victorian times and his story is told later.

Since the death of Issac Wilson in December 1899, the hall has passed from one owner to another, none staying very long. The coat of arms there are those of Sir Joseph Whitwell Pease who lived there with his family before moving to his new home at Hutton Gate Hall, another prestigious Victorian mansion. During the 1930's it was owned by the O'Neill family who gave the village its Cricket Ground after the death of Sir Arther Dorman when its ground in Grey Towers was no longer available. During the period of the Second World War it was a Nursing Home run by Doctor Dixon. After his death in the 1950's the hall again became vacant until bought by the Middlesbrough Council.

CHAPTER 7

The 18th Century Textile Industry In Cleveland

The Industrial Revolution assumed two distinct phases in Cleveland and although Nunthorpe itself always remained a rural farming community until the opening of the railway in 1853, it must have been greatly influenced by what was taking place in nearby Ayton and Stokesley. Some of its young people no doubt worked in the factories there and eventually settled in homes near them.

The first phase began when the textile mills were powered by the waters of the River Leven in the 18th century and lasted until the middle of the 19th century when steam powered looms of the West Riding and Lancashire could produce cloth much more cheaply. At its height the Cleveland industry was a very flourishing trade and the hand weavers and others from the villages far afield flocked to find work in Ayton, Stokesley and Hutton Rudby. They produced a particularly strong linen canvas suitable for ship's sails, huckaback for towels and a small amount of linen. They also imported hemp for sack manufacture and ropes.

Up to this time spinning and weaving had been a cottage industry right from prehistoric times when the women weighted down threads on their simple looms with stone weights such as those found on the Bronze Age site on nearby Barnaby Moor. During the Middle Ages every woman was expected to spin and if every cottage did not have its loom, a weaver in the village would weave her thread into cloth. He could produce a fine piece of homespun woollen cloth to be made into a man's smock or a peasant woman's dress. The fine linen thread would be spun and woven into a dyed cloth kerchief of clothes for my lady. When it was bleached a surplice for the parson or a cloth for the altar could be made. The country clothes would be dyed the soft shades of brown, grey, yellow and green produced by natural vegetable dyes but there were towns who were famous for a special dye, such as Lincoln green, to which the cloth could be sent for dyeing.

By the time of the Stuarts and early Georges the trade had become organised. The weavers and particularly their families worked long hours at their spinning wheels and looms in their own cottages. Even today in many old cottages there is a "spinning window" beside the old fireplace where the woman of the house could do her spinning in a good light beside a warm fire. In some areas the old cottages still retain a "weaving gallery" - a kind of verandah set up on the second storey of the cottage ensuring plenty of room to set up several looms for weaving cloths of various widths and at the same time enable the weaver to work in a good light. In this area, at Ayton and elsewhere, there is some evidence to suggest that the weaver had a special shed built at the end of the garth adjoining his cottage, where he and his family did their work. Before the mills were built, it was the usual practice for the agent of a wool merchant to call regularly on the weaver to buy his woven cloth, taking it to a small factory or workshop to be dyed, shrunk and made ready for sale on a market stall or in a shop. If flax had been woven, it would go to a bleaching mill to be made even whiter when laid out in long lengths in a sunlit field.

Wills and inventories of this time, before the coming of the factories, shows the weavers often farmed some land and were well respected members of the countryside. The weaving was a family concern with the wife and children doing much of the work while the man tended the farm animals and fields. One such weaver lived in Great Ayton at the beginning of the 18th century as this inventory shows:

Thos. Weatherill of Great Ayton Oct 27th 1713
Weaver
Purse and apparrell £5
1 mare and foal £7, 8 cows and 2 stirkes £23
1 little haystack and 2 little pikes £6
Wheat, oats and barley £8
2 old carts, 1 plough, 1 pair of harrows, 1 pair of horse gear £3
FOREHOUSE £1-10-0 Great Parlour £5. Little Parlour £11
CHAMBER £1 Milkhouse 10/-
In the WORKHOUSE one loom and geers belonging to her, one old bedstead with bedding and other small implements £1
1 swine, 6 hens and 1 cock, 6 geese £1-10-0

Total £66-10-0

But already in the early 18th century the Industrial Revolution was stirring in mens minds to change everything. In 1733 Kay invented the flying shuttle for the weavers, not long afterwards Hargreaves invented his spinning Jenny and the spinning and weaving machines were born, necessitating a factory life for the workers. These machines were powered by running water and after Watt's invention, steam power. Great mills were built along the river sides of the West Riding and with the arrival of cotton in Lancashire too. Here along the banks of the Leven and the Esk, small mills were erected. In Barne's Directory for Great Ayton in 1823, three Linen Manufacturers are listed, namely P. Hesselton and Son, Richard Lamb and Thomas Nattress. Two oil millers are listed, Phillip Heselton and Messrs. Richardson and Lawson. (Most of these mill owners were Quakers. The Richardson and Heselton families were later to found the Quaker School at Ayton and the Heselton family house on the Green became part of the school). A very interesting account of Great Ayton's linen industry was given by G. Dixon in his "History of Great Ayton School" (1891) -

"I must not forget to mention the bath. In a field at the end of the orchard garden was an old stone building known by the name of the bleach house. The Heseltons, the late owners of the estate employed many weavers of linen, huckaback (for towels) and sail-cloth. They bleached their yarn for the purpose in the grass field adjoining the building which was used for receiving it. Outside was a stream called the Dykes Beck. The idea was conceived that it could easily be converted into a bath-house and the water brought to it in drain pipes from the stream a short distance above.

The bath was chiefly used by the girls, the chamber above being a dressing room. There is a tradition that the old bleach-house was abandoned on account of a man losing his life by falling into the boiling chemicals".

A further extract gives an account of how the oil-mill worked:

"Adjoining the school premises was a mill known as the Oil Mill, the wheel of which was driven by the River Leven that flows through the school grounds damned back by stone steps over which the water flowed when not required at the mill. When wanted at the mill, a door was opened in the sluice which led down to the water-wheel. When there was more water in the sluice than the mill required it ran over a by-wash.

The oil-mill buildings were very old, said to have been at first a brewery (perhaps with malt kilns), afterwards a flax-mill. When we came to the village in 1841, it was used for expressing oil from linseed. A pair of edge-stones crushed the seed which was heated in small iron pans over a slow fire and kept from burning by revolving knives inside the pans; when hot, it was put into hair bags and placed between wedges made of beechwood, the upper ones driven by heavy stampers lifted by a revolving shaft and then allowed to fall on the wedge. When this was driven home, the crushed linseed was found pressed into a flat mess called oilcakes, sold to farmers for feeding their cattle. The oil ran down into tanks below the wedges. This oil when pumped into cauldrons and boiled with sulphuric acid, was called boiled linseed oil and was in great demand for mixing with paint. Phillip Heselton, senior, successfully established the oil business and carried it on to the time of his death, when it was leased to Saunders and Wetheral of Stockton, who also rented a similar mill at the west end of the village. When the new process of obtaining oil from linseed by hydraulic pressure so much more cheaply and efficiently came into use the two oil-mills were no longer required".

The oil being produced was linseed oil, used in paint manufacture and for other commercial purposes. The pressed seed produced cattle cake which may have helped in the production of such fine Yorkshire cattle.

The manufacture of linen was and still is, a labour intensive industry. The flax plant, its source, has to be harvested by pulling it up by the roots, then "retting" it. Retting involves soaking the plants, with their long stiff stems, until all the vegetable matter is softened and can be readily abstracted from the fine threads in the stems. Retting ponds from the 18th century can still be seen at Kirkleatham Hall, suggesting that some flax was grown in this area. The actual production of the thread, its spinning and weaving involves many complicated processes, many more than for the production of cotton or woollen goods. To produce very fine linen, special flax seed is sown and the plants pulled up before the seeds are ripe. However it was the coarser kind of linen which was generally produced here with a ready market for canvas for sails and huckaback towelling. The seeds too, were necessary to keep the oil-mills working. Most of the flax for the mills was imported especially from Holland and the Baltic and some considerable amounts of linen yarn. Trade figures of the late seventeenth and eighteenth century show how important were the imports of the flax and exports of the finished cloth from such ports as Stockton and Whitby. These figures abstracted from the port lists show the great surge of prosperity caused by first the enclosure and the beginning of the Agrarian Revolution and then the beginning of the first phase of the Industrial Revolution in this area.

Lists of Exports and Imports from the Guisborough, Ayton and Stokesley area 1638-1676:

EXPORTS - AGRICULTURE	1638-39	1665-66	1675-76
Butter (furkins)	8,599	30,871	42,600
Corn and Malt (quarters)	415	3,277	275
Calf-skins (dressed or tanned)	62doz	17doz	421doz

IMPORTS - AGRICULTURE

Corn (quarters)	1,970	140	450

TEXTILES - EXPORT

Woollen stockings (dozen pairs)	440	2,195	4,145

IMPORTS

Flax per cwt. (dressed & undressed)	89	75	385
Tow (for ropes)		440	2,195	4,145

It is possible to see evidence of a cornmill and the remains of an oil-mill today by taking a short walk behind the school at Great Ayton. Almost opposite the Library and Suggitts shop in the High Street is a footbridge across the river. After crossing walk up the path turning towards the left. Right in front is a waterfall composed of concrete steps which have replaced the original stone ones, with broken remains of a sluice gate beside it. A large stone house stands on the opposite bank and looks like a converted mill. This is the site of an old corn-mill. The footpath continues over several fields offering panoramic views of the hills and leads to a footbridge across the river. Before crossing the bridge continue walking up the riverside to a similar terrace of steps in the river from which a small mill-race leads back towards two stone buildings at the top of the field and in the school grounds. These are on the site of the oil-mill just described and a flax-mill which was also owned by the Heselton family.

Most of the mills in the area employed under forty people, whether producing textiles, oil or flour, but in a government survey of factories in 1839, when the industry was in decline, there are details of the people employed in a larger flax-mill at Stokesley.

"*Stokesley - 2 mills, one working and one empty. The mill working employs 139 persons, 72 of them women and girls and 67 men and boys. Of the girls 49 are under 21, of whom two are under 10, 10 under 12, and 15 under 15. Of the men and boys 45 are under 21 one of them being under 10, 15 under 12 and 21 under 15. The mill is worked by one steam engine of under 30 horse-power*".

This terse report reveals another aspect of industrial life in this early 19th century - the condition of the factory workers and the poor. The fact that this survey was made and the ages of the workers given, reveals a concern for this section of society instigated by the great Victorian social reformers like Lord Shaftsbury (1801-1885). Even here in rural Cleveland weavers and farm labourers had been forced by the introduction of machinery to leave their villages to find work in the factories of small country towns. Although the poverty and degradation of the poor in the large cities was mercifully not experienced here, there were still many mothers who were forced to send their children out to work at an early age. To have to accept the Parish Relief was regarded as degrading and the journey to the workhouse, if one was rendered homeless by eviction, was to be avoided at all costs. Had they but known it, the social reformers were stirring the conscience of Victorian England and Charles Dickens was using his pen to expose the social evils to a wide public so that their descendants would reap the benefit of free education and the Welfare State.

Now where was the market for all the thousands of yards of canvas produced? The answer, of course, was for the ships being built at Yarm, Stockton and Whitby. The 18th century saw a great expansion in trade following the sea routes to the other side of the world both eastwards and southwards opened up by such great explorers as Captain Cook and his friend Commodore William Wilson (who married the sister of Ralph Ward Jackson, the diarist) and retired from the sea to live in Ayton. Such voyages through uncharted seas whether round the Cape of Good Hope to the Far East or the newly discovered Australia, needed strong, sturdy ships manned by a hardy crew under a skillful captain and a massive amount of linen canvas sails.

Knowing the worth of the Whitby shipbuilders in constructing strong sturdy ships, it was to them that Capt. Cook gave his Naval Commissions to prepare for his hazardous voyages. The supply of canvas needed for equipping the ships built in those busy Whitby yards was more than the local sail-makers could cope with. In Young's "History of Whitby" (1817) there is this interesting paragraph:

"There are 4 sail-lofts (in Whitby) at present. Before 1756 the Whitby sail-makers procured the canvas from other places. There are now 3 manufactures for canvas; the first was begun about 1756 by the late Mr John Saunders; it comprises of three branches, one near the Market Place containing 16 looms and one in Tate Hill containing 16 looms and one in Guisborough of about the same number. In each of these manufactories flax dressing is carried on as well as weaving; to which I may add bleaching. Till lately the spinning was all performed in private homes; as a great part of it still is".

This was by no means the only linen mill in Guisborough.

In the 18th century, weaving of wool as well as linen was second only to agriculture in the economy of the town. As early as 1695 there is evidence of the linen trade here in the inventory of Thomas Brignall of Guisborough who left three looms in his workshop and in that of William Young of Stokesley dated 1694, his trade being given as that of "Linning Weaver". Daniel Defoe visiting Guisborough in 1725 mentioned that the town had "a very good manufacture of sail-cloth" and William Ward had set up "a manufactory for sail-cloth to give work to the poor people". William Ward (1648-1718) was the father of Ralph Ward the man of business previously referred to. This mill must evidently have flourished for a long time for his grandson Ralph Ward Jackson tells of visits to it in his diary.

It is an exciting thought that some of the sails on Captain Cook's ships may have been made from canvas manufactured near here. Maybe even the threads may have been grown in fields of blue-flowered flax where corn is growing, nearby!

Besides Whitby the other local market for sail-cloth produced at this time was the shipbuilding yards beside the River Tees. During the Middle Ages, Yarm was the most important riverside port in the area for it was there that the main road, running South through to York and North through to Durham, crossed the Tees over Yarm Bridge. This enabled goods to be moved easily in both directions. However as trade and commerce increased so the ships grew larger. Ships were built and repaired up to the 18th century, in time the ships needed by the increased trade, were so large that they found great difficulty in negotiating the shallow winding River Tees to its sandy estuary and the open sea. Trade declined at Yarm and shipyards were set up at Stockton. Small ships were still being built at Yarm when the Cleveland Linen mills were in full production but larger ships were built lower down the river on both sides at Stockton. The ships also needed to be fitted with ropes. A great deal of tow was imported. Among the list of manufacturers given in Baine's Directory 1823, are Thos. and John Mease, flax and tow spinners, and John Barnard, rope and twine maker at Stokesley, while at Guisborough was a rope maker named John Corney in the Market Place and later William Smith is listed as a rope maker in Westgate.

In 1771 the merchants of Stockton built a bridge across the river, having found that the ferry service used hitherto to have been wholly inadequate for the increased trade. As the tall masted ships could no longer go beyond this point, shipbuilding at Yarm virtually ceased. For the next fifty years, the shipyards at Stockton flourished and would be a ready market for the canvas and ropes which Cleveland mills produced. In retrospect the mind boggles at the thought of all the thousands of yards of canvas needed to equip a fleet of ships like those which Nelson commanded at Trafalgar but it is interesting to speculate that some of the canvas may have been made near here!

When Charles II came back to England in 1660 after living in that most extravagant and elegant court of the Sun King Louis XIV of France he brought with him a sense of style and a love of culture which had been unknown before in this country. During the latter part of the 17th century and during the 18th century a period of peace and prosperity opened up which allowed not only trade to develop but for those who could afford it, the building of beautiful homes and furniture which we can cherish today. In this area it is reflected in the beautiful Georgian houses built by prosperous merchants and mill owners particularly in Yarm and Stokesley, over which their respective Civic Societies keep a watchful eye. Ormesby Hall, so very elegant, yet small enough to be a happy family home was built in 1740 and is now National Trust property. Kirkleatham Hall with its famous alms-house and church with its mausoleum was the home of the Turner family for three centuries. It was built earlier but underwent extensive alterations during this century. Nunthorpe Hall itself has this same elegance and fine proportions though built in the Regency style a little later in 1821.

Undoubtedly the whole of the village would share in this period of peace and prosperity. With increased population in the area the extra food produced by the new methods of agriculture would provide a ready market for the gardeners and farmers. There was plenty of work for the young people should they wish or need to go to live in Ayton or Stokesley. This seems to have happened in Nunthorpe and Marton at this time for the available statistics show that the number of households from 1674 to 1801 did not change. In 1674 a Hearth Tax was imposed whereby a householder was taxed according to the number of hearths in his home and the householders in each place listed. In 1801 the first ever census of the whole country was undertaken so it is possible to access the rise in the number of houses in a place between these two dates.

The following list gives the data for the places in this district:

	Households 1674	Houses 1801	Population 1801
Guisborough	214	303	1719
Stokesley	122	334	1369
Ormesby	50	74	357
Marton	79	80	342
Nunthorpe	17	17	132
Marton	9	3	27*
*(last record)			
Middlesbrough	15	3	25

As can be seen from these figures the size of Nunthorpe and Marton remained static. In another list Nunthorpe,

Little Ayton and Newby are shown in 1801 to have under 10% of their population engaged in "trade, manufacture or handicraft". This could only mean that these villages were purely agriculture and their farms supplied the extra food needed for the increased population in the area. The figure of 132 people seems a large number for 17 households averaging almost eight. There may have been some large families but it seems more probable that at the hall and on the farms were many servants and labourers living in them.

How the people must have rejoiced when the mail-coach brought the news that Wellington had defeated Napoleon at Waterloo! Yet the end of the Napoleonic Wars ushered in a period of recession in world trade and poverty among the people of Europe. Canvas for ships sails was never needed in such large quantities again and by the middle of the 19th century no textile mills were left working in the Cleveland area. On 27th September 1825 the first passenger railway in the world was opened between Stockton and Darlington. This was the trigger which launched the Railway Age and created the great Age of Steel which was to engulf Teesside for the remainder of the century and beyond.

Friends Meeting House 1700
Rebuilt 1772

Heselton's house
built 1760

Friends Meeting House, Great Ayton

This drawing was done by Ruth Gaudie, a well-loved Quaker lady who lived for many years in Nunthorpe. She said she was descended from Quakers who had been converted by George Fox himself. When ninety years old she published a book of drawings and notes under the auspices of Stokesley and District Study Group 1982 entitled "*A Visual History of Great Ayton*".

CHAPTER 8

Culture And Religion In The 17th & 18th Centuries

"The Spirit of Man is a candle lit by God"

In the previous chapters consideration has been given as to how the people lived long ago in their homes, villages and Cleveland townships, and the joys and troubles which beset them from time to time. We have seen how, as individuals, they earned their living and what things they left behind them but have given little attention to their thoughts and beliefs. Thinking nationally this leads into an enquiry into what is meant by the "English Way of Life" and its cultural and spiritual basis. It was in these two centuries that England began to establish herself as an important nation and became "Great Britain" with its Empire in the 19th century. During the Middle Ages English thought, like that of the rest of Europe, had been largely dominated by the Roman Catholic Church and the feudal system. There was also constant friction not only with France but with Scotland. During Tudor times the feudal system had collapsed and the break with Rome resulted in the establishment of the Church of England. Finally after the death of Elizabeth I the thrones of England and Scotland were united under James I. The times were ripe for further development and expansion of power. Yet this change did not result in anything like the trauma and violence of the French Revolution or the religious wars of Central Europe although there was a Civil War and a Commonwealth which lasted for nine years. It was the Englishmen's love of his own countryside and an innate ability to achieve compromise which saved the land.

George Trevelyan gives an expert's view of this in the following quote from his book "English Social History".

"Foreigners were astonished at the love of the English gentry for rural life. Every gentleman, they remarked, flieth into the country. Few inhabit cities and towns; few have any regard for them. Though London might already be the greatest city in Europe, England was still in its essential life and feeling a rural community, whereas in France and Italy the Roman had deeply implanted a civilisation of the city that drew to itself all that was most vital in the life of the surrounding province. The place for the Squire, whether he were rich or poor, was at home in his manor house, and he knew and rejoyced in the fact.

Owing to the habit among the gentry of apprenticing their younger sons to trade, our country avoided the sharp division between a rigid caste of Nobles and an unprivileged bourgeoisie which brought about the French catastrophe of 1789. The manor house, its hospitality open to neighbours and friends of many different classes, was not ashamed to acknowledge a son in trade, beside another at the Inns of Court and a third perhaps in the family living.

Recruits from the landed class were constantly entering town life, while money and men from the towns were constantly flowing back to fertilize the countryside. Throughout Tudor, Stuart and early Hanoverian times, successful lawyers formed a large proportion of the 'new' men who introduced themselves into the country circle by purchase of land and by building of manor houses".

It may be recalled that William Pierson who bought Stokesley Manor and married Ann Bradshaw of Nunthorpe Hall in 1690 was a lawyer of the Middle Temple in London. As well as the 'Squire' there was also the "Yeomen of England" a type of person unknown on the continent, and peculiar to our society. George Trevelyan thus defines the yeomen farmers, such as those of Nunthorpe and Marton whose inventories were considered.

"The term 'Yeoman' covered at least three different classes, all now prosperous, the free-holder cultivating his own land; the capitalist farmer who might be a tenant-at-will; and the peasant who was lucky enough to enjoy a secure tenure at an unalterable rent. All these three types of yeomen might be cultivating either land enclosed by hedges or scattered strips in open fields. The wealth of many of them was derived wholly or in part from the fleeces of their sheep. The praise of the yeoman as the best type of Englishman, holding society together, neither cringing to the high nor dispising his poorer neighbour, hearty, hospitable, fearless, supplies a constant motif of literature under Tudors and Stuarts. And it corresponded to a social fact".

It was during this time of comparative prosperity from late 17th century and throughout 18th century that an English Renaissance came about making English furniture and ceramics pre-eminent in Europe. Their elegance and style are unsurpassed as is revealed in the prices paid for them in auction rooms today. Those who had the money were able to appreciate the talents of these craftsmen and employed them freely. Today we can see and appreciate these small halls of the gentry and the magnificent stately homes of the aristocrats amid beautiful gardens. They filled their houses with tasteful objects specially designed for them and around them created landscapes of great beauty. It was as if their appreciation of beauty was again finding expression in the country they loved and not the town. It is said that the "Spirit of Man is a candle". This candle certainly burnt brightly in the collective soul of the English nation during the 18th century in its appreciation of beauty.

The cottagers living in Nunthorpe, Ormesby, Great Ayton and Stokesley would know what was happening and see the beautiful silver, china, paintings and furniture in the manor houses and halls. Their prosperity might vary one from another but for each as they could afford it, their everyday dishes would be made of pewter instead of wooden platters. The country joiner now working to new designs would be able to produce tables and cupboards which would be a source of pride. Instead of the earth floor the forehouse or all-purpose kitchen-living room would now be covered over with red tiles or flagstones and the new parlour would have a homemade rug upon it. There would be a new mantelpiece over the fireplace and upon it an ornament or two, probably a fairing of coloured earthenware from Staffordshire or even a wooden clock. If the family were prosperous enough, an extra bedroom might be added to the cottage.

But man's aesthetical enjoyment of beauty, whether natural or man-made, is not the whole picture of man whether considered as an individual or in a society. The wise saying goes on "The Spirit of man is a candle lit by God and leads to God".

Unless man has a code of ethics and moral standards by which to guide his living the result is personal mental breakdown or social anarchy among mankind. The acceptance of this code which is a response to the light of the God like a candle within him might be termed religion whether orthodox or not. Our land is nominally Christian with its ideals of brotherly love and our best laws are based upon time. Whether one believes in orthodox religion or not, it must be remembered that this Christian ethic has inspired great movements dedicated to the amelioration of human suffering. To mention but a few - Lord Shaftsbury responding to his Anglican religious experience worked tirelessly during his long life to free the women and children of Victorian England from the slavery of their factory lives. Later General Booth, inspired by Methodism, founded the Salvation Army to serve the poor and needy. In our own time Oxfam was founded during World War II by the Quakers to relieve famine and social needs wherever found in the world, while Mother Theresa, a Roman Catholic nun, was awarded a Nobel prize for her work among the 'poorest of the poor'.

It was in this post Reformation period that the finest dissident Protestant sects originated as they broke away from the established church - the Church of England, but before considering the difficulties that entailed, another quote from Trevelyan's book will establish what was the attitude of the average Englishman adhering to the established religion:

"There was much in common between the squire, the lawyer and the yeoman. They were all men of the new age, not hankering after feudal ideals now passing away. And they tended to become Protestant, alike from the interest and conviction. They evolved a kind of religion of the home, essentially 'middle class' and quite unmedieval.

The tendency of Protestant doctrine was to exalt the married state and dedicate the business life, in reaction against the medieval doctrine that the true life of 'religion' was celibacy and monastic separation from the world. The permission to marry, conceded to the clergy under Edward VI and Elizabeth, was one symptom of this change of thought. The religious home was the Protestant ideal, with family prayer and private Bible reading in addition to the services and sacraments of the Church. These ideas and practices were by no means confined to the dissident Puritans; in late Tudor and in Stuart times they were the practice of Anglican families who loved and fought for the Prayer book. The religion of the home and of the Bible became a social custom common to all English Protestants. It was found most often, perhaps in the households of squires, yeoman and tradesmen, but it was widely extended among the cottages of the poor".

In 1615 the most significant book in British history was published, the Authorised Version of the English Bible. Under King James it was to be used in every church in the land alongside the Book of Common Prayer. According to the law every person was to attend the services held in the Parish Churches while a new Bible was to be placed and chained there. It also had great literary significance for its beautiful prose was to influence English language for generations to come.

Being written in his native tongue, an ordinary person no longer needed a parson to read it to him and interpret it for him. As has been stated in a great many homes it was read aloud to the family. For a time the people almost became Bible mad. They were thrilled by the stories they read and heard. After a time they began to interpret the words for themselves and did not always agree with the interpretation they had heard from the village priest. It is not difficult to imagine how bitter religious controversy occured. Men began to take sides and this was one of the factors which eventually led to the Civil War. On one side were the fanatical Puritans headed by the Parliament and the King with his Catholic Queen and Cavaliers on the other. As has been seen during the Civil War the villagers suffered most when troops were billeted upon them. During the Commonwealth their simple pleasures like singing and dancing were denied them so that they welcomed the pleasure loving, diplomatically wise, King Charles II with open arms. The English revolution was over.

In its aftermath the candle upholding the light of true Christianity was almost extinguished during the next century in the Church of England.

A period of woeful neglect of the parish churches followed; yet it is just at such low periods in the religious history of mankind that men of burning vision are born. Their dedicated lives, as it were, focus the holy light so that it illuminates and inspires other men's souls for generations to come. This dark period was no exception.

In my opinion there were three outstanding men of vision in the religious field born in this period. Two of them visited our area and their ideals were to have a profound effect on the people living here. These three men were George Fox (1624-91) the founder of the Society of Friends known as Quakers, John Wesley (1703-91) the founder of the Methodist movement, and William Blake (1757-1827), the mystic poet and artist. The influence of William Blake is not so apparent but his tender lyrical poems, full of compassion for animals and the poor exploited children of industry, inspired the great Victorian reformers and can still haunt their readers today. This gentle soul scarcely ever left his London home but his words are heard every month in almost every village hall and once a year in the Albert Hall when members of the Women's Institutes raise their voices to sing "Jerusalem". Both George Fox and John Wesley kept journals in which they recorded their visits to our corner of Cleveland. We know how the people living here had the opportunity to hear both men as they preached in the market places at Guisborough and Stokesley.

George Fox was a remarkable man in every way. In appearance he was strong and wellbuilt with piercing but kindly grey eyes. His loud vibrant voice, ideal for preaching in the open air and clean, neat appearance always impressed. His leather breeches and tall steeple hat became famous. At the court of King Charles II where feathered hats gave a flourish to stately bows, he obstinately kept his tall hat firmly on his head, much to that merry monarch's amusement. When asked why he did so, he gave this famous reply to the King "In my view, brother Charles, all men are equal in the sight of God and it is to Him alone I doff my hat". The King recognised his sincerity and became his friend. While still a very young man, he felt impelled to wander through the fells of northern Derbyshire and southern Lancashire seeking to solve the riddle of life and find the light of God within himself. After many months spent in these silent places in contemplation he found what he sought - "the Light which hears" and in his illumination recognised that this same light burned

Printed with permission of Library Committee of Religious Society of Friends – London

Swarthmoor Hall, Cumbria in the 19th Century

The Society of Friends (Quakers) was founded here in 1651 under the protection of Judge Fell and his wife Margaret.

George Fox

within all men irrespective of race, colour, creed or sex. He was to spend the rest of his life preaching this then revolutionary doctrine. These ideas were welcomed by groups of 'Seekers' who had settled among the quiet fells of the Pennines in the Yorkshire - Lancashire border and it is here that the first meeting houses of the Society of Friends were founded. From these early Friends, the Quaker missionaries known as the "Valiant Sixty" set out leaving home and kinsfolk, fired with George Fox's burning zeal to face persecution and even death in spreading his teachings far and wide.

On one of their first journeys two of these missionaries visited Guisborough, soon after the Society of Friends was founded in 1650. A small group there formed a 'meeting' and as was his wont George Fox himself went there in 1651 to follow up their work. His account of his visit there at this time is given in his journal as follows:

"And the next day I passed to Cleveland amongst those people that had tasted of the power of God but were all shattered to pieces and the heads of them turned Ranters. Now they had had great meetings, so I told them after that they had had such meetings, they did not wait upon God to feel his presence and power and therein to sit and wait upon him, for they had spoken themselves dry and had spent their portions and not lived in that which they spoke and now they were dry. They had some kind of meetings but took tobacco and drank ale in them and so grew light and loose".

He remonstrated with them with this result:

"But the heads of them all came to nothing but most of the people convinced and received God's everlasting Truth and stand a meeting to this day and sit under the Lord Jesus Christ's teaching, their Saviour".

Having dealt with his own people he then went on to tackle the established church and its priest:

"And so, upon the First day after, the word of the Lord came to me to go to the steeplehouse; and so when the priest had done, I spoke the truth to him and the people and directed them to their teacher Christ Jesus, their free teacher that bought them. An so the priest came to me, with whom I had a little discourse, but he was soon stopped and silent, after which I passed away, having had several meetings amongst those people".

Having dealt with Guisborough he then went on to Stokesley. They apparently had no group of Friends there but again on the Sunday he went to the church - the steeplehouse - as he called it. One can imagine the excitement among the people this engendered:

"And I was moved to go to Stokesley steeplehouse and when the priest was done I spoke to him as I was moved and to the people the Truth of God and they were moderate and I let them see their true teacher and how that their teacher was found in the steps of the false teachers and how the Lord was come to teach his people himself and the light which Christ did enlighten withal they might come to it themselves and so by it come to Christ; so when we were gone out of the steeplehouse into the street, the priest sent for me to his house and I sent to him and bad him come into the street among the people to try his ministry and himself, and it was in the snow in the winter, and he did not come and so I passed away in the Truth that reached in all hearts".

So in our mind's eye we see this tall wellbuilt young man of twenty six clad in a fine suit of leather, ignoring the snow and stormy weather as he confidently strides along the country lanes and over the wild moors. He visits the villages finding a welcome there among the common people and on a Sunday morning attending the village church to debate with the priest. He delivers his message and at quite a number of places meetings are established to be visited later.

Not only did he always speak out on purely religious matters for in this account of his visit to Staithes, which followed his visits to Guisborough and Stokesley we find the beginnings of the well-known Quaker concern with social justice:

"And then I went to the steeplehouse where was a high priest that did much oppress the people with tithes. And when I spoke unto him, he fled away after I had laid his oppressing of the people upon him. For if the people went a hundred miles off a-fishing, he would make them pay the tithe money, though they caught the fish at such a distance and carried the fish to Yarmouth to sell.

But the word of the Lord stuck with some of them so that at night some of the heads of the parish came to me and were most of them convinced and satisfied and confessed the truth. So the Truth began to spread up and down the country and great meetings we had".

In his journal Fox records that he again visited Cleveland after his visit to the county of Durham in 1658. Later as the persecution of the Quakers became intense he records how he kept in touch with the groups of Monthly Meetings here by sending letters and messengers. Following his first visit in 1651 a Meeting was settled in Guisborough under John Whitehead and the Quakers met in each others houses. By 1687 there was greater religious tolerance everywhere and the Quakers were able to buy a place of their own in Westgate although their Monthly Meeting had been recognised since 1669. Similar groups were established in Stokesley and Great Ayton about this time. A survey carried out by Archbishop Skelton in 1669 records a Monthly Meeting held at Stokesley in its lists of groups or conventicles that do not conform to the Church of England. No less than thirty seven Quaker Meetings were recognised in Yorkshire at this early date.

Before the Act of Tolerance in 1689, the Quakers were made the objects of a great deal of public abuse and persecution. They were brought before the Magistrates for non-payment of tithes to the Church. In the court they refused to remove their hats before speaking to the bench and refused to take the oath. This was regarded as an insult to the State, for which crime they were first heavily fined and later put in prison where many of them died. In all George Fox, himself, spent six years in prison. His worst experience was the two years 1664-1666 which he spent in foul conditions, first in Lancaster Castle and then he was removed to Scarborough Castle. It must have been a very traumatic experience for him, for he describes his imprisonment in great detail and the journey between the two places., As he rode with his guards on the long journey, he was so physically weak that he could scarcely sit on his horse. At first his treatment at Scarborough Castle was very bad. In his journal he describes his plight as being "as a man buried alive, in a damp cold room exposed to the wind, the sea and the rain" where "the water came over my bed and ran about the room, that I was fain to skim it up with a platter". Famous people came to dispute with him but no Friends were allowed to see him or bring him comforts. Yet no hardship could break his spirit or make him lose his composure. Instead he won for himself the love and esteem of his goalers and the governor of the castle, Sir Jordan Crosland. Not only was he properly housed within the castle but when the governor was obliged to go to London on Business, he tried to use his influence to procure George Fox's release. When he found that he could only be released on the orders of the King himself, George Fox wrote to His Majesty. After a time the order for release came from the King. It was brought by no other than John

115

Whitehead, the Guisborough Quaker. The journal continues the story as follows:

"So the governor received the order and the officers gathered together and discharged me and gave me a certificate as follows:

Permit the bearer thereof, George Fox, late a prisoner in
Scarborough Castle and now discharged by His Majesty's order, quietly to pass about the lawful occasions, without any molestation.
Given under my hand at Scarborough Castle this first day of September 1666.
J. Crosland, Governor of Scarborough Castle.

And I would have given the governor something for his civilty but he would not receive anything, and said, whatever good he could do to my friends he would do it and never do them any hurt and so he remained to do till he died.

And when the mayor of the town sent to him for soldiers to break up Friends Meetings, if he sent any down he would charge them not to meddle, but remained loving till he died".

Later George was to meet his friend again. In 1669 he visited the Meetings in Yorkshire with Margaret Fell, now his wife, and the journal records:

"And when I came into Scarborough the governor heard that I was to come to town and sent to me by one of his soldiers, and said surely I would not be so unkind as not to come to see him and his wife. So after meeting was done I went up to visit him and he was very courteous and loving".

Before leaving the subject of early Quakerism mention must be made of the early evidence we have of it locally. One feature of their faith was that they preferred to be buried in their own burial grounds and many of these have survived. Sometimes a farmhouse was licenced as a Quaker Meeting House and the one at Stokesley known as Quaker's Grove had a burial ground with tombstone attached to it until recently. At Broughton also was a farm called the Grange, licenced in the same way. The Quakers loved the quiet secluded places where they could pursue their silent worship undisturbed so today there are burial grounds to be found at Castleton, Lealholm, Bilsdale, Liverton, Moorsholm as well as those in use at Guisborough and Great Ayton. The Meeting House nearest to Nunthorpe is at Great Ayton and it has a very long history. Immediately after the Act of Toleration was passed in 1689 a meeting house at Ayton was certified to the Justices at Thirsk. The present Meeting House was built in 1700 and rebuilt on the same site in 1722. The Quakers believed fervently in education. Many Quaker schools were founded and still prosper today in numbers and standards. There are three prominent Yorkshire ones at Ackworth, York and Great Ayton.

Alec Wright, the local historian of Stokesley, who died in 1981 commented "Although Quakerism had declined in the twentieth century, it is still a vital force for good throughout the world".

With this statement I agree entirely, not only in material terms but in the basically more important realm of ideas.

The principles promoted by Fox and his early followers are still at work in the heart of man today. These principles are not now proclaimed in the market places but take the form of mass demonstrations by people seeking to embarrass governments into action or the quiet establishment of an alternative method of living.

Among such are:

1) The Peace Movement - for three hundred years a firm commitment by the Quakers - reconciliation at all levels rather than war and conflict. Many conscientious objectors in many countries have died in prison for this principle. Yet Quaker pacificism does not conflict with their humanitarian principles for Quaker Ambulance teams served the wounded on all sides of the conflict in both world wars. Oxfam, one of the largest and most influential charities of this country began as a result of Quaker concern in Oxford at the plight of the Greek villagers under German occupation in World War II.

2) Anti-Racist Movement. True Christians everywhere recognise that all men are equal in the sight of God, a principle proclaimed by George Fox which roused such fierce opposition from Church and State during the seventeenth century Yet even today in spite of great international organisations like the United Nations, in our multi-racial society, difficulties arise in its application at the grass roots of society.

3) Meditation. In the tense, busy world of today more and more people are turning to the peace and relaxation of meditation, such as that which has been practiced in the East for centuries. A seeking of "peace within" is surely a prelude to seeking "peace without". This is also leading to a mutual appreciation of people of differing traditions all seeking to find the One True God. Is this not truly a reflection of the Quaker "silent worship" which so puzzled Fox's contempories?

4) Spiritual Healing and Holistic Living. George Fox himself was a spiritual healer and many of his cures are recorded in his journal as well as spiritual healing meetings. Throughout the Christian Churches there is now a revival of interest in spiritual healing as people become disillusioned by the constant use of drugs. The simple way of life of the early Quakers with its insistence on cleanliness and a wholesome diet, eschewing tobacco and ale reflects the "nature cure" movement of today. George Fox recognised that mind, body and spirit must work in harmony if good health were to be maintained, which is the principle behind today's Holistic Living. Completely contrary to the spirit of his time he advocated that there should be homes for the mentally ill. The average seventeenth century citizen was bewildered by Fox's ideas but his principle of complete integrity in all business dealings he could understand and appreciate. The Quakers soon established a reputation of complete trustworthiness. A Quaker was a man whose "Nay" was "Nay" and his "Yea" was "Yea". This brought them respect and prosperity, although after a time, this same prosperity led many to desert the Quaker way of life in the later eighteenth century. What a revolution it would be in the world were this principle followed universally in business and politics in this twentieth century!

(Extracts from Fox's journal taken from Guisborough before 1900).

Now let us turn to John Wesley, the founder of Methodism. He too came and preached in Stokesley and Guisborough almost a century later and caused a great stir. On the whole he was ignored by the gentry of the area but they may have been among the crowds listening as was Ralph Jackson, the diarist, who records hearing him in Guisborough:

"General Hale invited me to go with him to hear Rev. John Wesley preach extempore for half and hour - an excellent and effective discourse".

Wesley was then an old man of eighty five and it was his last visit in 1788. George Fox had found his followers among the yeomen farmers, the craftsmen and small business men who had sufficient education to read their Bibles and speak and think for themselves. John Wesley, living a century later in a very different cultural and religious climate appealed to the labourers, factory workers and small shopkeepers living in towns and country villages caught up in the Industrial Revolution. They listened to his simple message gladly. They might not all be able to read or write but they built chapels for him and in them sang with joy the beautiful hymns written by his brother, Charles which we still sing today. John Wesley was born in 1703 and died in 1791 so that his life spanned the eighteenth century and he saw the whole landscape transformed as he travelled the length and breadth of the country. He saw villagers with their families forced to migrate to overcrowded towns to earn a living and often live in miserable conditions. He was an ordained minister of the Church of England but he lived in an irreligious age. He saw his vocation was to go out to the people and minister to them in love and hope, by giving them God's message in a language they could understand. His indomitable spirit and deep religious faith gave to his preaching an irresistible appeal to all who heard him. Unlike George Fox and his early followers the new Methodists did not suffer cruel persecution and imprisonment but were nevertheless regarded as non-conformists and therefore with suspicion by the authorities. The people gathered in crowds whenever and wherever John Wesley preached. They would even gather to hear him before they went to work at five o'clock in the morning, The records in the journal show that one morning while visiting a village on the Yorkshire coast, he preached a sermon to people assembled on the sea-shore at 4.30am at their own request. The night before he had preached there on a "warm still evening to a multitude of people as the sun was setting". It was almost a Biblical setting reminiscent of his Master.

For fifty two years John Wesley journeyed up and down the country on long preaching missions. Our part of the country seems to have been one of his favourite haunts. He went to Yarm no less than nineteen times. When he went there Stokesley and Hutton Rudby at first and later Guisborough were included in his itinerary many times. There is no record of his preaching on the Green at Ayton, though he must have passed through many times.

He had special friends with whom he used to stay while in the area. His first visit to the district was in 1745 at the invitation of Mr Adams of Osmotherley, with whom he stayed on all the subsequent visits. In his journal he states that he and his host arrived back from Northallerton between nine and ten in the evening. On their arrival they were met by a crowd gathered to hear him preach and again he was preaching to them at 5am in the morning. He wrote of his hearers "many of them I found either were or had been Papists. Here am I brought without any care or thought of mine into the centre of the Papists in Yorkshire". He came again to Osmotherley in September and October the same year and visited Mount Grace Priory. Two years later he was back and with the approval of the vicar he preached in the Parish Church. But when he returned six weeks later he was not allowed to preach in the Church for the Anglican authorities had not approved of his preaching there.

Another favourite house was the home of Mr Merryweather at 17 High St, Yarm. While visiting there he was seen by a little girl who later described him as wearing a black cassock, black silk stockings and shoes with silver buckles. He travelled to Yarm in a lumbering old coach which had a bookcase inside it. Some of the earliest local preachers were attached to the first chapel founded there. John Wesley's first visit to Yarm was in 1748 but not till 28th November 1752 did he come to Stokesley where he preached "not without many threatenings from the authorities". He went on to Hutton Rudby, then a large prosperous village with several textile mills. Thereafter his visits to Stokesley were almost biennial until his last visit in 1790 at the age of eighty seven. The congregation at the chapel only built up slowly, unlike that of Hutton Rudby but when he visited Stokesley in 1784 he was able to write in his journal that he found "the word of God at Stokesley more livelier than it had been for many years". It is thought that he used to stand on a small stool for preaching, for one was left behind by him in the square at Stokesley and is now in the John Wesley Museum.

He did not visit Guisborough until 1759, that is seven years after first visiting Stokesley. A glance at a road map of the time will suggest the reason. On leaving his friends in Osmotherley to go to Yarm he could travel as far as the Tontine Inn where by taking the right fork of the road he could proceed to Stokesley and Hutton Rudby. Having finished his visiting and preaching in these places he could re-join the good turnpike road to Yarm. His method seems to have been to preach to the people of a town or village and when a number had been converted, form them into a "meeting" from which a church could be built up. Subsequent regular visits gave them help and encouragement. When he felt they were well established he would then visit another area and do the same.

On his first visit to Guisborough he noted that he preached "to a lovely congregation in a meadow near the town". Wesleyan Methodism there began a year later when a group of believers made a declaration signed by twelve members to meet in the house of Thomas Corney. Two years after his first visit John Wesley gave this account in his journal of his next visit:

"Monday June 22 1761 - Rode on to Guisborough. The sun was burning hot, but in a quarter of an hour a cloud interposed and it troubled us no more. I was desired by a gentleman of the town to preach in the market place; and there was a table placed for me but it was in a bad neighbourhood; for there was so vehement a stench of stinking fish as was ready to suffocate me and the people roared like the waves of the sea; but the voice of the Lord was mightier and in a few minutes the whole multitude was still and seriously attended while I proclaimed "Jesus Christ" made of us God unto us wisdom and righteousness and sanctification and redemption". It should be noted that he would be standing not far from where the Market Cross in Guisborough now stands and near the old tollbooth which was on the site of the Town Hall. Here were the fish shambles which on a warm summer's day before the days of refrigeration, would indeed smell.

From Guisborough where he probably changed horses he extended his mission to Whitby and the coastal towns and villages, travelling in his 'lumbering coach', or riding alone, either along the coast road or over the moors. What a tiring shaky journey it must have been along those rough roads and up and down those long steep hills whichever way he went! He came many times to Guisborough as in 1774 when he records:

"In Guisborough I was constrained to preach abroad and the whole multitude was as silent as the subject - death. I never before had such an opportunity at the place. In the afternoon through miserable roads we at length got to Whitby".

Guisborough Market Place 1762

John Wesley first preached at Guisborough Market Cross on June 22nd 1762. It was a hot day and in his Journal he complains that "there was so vehement a stench of stinking fish as was ready to suffocate me". The picture shows the building which was "The Cock Inn" where Ralph Ward Jackson used to meet his cronies. It is now the Bank shown on the right hand of the picture. It's imposing doorway and the archway leading to a yard show it once to have been a inn.

All Saints Church, Great Ayton

A sketch of the interior of the old church at Great Ayton showing the boxed pews and three-decker pulpit. This is the Church of the Rev. Ralph Jackson who gave his report on the parish in 1743. He would preach here but not from this pulpit for the church was not fully restored till 1788 by the Marwood family.

He had amazing vitality even in old age, for in 1786 and 1788 when eighty five years of age he records:

"At eight I preached to a lively congregation at Stokesley with much liberty of spirit and at Guisborough to one far larger and equally attentive. In the evening I preached at Whitby in the new house, thoroughly filled above and below".

Two years later he came again to Stokesley for the last time on Friday 18th June. But, even his iron constitution was beginning to crack under the strain, for only ten days later, he wrote this sad entry in his journal:

"This day I enter my 88th year. For above 86 years I found none of the infirmities of my old age; my eyes did not wax dim, neither was my natural strength abated. But last August I found almost a sudden change; my eyes were so dim that no glasses could help me. My strength likewise quite forsook me and probably will not return in this world; but I feel no pain from head to foot, only it seems nature is exhausted and humanly speaking, will sink more and more, till the weary springs of life stand still at last".

He died the next year.

John Wesley was in essence a simple sincere man, carrying out his vital God-given mission with power and humility based on service and helped greatly by the genius of his equally humble, quiet brother Charles, the hymn writer. He had no idea that he was founding a world-wide movement which would be a great power for good in the coming centuries. Nowadays in Britain it has lost a great deal of its support especially among the so called "lower classes" but it should be remembered that when General Booth founded his Salvation Army he was first inspired by a splinter group of the Methodists called the "New Connection" in late Victorian times. Along with other non-conformist churches like the Baptists, it was taken to the United States where it took root and has greatly influenced the development of the towns and villages there, especially in the Middle West.

In 1953 at the time of the Coronation it came as a surprise to learn that the popular Queen Salote of Tonga was an ardent Methodist. When Queen Elizabeth and Prince Philip visited her son, now King of that remote island they were invited to a service in the large Wesleyan Church there and heard the children and congregation sing the familiar hymns of Charles Wesley. The man whose inspired preaching began all this, came many times to this area to give his message to the people living where we live now. Within him the candle lit by God did indeed shine brightly and its light literally reached the ends of the earth.

In the 18th century all people were bound by law to attend the Church of England services. Tithes were imposed on all property for the upkeep of the state church. Those who for reasons of conscience did not conform were termed recusants and a strict watch was kept on their activities by the ecclesiastical authorities. Besides the Roman Catholics, Quakers and Methodists already mentioned there were also Baptists, Congregationalists (at first called Independents) and Presbyterians also active in the area. As early as 1653 in Stokesley the first Calvinistic Baptist Community in Yorkshire was founded. The leader was William Kaye who was baptised there along with nineteen others. In 1702 the Presbyterians met at the house of Mr John Coulson of Newby. Earlier at Ayton Hall, a Scots Presbyterian minister was chaplain to the Lord of the Manor during the Commonwealth (1649-1660) and served the first Presbyterians to be gathered there. In 1743 a Presbyterian meeting house was built in the grounds. Though no longer used for religious purposes the building can still be seen there.

The Independent or Congregational Society was active in Guisborough at the end of the 18th century, their first meeting under the care of a lay preacher being in 1802. By 1811 they were sufficiently well established to build the small Ebenezer Chapel in Westgate. Though much modified it still serves the Guisborough Congregationalists and Presbyterians, now united under the name of the United Reformed Church. It is Guisborough's oldest Chapel.

To the authorities of the Established Church our area must have seemed to be a hot bed of dissension - or was it simply a symptom of the basic independent spirit of the typical Yorkshireman?

Now what effect was all this likely to have on the Nunthorpe and Marton villagers? The truth is, probably not very much. Of course they would be there in the crowds listening to what the visiting preachers had to say and expressing their opinions about what they heard. Like the Archers of fictional Ambridge, farmers are notoriously conservative (both with a large and a small C!) in their outlook. They would attend church every Sunday and the beliefs of others would be a matter for comment in pub and home. In any case they had an absentee landlord and he was a dissenter himself!

How necessary was the missionary work of Charles Wesley and the other non-conformists is revealed in a document which has come down to us. It is a report dated 1743 on the parish of Ayton West (which included Nunthorpe) made before the expected visit of Archbishop Herring's representative when he was making an ecclesiastical survey, being just before Wesley's first visit to Osmotherley in 1745. It is quoted in its entirety because it reveals so many interesting aspects of church life at this time and will be of particular interest to those familiar with church life now.

Ayton (West)   Cleveland

I   We have in our parish one hundred and forty families; seven of which are Dissenters; three Presbyterians of Non-conformists and four Quakers.

II   We have two licensed Meeting Houses in our parish; one a Presbyterian Meeting House, the other a Quaker Meeting House, both of which sort of Dissenters assemble once every week. Mr Andrew Porteous teaches in ye Presbyterian House. None among ye Quakers but Travellers.

III   There is one Public School in our Parish, and generally twenty or thirty children are taught in it. Due care is taken to instruct them in the principles of ye Christian Religion - according to ye Doctrine of ye Church of England. They are duly brought to ye Church, as ye Canon requires.

IV   There is not in our Parish, any Alms-House, Hospital or other Charitable Endowment, nor any land for ye Repair to our Church or to any other Pious Use.

V   We have no Rector or Vicar in this Parish; The Glebe Lands, Houses, Orchard Gardens, Tythes etc are all invested in the Hands of Chomley Turner Esq Impropriator.

VI   As I am ye Residing Curate, I am duly qualified according to ye Canons in yt. behalf. I do not live in ye Parsonage House. The allowance made me is Thirteen pounds, six shillings and eight pence yearly.

VII   I do not know of any who come to our Church yet are not Baptised or that being Baptised and of a

Competent Age are not confirmed, only those who design to offer themselves for Confirmation at Stokesley.

VIII The Public Service is read in our Church twice every week, once every Lord's Day and once on Wednesdays. The Curacy is so very inconsiderable. I am obliged to attend to another small Curacy to maintain myself and family.

IX I only Catechise during ye Season of Lent, Sundays and Wednesdays. None of ye Parishioners refuse to send their children or servants to be instructed.

X The sacrament of the Lord's supper is administered five times every year; we have in our parish two hundred and twenty four Communicants; about fifty or sixty usually receive. One hundred and two received Easter Last.

XI I give open and timely warning of ye sacrament before it is administered. The parishioners do not give in their names as not being Customary in this place. I have not refused ye sacrament to anyone.

Ralph Jackson
Curate of Ayton
Univ. of Edinburgh M.A.

C.W. (Churchwardens)   Nicholas Richardson
William Cotham.

(A note at the bottom is added evidently at a later date)

Presented for fornication - C.D. - bastard child. Excomd. 29th July 1744, pardoned 13th Aug. 1744, confessed the crime with A.B. and did penance.
In a similar document concerning another parish, Osmotherley is this report:

Presented for Ante-Nuptual Fornication - A.B. with C.D. (his wife) they did penance.

It is thought that the other small curacy to which this poor curate administered was the chapel in Nunthorpe Hall. Elsewhere it is stated that the fee for this was £10 per annum paid by the Roman Catholic Pierson family who owned it.

On reading this official report, no doubt reactions will differ, but all must feel great sympathy for that poor sincere man, loved by his parishioners and yet so exploited. The exploitation is embodied in the word "Impropriator". The dictionary definition of impropriate is "to place tithes ecclesiastical property in lay hands". Before the Reformation the payment of tithes was in ecclesiastical hands but the owner of a piece of land or village could grant their payment to a monastery. Thus the tithes from the land in Nunthorpe owned by the Meinhill family of Whorlton Castle in the 12th century were granted to Whitby Abbey. After the dissolution of the monasteries the right to the tithes being paid by a village through the parish church could be purchased. Then the "impropriator" and his heirs were responsible for the cost of running the church and the salaries of the clergy. This system did not cease altogether till 1936.

In this case their impropriator was Mr Chomley Turner who lived at Kirkleatham Hall. He had married Jane Marwood of Busby Hall near Stokesley. She was the only child and heiress to the estate which traditionally held the impropriatorship of the parish of Ayton. So it passed to her husband. In this year of 1743 he was a very unhappy man for his only son William Marwood Turner had died while away from his home doing "the grand tour" in Italy. In his memory his grieving parents rebuilt the church at Kirkleatham with its famous

Mausoleum. This couple were made further unhappy when their only daughter eloped with a Dutch officer who had billeted at the Hall during the 1745 Jacobite Rebellion. She was promptly disinherited but eventually her descendants inherited the property. When Chomley Turner died his brother and heir erected a life sized marble statue of him in the church, and beneath is a long epitaph in the manner of the period extolling his virtues. Whatever may have been his merits the parishioners of Ayton had little to thank him for. When great renovation of the church at the end of the century took place, it was in the hands of the Marwood family of Busby Hall. No wonder Jane Austin writing at the end of the 18th century made Mr Collins, the curate in "Pride and Prejudice" so obsequious to his patroness! It must be also pointed out that in contrast to the beautiful alms-houses built by the Turner family at Kirkleatham still standing, in Ayton there was no provision for the sick, the poor or the aged at all.

The educational facilities as revealed in this document were very meagre. The one school referred to is The Postgate School built in 1704 and endowed for eight poor boys, the rest of the twenty to thirty paying a small fee. How fortunate was James Cook to have had the opportunity of attending here! The master taught the boys reading, writing and arithmetic while religious instruction was given by the curate.

In view of the great interest and support for the Quaker movement in the century before, it is surprising to find that there were in 1743 only four Quaker families living in the district. It is true that their activities too were at a low ebb and ripe for the reforms which came later.

In spite of his lack of a vicarage and his poverty, Rev. Ralph Jackson, the curate seems to not only have carried out his duty with due care but to have won the love and respect of his parishioners for they supported him well. Out of his flock of one hundred and thirty three families, one hundred and two received Communion on Easter Sunday. As is tradition of the church that the clergyman receives for himself the Easter collection, one hopes that the prosperous farmers and their wives gave generously. Although Rev. Ralph Jackson would not benefit, the financial situation of these poor parsons did improve towards the end of the century when in 1774 a grant was paid from a national fund known as Queen Anne's Bounty. With it a piece of land of about five acres on Easby Lane was purchased, the rent from which went to the curate of Ayton parish.

The life of a curate in a country parish like Ayton must have been a very lonely one. The bishop never came to the parish, the nearest visit being to Stokesley where he held the confirmations. Even the curate's institution into his new parish was held at York. The neglect of parochial care continued in Ayton later in the 18th century for the Rev. Ralph Jackson's successor, Anthony Hastwell, was only a young deacon. He appears to have run the parish and administered communion from 1756 although he was not ordained or instituted till 1761. He served the parish for almost forty years and so would be able to play his part and enjoy the revival in both spiritual and material terms which resulted in the restoration of the church in 1788-90.

Before going on to examine that restoration there are two more items shown in this document of 1743 which are of interest, the implication of the moral note added later and the position in the parish of the churchwardens. The note said:

"Presented for fornication C.D. bastard child. Excomd 29th July 1744, pardoned 13th Aug 1744, confessed the crime with A.B. and did penance".

The couple evidently left Ayton and possibly went to his home village where they were married. That, however did not let them off the hook for there is this note in the record of the parish of Osmotherley: "Presented for Ante-Nuptual Fornication - A.B. with C.D. his wife, they did penance". Now what did being "presented" and "doing penance" for misdemeanours mean? In the "Stokesley Selection" this is explained. The sinner had to attend Sunday morning service and stand in front of the congregation. He had to be "bareheaded, barefoot and bare legged, having a white sheet wrapped around him from the shoulders to the feet and a white wand in his hand and stand upon a form, before the pulpit" and say a long prayer of contrition. What was meant by "presentation" and how did this piece of church administration work at parish level. In his own inimitable way Roland Parker tells us in his book "The Common Stream"

"If this and other villages in the neighbourhood had little sympathy for the Crown, they had even less for the Church. For this the church itself was largely to blame. I do not mean the parson. No, the trouble was with the Archdeacon, backed by the Bishop, vigorously striving to maintain ecclesiastical control over matters which in many cases ought really to have been left to the individual consciences and common sense of the villagers. The result was a constant niggling, backbiting., prying into private affairs, which did not raise moral standards one little bit, rather the reverse. The churchwardens joined in the witch hunt, if only to save their face and divert official structure for themselves. Then as the churchwardens had their hands pretty full with looking after the more mundane affairs of the village, two inquisitors were appointed whose specific duty was to spy out and report the moral and religious shortcomings of their neighbours".

Then he gives some examples of the kind of sins these villagers committed and for which they were "presented" from the Visitation records of his area. For example:

William Yule has not received communion for a year and more.

Elizabeth Owsten of Foxton is vehemently reported to be with child.

Mr Meade was presented for not receiving the Communion at Easter.

Mr Brampton (vicar) was presented "for not catechizing our servants and our children neither have we any minister resident in our parish".

Edward Lithell of Melbourn was presented "for being at Foxton Fayre on the Sabath daye".

"Neither the vicar nor his curate do use the Clokes appointed for them".

Nicholas Campion presented "for carting upon Hallowmas daye".

Thomas Adleson presented for "suffering of play in his house ye 29 December being Sunday".

But this reveals a most unseemly row in church:

"Mistress Meade was presented for going out of the church two Sundays together and being called back by the minister shaked her hands at him and spoke some contemptuous speech against him and so went away".

Roland Parker concluded this section on presentation in his book by telling an anecdote about one Valentine Phipps, a notorious character of the village of Foxton in the 17th century:

"It was inevitable that sooner or later Valentine Phipps should find himself in an unholy rumpus. It came in 1638 when, under the influence of drink, he addressed one of the churchwardens, George Wells, as a "base rogue, a base rascal and whoaremasterly rogue". That is what Wells said he said, I doubt whether the whole of Phipps' speech was reported. Phipps was charged with absenting himself from the church on

thirteen consecutive Sundays and holy days, and that he was seen "riding upon horseback on the Sunday towards St. Ives market to buy Cattell". When told that he would be reported to the Archdeacon he answered that it was his trade and added "I care not a turde for Dr Eden and his court. No right minded person could condone the behaviour of a drunkard who did fall off his bed, most beastly spew, defile and bewray himself". But it soon became evident that many people in the village shared Phipp's views on ecclesiastical authority".

It must be remembered that before the Industrial Revolution at the end of the 18th century England was a land of villages and each parish responsible for its own affairs. The average villager during his whole lifetime did not often go beyond the boundaries of his next parish and so the authority of the parish officials were of great concern to him. If in Ayton, for example, he were to get drunk and behave in a disorderly fashion, he could find himself locked up in the Round House which was situated at the Stokesley end of the old Ayton Bridge or be put in the stocks to be mocked at and pelted with rubbish. If one of his animals strayed, it could be put in the village pound and he could not get it back without paying a fee. If he tried to get it back himself or refused to pay the fee, he could face a serious fine. The overseeing of all these bye-laws was part of the duties of the parish officials. No doubt in the absence of any newspapers and other media, their doings and the doings of everybody else in the village were of interest to those gathered round the village pump or in the churchyard after morning worship on a Sunday.

Collectively these officials met as a group known as the Vestry and were elected by the villagers every Easter. Let us turn once more to the document giving details of the parish of Ayton in 1743. The document is signed not only by the curate but also by the churchwardens. In the mid eighteenth century their position was very different from their purely ecclesiastical status of today. Roland Parker in his book "The Common Stream" gives a very lively account of the function of the churchwardens and other village officials at this time:

"Norminally the affairs of the parish were under the control of the Vestry (elected at an annual meeting of the villagers each Easter). In practice all the work was done by a mere handful of men, answerable to the Vestry for some of their actions, to the Justices of the Peace and the Chief Constable for the rest. These parish officials did not make the laws; they simply carried them out, but in such circumstances that it often appeared to the villagers that they WERE the law. When one considers that a great deal of what nowadays is done by Parish Council, Rural District Council, County Councils and Government Departments was in the eighteenth century done by a few unpaid local officials in every parish, one cannot escape the thought that those officials must have been men of outstanding qualities. And I believe they were. They were honest, public spirited, thrifty, hard working, hard headed, hard hearted or compassionate as the circumstances demanded, conscientious, shrewd good fellows. Not all of them all the time, but most of them, most of the time. They were not necessarily men of education. So long as two of their number could read and write and do simple arithmetic on paper, then they could manage the clerical side of their business and do it with and economy of paper work which modern administrators might well envy or emulate.

Their paper work in fact consisted of one single book, in which they wrote their accounts from time to time, page by page until the book was filled. One such volume, only one, of the Overseers and Churchwardens Accounts for Foxton (his village) has survived. It covers the period from 1770 to 1795".

Great Ayton parish is more fortunate for as Dan O'Sullivan in his book "Great Ayton" records the Great Ayton Churchwardens Accounts for the eighteenth and nineteenth centuries are kept at the County Record Office in Northallerton. This is no small measure due to the Rev. Robert Kettlewell who had the first volume in 1734-44 bound at his own expense in 1937 and who researched them for his book "Cleveland Village". The entries are short and cryptic but with a little imagination a great deal of information about the village life at that time emerges. It was the Elizabeth Poor Law which set up this system which would operate with two churchwardens, two overseers and a constable, assisted by a surveyor of highways or waywarden. All were voluntary posts. The churchwardens were responsible for the maintenance of public buildings such as the church (and later the school) the stocks and Round House. With the overseers they administered poor relief and the care of orphans. The problem of vagrants was a thorny one, not easy to administer justice with compassion. Each parish was responsible for its poor for which a Poor Rate was levied. If for example a poor young woman with her child wandered into the parish looking for her husband she could not be allowed to stay to be a burden on the rates of that village. It was the constable's duty to see that she was moved on the next day.

The post of a constable was a very unpopular one and needed coersion for anyone to do it for a minimum of a year. How difficult it must have been to put a neighbour in the stocks or the Round House for being drunk and disorderly or forcing a poor man to pay a fine when releasing his straying cow from the village pound! Yet there is evidence that these poor "willing horses" serving the parish sometimes enjoyed themselves at the parish's expense. For example at the time when according to Rev. Ralph Jackson's report communion was only celebrated five times during the year, there is this item in the Great Ayton account book, typical of others:

"1734 26 quarts of wine got at John Burdon £2-3-4d".

Each year a considerable sum of money was spent on the Costs of the Visitation and this included a dinner with ale for those attending. The company included the parish clerk and the sidesmen from Nunthorpe and Little Ayton.

April 29
To 5 Diners at Visitation   12s.6d.
Lickor and the waters   £1-13s.6d.

Towards the end of the 18th century the church authorities everywhere awoke to their responsibilities and a wave of religious fervour swept over the country. In the 1770's when the countryside was prosperous civic pride was aroused and the parish churches whose fabric had scarcely been touched since Tudor times were strenuously restored. Nowhere is it more so evident than in the Cleveland area. The old Saxon church of All Saints was gutted to give it a typical Georgian interior in 1790 by the Marwood family and its parishioners. The walls were plastered and colour-washed ready for the marble memorial plaques. One of these with its white square base and triangular black ornamentation on the top is to commemorate Captain Wilson, the explorer friend of Captain Cook. A three-decker pulpit with sounding board was built and the font given the then fashionable pyramidical cover. Typical Georgian box pews were put in and at the west end of the church a musicians gallery supported by round columns. Here the musicians would play their instruments such as violins, a cello and wind instruments such as a clarinet and trumpet. While with them would sit the choir. When the congregation were singing they would turn round to face the band and choir. According to Ruth Gaudie in "A Visual History of Great Ayton":

"In 1858 the choir felt they were too conspicuous and consequently some brass rods were set upon the gallery front, with red curtains suspended from them.

The first organ was presented to the church in 1840 by John Rigg of Manchester, who is reputed to have originated in Ayton. This organ was designed to play certain tunes by means of turning a handle, in barrel organ style. However some of the tunes were considered by the vicar, Rev. J. Ibbotson to be too lively so he had a new set put in. In 1856 another organ was presented to the church by Mr Marwood of Busby".

The gallery was reached by a flight of outside steps and a door breached in the north wall. During a later restoration the gallery with its outside steps and pillars were removed but there is a photograph in the church to show what they were like. The singers each had their own candles and the church would be lit at night by Georgian type candelabra. The outside appearance of the church was greatly changed when the coloured medieval windows were removed and plain round-headed sash windows were put in known as "Cleveland Churchwarden". A church tower was built in 1788 but demolished when a Victorian restoration took place a century later.

Another larger church to be transformed in this way was Stokesley Parish Church in 1771 and Alec Wright, the local historian, who lived in Stokesley left us this comment upon it:
"*The appearance of the new building followed the style of many other Cleveland churches then undergoing a wave of "restoration" or rather desecration, since named "Churchwarden Gothic". The interior walls were plastered and colour-washed; there would be large box pews bearing the owner's names, tall round-headed windows, filled with small paned, heavily sashed, plain clear glass, probably a three-decker pulpit and the Commandments and Lord's Prayer painted on large wall boards for all to read, learn, mark and digest".*

With the revival of church building went a revival of interest in spiritual matters and the low period for the Anglicans at church and the Quakers in their Meeting House passed.

One feature of Ayton village life has been the harmony which has always existed amongst the various religious sects. With the coming of the Industrial Revolution came the Quaker industrialists and a great influx of people which in turn led to the founding of the Great Ayton Quaker School and the building of the new parish church of Christ Church. But their stories belong to Victorian times and the next part of this book.

Before continuing the story of this area of Cleveland into modern times let us take a backward glance at it through the eyes of two very early writers - William Camden who came in 1695 who may have met some of the people whose inventories we studied and the other a friend of John Graves, the Cleveland historian of Yarm, visiting almost exactly a hundred years later. Each of them did the traditional thing and climbed Roseberry Topping to admire the view. The mountain would have been a little higher for them, being before the landslide which spoiled the conical shape. Each was duly impressed and wrote about the experience.

William Camden wrote:

"*Next Ounesberry Topping; a steep mountain and all over green, riseth so high as to appear at a great distance; and it is the landmark that directs sailors and a prognostic of weather to the neighbours thereabouts; for when its top begins to be darkened with clouds, rain generally follows. Near the top of it there issues from a huge rock a fountain very good for sore eyes and from hence the grassy hills, green meadows, rich pastures, fruitful cornfields, rivers full of fish, the creeky mouth of the Tees, shores low and open, yet free from inundation and the sea with ships under sail rendered the prospect very agreeable and entertaining".*

Writing in his "History of Cleveland" published in 1808 Graves gives this account of an excursion up Roseberry Topping by a party of his friends:

"After a tedious labour of near an hour up the steep ascent, we reached the rocky summit from whence the most entrancing prospect opened to our view. Before lay extended the beautiful vale of Cleveland, with the county of Durham, woods, meadows and cornfields, interspersed with views of rural villages, farms and gentlemen's seats, some of which by their whiteness gave an animating gaiety to the scene. The River Tees is seen winding through the valley with stately ships on its bosom, which give additional beauty and variety to the prospect. To the east we had the first view of the sea, covered with ships, whose glittering sails, now fully bosomed to the wind, now eddying to the breeze, formed various shades, contrasted by the sunbeams as they stood in different directions to the enraptured sight. To the south the prospect is bounded by a chain of hills rising behind each other in towering height, which seem to vie in lofty majesty with that on which we stood; the whole composing such a scene of beauty and sublime grandeur as can seldom be found united in one view........

We left this delightful prospect with regret, highly gratified with our excursion, the impression of which will dwell upon our minds as long as the faculty of recollection remains unimpaired".

They obviously enjoyed a very pleasant afternoon but only in the confident 18th century could its appreciation have been expressed with such verbosity! By the way, did he have a telescope to see those ships?

Now let us leave this peaceful country scene as it sleeps in its rural innocence, just before it edges into the 19th century and the energetic bustle of Victorian England.

CHAPTER 9

Life On The Banks Of The River Tees In The Early 19th Century

Looking round the Dorman Museum in Middlesbrough one's attention is attracted to a very large framed map showing a detailed plan of the proposed canal to be dug between Stockton and Darlington. Although this plan never came to fruition, it highlights the concern of the business community regarding the best way to convey heavy goods in the opening years of the 19th century. This was the Age of Steam and coal had assumed the same importance as a source of energy that oil enjoys today. Plenty was being produced in those railwayless, motorless days but its export and transport was a great problem. The most obvious route to London and elsewhere was via the River Tees but here lay the nut of the problem. Its course wound in great loops, wide and shallow, choked with shifting sand-banks. Near its mouth entered the sea along three sand-choked channels each with its sand-bar. On each side of the estuary were salty marshes and "clems" (or "slems"), sand-banks covered by tidal waters. Without great changes no transport by large ships was possible.

The inhabitants of the villages lining the river bank were all able to make a good living by pilotage and gathering a rich harvest of cockles, mussels, crabs and lobsters. There were also sandy islands called "batts" upon which rough grass and willows grew which provided a splendid habitat for wild life. Seals and wild fowl of all kinds thronged the area. Small rowing boats acted as ferries conveying passengers and goods from village to village and bank to bank across the river. On an early Victorian map these villages are named as Portrack, Newport, Cargo Fleet or Cleveland Port. When the tide was low, it was possible to cross the river where it narrowed near Newport by riding on horseback, as my great-grandfather did on one occasion or over the stepping stones at its narrowest point. At one time these large stones stood by the gates of Albert Park.

A good description of the river as it was before the 19th century is given in the first chapter of the "History of the Tees Pilots" by D.S. Hellier. It paints for us a scene of unspoiled natural beauty where leafy banks line a river full of trout and salmon for the fishermen but which could be full of peril for men who were not aware of its dangers. Pilots who knew every shift of the sand-banks, tide and wind were essential. At the head of the largest loop was the small port of PORTRICK from which fish was exported. The name was later changed to PORTRACK for a very important reason. The small shallow vessels of the Middle Ages and Tudor times had managed to negotiate the river, albeit with difficulty, up to Stockton and Yarm but as the vessels grew larger, sailing up and down the river on the tides became very hazardous. Indeed, many vessels were wrecked and sailors drowned in stormy weather before crossing the sand bar across Tees Bay into the open sea. To help to navigate these vessels round the largest loop, men and boys were employed to pull them round the river bend until tide and wind should make it possible for the ships to sail to the river mouth. This procedure became known as "Tracking" and the place - the Port of Track - PORTRACK. Here it was also possible for a ship to be overhauled which was usually done in winter. Its sails could also be renewed or repaired in one of the sail-lofts. This no doubt was one of the outlets for the products of the Cleveland linen mills.

With the advent of the larger sailing vessels it was often found necessary to transfer their cargos to small flat-bottomed boats for their journey further up the river to Stockton and Yarm.

Eventually at the beginning of the 19th century a group of Stockton and Darlington business men sought to improve navigation along the river by cutting a channel across the large Mandale (Thornaby) Loop. In 1810 the cutting was made, thus shortening the river channel considerably and at the celebratory dinner in Stockton Town Hall to mark its opening, a most important discussion took place. Some wished to examine the feasibility of building a canal between Stockton and Darlington while others sought daringly to examine the possibility of building a railway which would pull the coal trucks by the newly invented locomotive of the Mr Stevenson of Newcastle. It was decided to set up a committee to look into the merits of the two projects in detail. The committee was chaired by Edward Pease of Darlington and five other Quaker business men served with him.

This committee it was who built the first railway in the world to carry goods and passengers. After obtaining Parliamentary sanction they became directors of the famous Stockton and Darlington Railway Co. With much excitement on the 27th September 1825, the first trucks carrying goods and passengers opened the line between the two towns. Coal could now be exported from the coal staithes being built at Stockton but alas for the passengers! After the first thrilling ride, sitting or standing in trucks on the first day, for many years, the only way they rode on the railway lines, was by being pulled along by a horse in a coach fitted with suitable wheels and carrying four inside passengers and eight outside. For several decades the railway was no threat to the trade of the stage coaches!

In 1826 a Tees Coal Company was formed financed by Thomas Richardson, a Quaker cousin of Edward Pease. He lived at Great Ayton and later in 1841 became the founder of Great Ayton Quaker School. However it soon became clear that the river at Stockton was too shallow for large ships and the company would fail. Thomas Richardson insisted that the railway must be extended further down the river where larger ships could berth at the coal staithes there. Not without some difficulty and making an undertaking to improve the river between Stockton and the river mouth, was the necessary Parliamentary sanction obtained.

The site which the directors had in mind, was a low hill situated just round the last bend in the river before it opened out into the wide sandy estuary of Tees Bay. In the Middle Ages the hill had been crowned by a small priory. That was now in ruins and incorporated in the farmhouse which stood in the middle of a prosperous farm. Middlesbrough Farm was owned by William Chilton of Billingham who might be persuaded to sell. The tenant farmer was John Parrington. At last on 18th

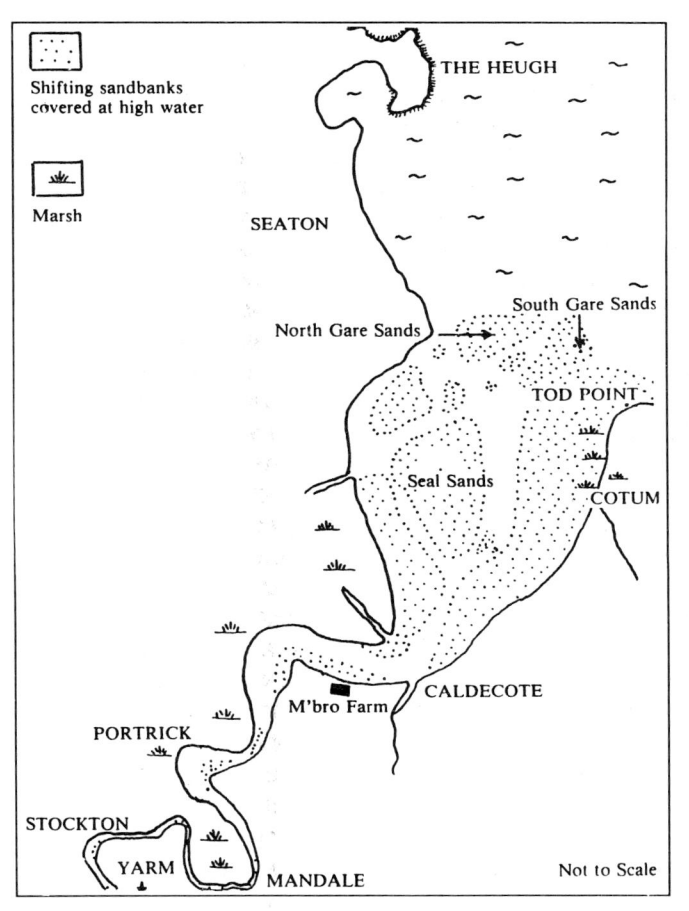

The River Tees (Circa 17th Century)

This map dating from the 17th century shows the shifting sandbanks and winding shallow stream which made the improvements in the 19th century so vital.

The River Tees 1982

The modern navigable River Tees showing its deep safe channel and the land reclamation of most of the sand banks, especially on the north bank. Compare this map with the previous one of the 17th Century River Tees.

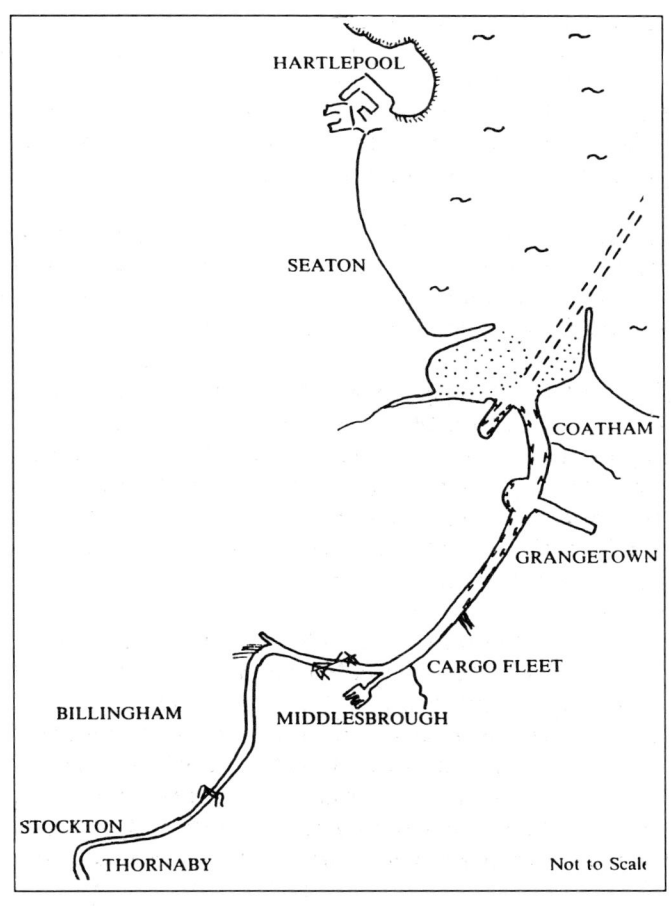

133

Early Middlesbrough Industry – Coal

Middlesbrough Branch Railway was opened December 27th 1830 for the purpose of carrying coal to the coal staithes at Port Darlington (now Middlesbrough). The "Globe" engine designed by Timothy Hackworth pulled the first wagons (shown left). Colliers took coal to London. The collier brig "Middlesbro" shown here was built at the local yard of James Laing in 1833.

From the book "Vintage Middlesbrough" by Norman Moorsom

August 1828 Joseph Pease, the very enterprising son of the Stockton and Darlington Railway Co. Chairman, and other interested Friends, went to inspect the site and report back. The journal of Edward Pease gives us a very clear account of this journey which was to change his life.

Besides the business purpose of the trip Joseph, then a young man, gives some interesting details. They rose early and sailed round to enter the Tees Mouth. As they sailed along they saw seals basking on the sand-banks and a woman shrimping at Newport. After inspecting the site they paid a visit to a pretty village called Cleveland Port (now Cargo Fleet) from where ships sailed laden with the produce from the farms and mills of Cleveland. Here the party ordered a breakfast of ham and eggs with tea and coffee, a sumptuous meal for tenpence each including tip!

In view of what was to come later his assessment of the site and its potentiality make interesting reading. In his journal he says that he was:

"Much pleased with the place altogether. Its adaptation to the purpose far exceeded any anticipation I had formed, the rising piece of land on which the Farm House of Middlesbrough stands is peculiar as there remain many traces of the mound having been the site of more important buildings, there is a Burial Ground to which a very invincible tradition asserts a Church or Chapel was attached in olden times, whether it stood where the waves now flow may be disputed but it does not seem improbable as remains of such an erection are visible. Imagination here has very ample scope in fancying a coming day when the bare fields we then were traversing will be covered with a busy multitude and numerous vessels crowding to these banks denote the busy Seaport. Time, however must roll many successive annual tides were so important a change is effected, but who that has considered the nature and extent of British enterprise, commerce and industry will pretend to take his stand upon this spot, and pointing the finger of scorn at these visions exclaim, that will never be? If such a one appears, he and I are at issue. I believe it will".

The story goes that the reaction of John Parrington, the last tenant farmer of Middlesbrough Farm, to these ideas was very different. During an after dinner conversation in the old farm house a friend said to him:

"I suppose the Quakers of Darlington are about buying your farm to build a town here"

That remark must have shocked Parrington for he replied:

"Build a town here! What build a town at this out of the way place! Why it is said that time works wonders, but you may depend upon it, if ever a town is built here, I'll be hanged if I don't turn this house into a public house and hoist the sign of the 'Quaker Arms', as I suppose if a town is built here it will be a Quaker one".

Strangely enough after the Quakers had bought the Middlesbrough lands, John Parrington went to Grange Farm, the site of the present Grange road and the Middlesbrough Farmhouse was taken over by Robert Manners who transformed it into the Middlesbrough Inn and Brewery. His brother John Manners became the first Surveyor for the new town.

On 11th May 1830 Joseph Pease and his partners signed the title deeds to the Middlesbrough Estate for £45,000 consisting not only of the Middlesbrough Farm lands but also the adjoining Monklands Farm, an area of 488 acres 18 perch, upon which the new town and port were to be developed. The Quaker business men were all relatives of the Pease family and were known henceforth as the Owners of the Middlesbrough Estate. The whole enterprise was to be under the direction of Joseph Pease who rapidly set about putting his plans into execution. He was ably assisted by some remarkable and energetic young men. Richard Otley, the land surveyor to the Stockton and Darlington Railway surveyed and managed not only the construction of the railway from Stockton to Middlesbrough including the building of a railway bridge over the Tees, but also the coal staithes at the riverside at Middlesbrough. On 27th December 1830 the station and coal staithes were opened with great celebrations and the first cargo of coal shipped in S.S. Sunniside on January 31st 1831.

The man who superintended the shipment was William Fallows later known as the Patriarch of Middlesbrough. He was the shipping agent to the Stockton and Darlington Railway and was sent to Middlesbrough in 1830. He organised the exportation of the coal and became known as the Harbour Master. In the same year, after the first coal shipments, he formed a steamship company which ran the "Majestic" to and from London for many years.

Trades and industries began to gather rapidly round the budding port. The first industry of any size was Laing's shipyard where the first wooden ship, a collier brig of 2000 tons, named the "Middlesbrough" was launched in 1833. This enterprise was joined in January 1834 by the Middlesbrough Pottery founded by Richard Otley and soon to be associated with Isssac Wilson of Nunthorpe Hall. Ancillary trades such as mast and sail makers, rope makers, shipchandlers as well as the pilots were joined by the service trades such as shopkeepers of various kinds, publicans and those trades associated with the necessary housing which was rapidly going ahead.

Joseph Pease with his surveyor Richard Otley had drawn up plans for the new town very carefully. It would house five thousand people, covering thirty two acres and be situated between the river and the railway. In those days workmen always lived near their place of employment and managers likewise. There was to be a market place in which a Town Hall and Church were to be built and around it grid formation were the North, South, East and West Streets for the workers. On the outskirts were the large terrace houses, with gardens at the back where the owners and managers lived. Roads were laid out according to the plan and plots of land where the houses were to be built, were sold. The first house to be built in the new town belonged to Mr George Chapman. It was situated in West Street, built in 1830 and demolished in 1960. The plaque stating this fact is now kept in the Dorman Museum. Next door to it was a public house known as King William IV, no doubt a necessity for the building workers, giving refreshment and accommodating visitors to the new town.

As William Parrington had jokingly hinted, the Quakers tried to enforce their moral standards upon the new town. This was certainly in the best interests of the townspeople for as yet there were no municipal officers, but it is very interesting to see how they went about it. On February 8th 1831 the Owners drew up an Indenture outlining the details of what was required from those intending to set up house in the new town. For their part the Owners agreed "within four years to macadamise intended streets and public passages, construct causeways and footpaths of durable material, construct sewers, conduits, gutters, sinks and water courses and construct a road of forty feet". The would-be townsfolk were asked to comply with certain rules which they hoped would ensure a happy community spirit. People must sweep their pavements, not let out ferocious dogs unmuzzled or drive without reins. They must not drive furiously coach, chaise or wagon cart. A stage coach must stop just long enough to take up or set down passengers and not loiter. The letting off of musket, gun or pistol, making a bonfire, squibs, rockets or fireworks or sliding on any pavement are all barred. No dung, filth, rubbish or any offensive matter must be thrown on to public highways. They must not bait or cause to be baited any bull or bear or throw any cock or fowl in the manner known as cock throwing. They must not play football or other games to the annoyance of the public.

All those paying a poor rate of over £5 per annum should meet every first of July and appoint a committee of seven. This committee would appoint a Surveyor. The Surveyor had to inspect streets and repair the same, make all contracts, calculate and collect the rate, keep proper books and prosecute all offenders. John Manners became the first Surveyor.

In this way the seeds of the new town and port, envisaged by Joseph Pease and his partners, were sown and grew rapidly. The coal exporting industry fulfilled all their hopes but the silting up of the river near the staithes made it necessary to build the Middlesbrough Docks in 1842. This was quite justified when they shipped one and a half million tons of coal during the first year. From 1833 Laing's Shipyard was building a succession of wooden ships, later to be replaced by iron ships and this brought prosperity to the ancillary trades connected with shipping. A shipping company conducted a regular trade with London and elsewhere and among the local shipments was the earthenware crockery made by the Middlesbrough Pottery Co., founded in 1834 by Richard Otley, who was soon joined by a young cousin of Joseph Pease from Kendal, Issac Wilson. He took control in 1844 when it became known as the Middlesbrough Earthenware Co., and from 1852 till it closed in 1887 it was known by the name of Messrs Isaac Wilson and Company. Any surviving pieces of pottery are now collectors items and can be dated by the company names.

In his "History of Cleveland" published in 1846, John Walker Ord gives us a fascinating glimpse of life in the first decade of this new town. He concludes his account by remarking:

"In 1829, according to "White's Gazetteer" it had only about forty inhabitants but in 1841 the population has reached the amazing number of five thousand, seven hundred and nine! The increase of voters in the election of members of Parliament for the North Riding is one hundred and three".

Ord is always concerned with the ecclesiastical aspect of local history and so gives us details of the small Benedictine Priory or cell which had stood on the site of the new town. He suggests that this medieval priory was built on the site of a cell founded in early Saxon times by St. Cuthbert. He quotes twenty one charters of grants of land dating from its foundation in 1130 on land granted by Robert de Brus II. Until the 19th century the Middlesbrough lands were in the parish of Acklam.

In 1836 the inhabitants of the new town decided they must build a new church. It was to be named St. Hilda, after the patron saint of the old priory and Ord gives us a description of how the people went about raising the money:

"In 1836 a new church dedicated to St. Hilda was proposed to be erected on the site of the ancient chapel of which indeed the unenclosed burial ground had been occasionally used to that time. This elegant edifice cost the sum of £2500, of which £1200 was obtained from a bazaar and £500 from the Church Building Society. The Archbishop of the diocese also contributed £100. Thomas Hustler Esq (of Acklam Hall) £100 and Thomas

Richardson Esq and partners the site of the building.

The bazaar proved a brilliant and successful experiment, the most influential and distinguished ladies in Cleveland having on this occasion consented to preside at the stalls.

The first stone was laid by the Lady of Thomas Hustler Esq of Acklam Hall and the building completed in 1840. On September 25th 1840 the church was consecrated by the Lord Bishop of Durham, assisted by the clergy of the district, on which occasion a splendid cold collation was prepared at the Exchange.

Previous to this, chapels had been erected by the Unitarians, Wesleyans, Calvinists and Ranters''.

What a bazaar that must have been! Also how sad to think that the social climate of the latter part of the 20th century has led to the demolition of this fine building!

While giving details of the town, around 1840, he says:

"There are numerous excellent shops for merchandise, 4 public breweries, 3 iron foundries, in one of which 400 persons are regularly employed. There is also a sail-cloth manufactory in which the cloth is woven by patent machinery to a very considerable extent: an extensive manufactory for pottery and earthenware and extensive brick and tile yards for which clay of excellent quality is found and employing upwards of 300 persons. Of these bricks the whole of Middlesbrough, the Exchange excepted, is built''.

In the first decade of the new town, trade flourished and the enterprising business men built for themselves a fine Exchange building which was opened by Royalty in 1837 in the person of the Duke of Sussex, an uncle of the new young Queen Victoria. Sussex street was named in honour of this occasion and the Exchange still exists, being now the Custom House in Queen's Square. But even they could not have foreseen the consequences to the whole area when, in 1839 Joseph Pease met two young and ambitious business men in Newcastle. They were Henry Bolckow and John Vaughan, ideal partners and brothers-in-law. Henry William Ferdiand Bolckow (1806-1878) was born in Sultan, Mecklenburg, Germany, the son of a country gentleman. Having been sent, as a young man, to Newcastle to learn business methods, he had decided to settle there. So successful had he been there that he had just sold his business interests for £50,000 and was looking for a suitable investment for this money. He met John Vaughan (1799-1868) a Welsh engineer trained in the Welsh ironworks, who dreamed of establishing an ironworks. The friendship between the two young men was further cemented when John Vaughan, who was a widower with two sons, married Henry Bolckow's sister who was a widow with three children. It was at this point in their lives that they met Joseph Pease who persuaded them to build a new ironworks in his new town of Middlesbrough.

These first ironworks of Messrs Bolckow and Vaughan were opened in August 1841. They consisted of a forge, a foundry and a rolling mill. At first the pig-iron came from the blast furnaces which they owned at Witton Park in Durham. It soon became obvious that there was a serious shortage of iron-ore, their only source being that which was shipped from Whitby. However all this was changed when John Vaughan made his dramatic discovery of iron-ore in Eston Hills, only four miles from the works. Many versions of this find have been told but fortunately there is an exact account on record given by the engineer John Varley who was with him at the time. It reads as follows:

"Mr Vaughan and myself, having gone to examine the hills for the most suitable place for boring, we decided

to ascend to the east, adjoining Sir J.H. Lowther's ground (Wilton Castle Estate) and so walk along to Lady Hewley's ground to the west. In ascending the hill in Mr C Dryden's grounds we picked up two or three small pieces of iron-stone. We therefore continued our ascent until we came to a quarry-hole from whence this ironstone had been taken for roads, and next on entering Sir J.H. Lowther's grounds to the west, a solid rock of ironstone was lying bare upwards of sixteen feet thick. I need scarcely say that, having once found this bed, we had no difficulty in following the outcrop in going westwards without any boring as the rabbit and fox holes therein were plentiful as we went. We also examined the place in Lackenby Banks, squared down in 1811 or 1812 by the late Mr Thomas Jackson of Lackenby.

The period from 8th June 1850 till the middle of August following was occupied in completing arrangements for opening out this ironstone and the first trial quarry was begun on the 13th August 1850. A temporary tramway was soon laid down and by the 2nd September 1850 the first lot of seven tons was brought down in small tubs to the highway-side, from thence carted to Cargo Fleet and thence again by rail to Witton Park Ironworks, being about three weeks after actually seeing the ironstone and by this method 4041 tons were sent away by the 28th December following''

Before launching into the history of the ''boom'' period which followed this discovery and made Middlesbrough a great Steel Metropolis let us take a final backward glance at the life of the inhabitants of the new town and in particular how they travelled.

In her book ''The Story of Cleveland'' Minnie Horton gives a fascinating picture of travel by rail during these early years.
''When George Stevenson had run the first passenger train in the world from Stockton to Darlington in 1828, it became generally thought that the steam engine continued carrying passengers daily from then on - but this is not the case. The Owners were mainly concerned in carrying merchandise. Indeed Stevenson's engines proved not strong enough for the continual heavy loads they were expected to pull. At one time the Directors of the Railway Company considered using horses only and they did do this to a great extent. It was ten years before the passenger coach was drawn by a steam engine. When the Stockton and Darlington Railway had been extended to Middlesbrough in 1830, the first railway station was a wooden hut at the end of the coal staithes. When not required it housed the solitary coach which was built in the shape of a stage coach but was fitted with flanged wheels. It was named "The Majestic" and it was drawn by a horse which was not noted for is speed. Each morning Mr Brown, the driver of the railway coach used to walk in a leisurely fashion from where the horse was stabled, blowing his horn as he went. He was never in a hurry and gladly waited for any passenger he saw coming down the road. The railway coach made three trips a day each way between Middlesbrough and Stockton. No one knew the time the railway coach would take on the journey for if it got behind a number of coal wagons its speed dropped to something like a walking pace!"

By the time the railway had reached the end of its first decade in 1840 improvements had made a proper timetable possible. It was drawn up as follows:

Railway Coaches

To Stockton hourly, Darlington every two hours;
To Auckland, St Helen, at 12 noon and 4 aft.

Presumably the trains went approximately on the hour! By 1840 the town envisaged by the young Joseph Pease was becoming well established and a street directory was compiled. There were now fifteen streets and a central square dominated by a fine church. The households are listed with the trade or occupation of the head of each by the side of his name. These number two hundred and sixty three and every trade and profession is represented. Besides the manual workers and craftsmen and craftswomen of every description are the shopkeepers, two Academy proprietors presumably having a school in Stockton Street, a police officer, three attorneys and managers of the National and Provincial Bank and the Norwich Union Fire Office. As one would expect there were a great many "master mariners" and other trades connected with shipping. John Parrington is listed as "Farmer (Grange)" and Joseph Kipling as also listed as a farmer, possibly employed by him. Around the new town the cows still grazed in the fields as can be plainly seen in the picture now hanging in Middlesbrough Central Library, painted in 1832. Southfield road in its name perpetuates the boundary of Grange Farm which set the limits to the new town.

One feature which stands out in this directory is the number of inns. There are twenty eight in all with no less than four in Durham Street. So many had seafaring names such as "The Lord Nelson"; "The James Cook"; "The Mariner's Arms"; "The Sailor's Return"; that there is no doubt who were their best customers. For the more selective clientele there was "The Middlesbrough Hotel".

It was from this hotel that the stage coaches started which were the usual mode of travel. Here is part of the timetable:

Coach - from the Hotel

"The Union" - to Whitby, Scarborough etc at $^{1/2}$p. 10a.m. daily in summer; and on Tuesday, Thursday and Saturday in winter.

The thought of riding on top of a coach, embarking on a journey across the moors, not only to Whitby but to Scarborough on a winter's day at half-past ten sends shivers down the spine! Then there was the prospect, even at the best of times of walking up those long steep, unmodernised banks, Ormesby Bank, Birk Brow, the Jolly Sailors Bank, and the dreaded Blue Bank on the way to Scarborough! Yet these were the days when travellers like "Mr Pickwick and the Pickwick Club" our Victorian forefathers, thought nothing of it.

If you wished to go to London in relative comfort you could go by a Steam Packet called "The Emerald Isle" which left the port every Wednesday an hour before high water. Goods were carried by horse-drawn carriers'; carts which left two of the inns on Wednesday and Saturday going to Whitby and Guisborough and to Lofthouse (Loftus) and Staithes on Monday and Thursday. Presumably parcels were dropped off at the inns en route.

(A full list of the 1840 Middlesbrough Directory and a further account of travel in the early days of Middlesbrough can be found in "The Birth and Growth of Middlesbrough" by Norman Moorsom from which the above details have been taken).

Thus was launched the "boom" period which created the modern Middlesbrough, first to the south of the railway line and then ever wider, engulfing the old villages of Acklam, Leventhorpe (Linthorpe), Portrack and Newport, a process still continuing today. These mid Victorian decades were years of great industrial change and expansion but also meant a great deal of hardship for those whose traditional skills were no longer needed - the "Hungry Forties". Here was work in plenty so miners came from Wales and Cornwall to open up the iron mines not only at Eston but Normanby, Loftus, Skinningrove, Upleatham, Skelton, Lingdale, all round the Guisborough hills and Roseberry Topping. In this way Great Ayton with its satellite, Nunthorpe, were hurled into the bustling Industrial Revolution. In these early Victorian times workpeople flocked to Teesside at a phenomenal rate - labourers from the farm lands and mills where machinery was taking over. Labourers in their hundreds fleeing from the Potato Famine and starvation in Ireland came here and in time built a cathedral for their Roman Catholic worship. Tradespeople of every description came to serve this growing community. Businessmen throughout Britain poured their money into the ironworks, mines and docks when they became Limited Companies and investment was possible. The largest ironworks, Bolckow and Vaughan, became a Limited Company in 1864. Ironworks, docks and ships were built; the river was dredged and deepened, its sand-banks and estuary bars, which for centuries had hindered shipping were blown up and the river water contained in one channel lined with stout walls made from the hard durable waste slag of the furnaces. Of course social problems abounded, the greatest of which was housing for this great influx of workmen and their families. However large deposits of suitable clay for making bricks was found near at hand so that brickworks could easily be established. Far too quickly for health and comfort street after street of small cottage homes covered the marshy land at Newport (now the industrial estate Cannon Park). In this mid nineteenth century such was the pressure for accommodation that it was said that "the beds were never cold" for, as the day workers vacated them in the morning, the night shift workers lay down to sleep during the day.

The demand for iron and steel seemed insatiable for "railway mania" at home and abroad was at its height. There was a great demand for lines and railways, girders for bridges and railway stations, plates for the new ships, pipes and machinery of all kinds using literally millions of tons of ironstone annually from the mines of Cleveland. The youngest borough in England, Middlesbrough, grew by the end of the century to become the greatest iron and steel town in Europe. But shall we leave this rumbustious, bustling scene with its wealth and poverty and its great social problems, to look once more at the peaceful countryside up on the hills so near its doorstep.

In rural Cleveland the landowners and property owners viewed the activities down by the riverside with its influx of new work-people, especially from Ireland, with alarm. Joseph Pease and his Quaker friends might draw up a list of regulations for the new town but the influx of young men seeking work meant not only a lively place but one where drunkenness and fighting were inevitable. The police force as we know it today was to come. Robert Peel, the Home Secretary introduced the first policeman to the streets of London in September 1829. They were unpopular and only very slowly were policemen introduced into the rest of the country. To deal with the day-to-day problems of law and order in the 1830's, Middlesbrough had a remarkable parish constable. He and his trained dog Nettler, were the terror of trouble makers. By 1841 Mr Old had become an official policeman and had three assistants. When there was trouble, especially among the Irish navvies, from fighting or being senseless through drink, the policemen would push the man to the police station in a shopkeeper's handcart. If the drunken man was too aggressive he was put in the stocks in Queen's Square to cool down. Nevertheless the policemen found it advisable to walk down the dark streets three at a time.

It was, therefore, little wonder that the local gentry with their large estates and woods filled with game sought to protect themselves. A recently discovered document reveals that in defence they set up what might be called "a self-protection" society under the chairmanship of the Earl of Zetland. It was officially called "Cleveland General Association for the Protection of Persons and Property, the Prosecution of Felons and Prevention of Poaching and Vagrancy". Its inauguration took place at the Town Hall in Guisborough on 19th December 1839 and its rules formulated. The aim of the association was set out in Rule 5.

"That the Association will use every endeavour to detect and prosecute to conviction any person or persons who may be guilty of Felonies, Robberies or Petty Thefts, Assaults, Breaking down Fences and Gates, Trespassing upon Property, Cutting down young Trees or Underwood, Breaking Windows or committing any other Malicious Trespass or Misdemeanour - and all persons Encamping on the roadsides or committing any act of Vagrancy".

Modern readers will note how seriously the "vandalism" of those days was regarded. This damage to property would not be done by mindless hooligans out of mischief but probably by a man persuing a hare or pheasant for a meal for a hungry family or to fill an empty grate in winter. Nor were the road users exempt as Rule 7 reveals:

"And further that this Association will proceed against all Farmers, Servants, Coachmen and others who may be detected in driving their Wagons, Carts and Carriages, furiously or negligently on the Turnpike Roads and Highways, so as to endanger the Lives and Persons of Her Majesty's subjects".

This last sentence must have a familiar ring to offending motorists today but a successful prosecution would not end with a fine or ban from driving. These were the days of very harsh laws especially against the poor and hapless. The law was in the hands of the all-powerful magistrates living in their stately homes. A man might be hung in the gallows for stealing a sheep and transported for poaching a pheasant or a salmon. Transportation, like the unjust clearances taking place in the Highlands of Scotland at this time, provided a strange quirk of history. Convicts or not, these countrymen were ideal people to send to the new-found colonies of Australia and New Zealand. They were the ones who knew how to live off the land and were inured to hardship. In order to catch the offenders the Association were to appoint two policemen mounted on horses, one living in Guisborough for the East Langbaurgh district and another at Stokesley for the West Langbaurgh district. It might well be asked how two policemen, even when mounted on horses, could effectively police an area which stretched from Yarm to Loftus. A little reflection might reveal that apart from the long list of members of the Association, whose property covered the whole area, in all the country towns, were other men who could be called upon. Each hall or mansion had gamekeepers, gardeners, manservants of all kinds, labourers and estate workers. These could be called upon to help in any situation at any time. In other words the police constable could provide himself with a "posse" like any Marshall in Dodge City in any Western film.

This was, as it were, a small foreshadowing of what was to come. The discovery of ironstone in large quantities in the Eston Hills opened the first phase of the industrialisation of the whole of old Cleveland. With it gradually the three small rural communities of Nunthorpe, Marton and Ormesby lost their focus on agriculture and became as it were satellites of the industry which had built up on both sides of the Tees. By the end of the century Acklam, Leventhorpe (Linthorpe), Portrack, Newport and Cargo Fleet communities had been engulfed. This century the wave of urbanisation has swept southwards. So now we will trace the story of how that happened.

CHAPTER 10
The Coming Of The Railway

Had one stood on the top of Roseberry Topping in the fateful year of 1850 to admire the countryside all around, as the friends of Rev. John Graves had done about fifty years before, one would find little had changed since then, just smoke rising from the rolling mills and pottery works by the river with perhaps puffs of smoke from the steam packet as it chugged its way through the sailing ships. But great changes were on the way. Within three weeks of its discovery, the ironstone on Eston Hills had been quarried and carted to the ironworks. Immediately plans were put into action to survey the adjoining Cleveland Hills. Businessmen eagerly put up the necessary money to open new mines in the whole area and build railways to bring it to the furnaces which were erected near the river. Codhill Mine at Hutton Lowcross was the first mine near Guisborough to be opened by Joseph Pease and his son in 1853. At the same time a mineral line was built to link it with Middlesbrough and opened the same year. Within another year the line had been doubled and this is the track which runs through Marton and Nunthorpe today. At first the Darlington and Stockton Railway Co. who naturally built the line, were most reluctant to carry any passengers. No doubt due to the presence of one of its directors Mr Isaac Wilson of Nunthorpe Hall, passenger services began to run on 25th September 1854. Nunthorpe Station was built and its first station master appointed.

It must be remembered that these were very significant years in the history of Victorian Britain. In 1851 the Great Exhibition at Crystal Palace established our country as the greatest industrial nation in Europe and the centre of a mighty Empire. In this year too, a census was taken which reveals a good deal about the farming community of Nunthorpe before the changes which its railway link was about to bring about.

At the beginning of the 19th century the Hall and Nunthorpe Estate had been bought by Thomas Simpson. He rebuilt the hall in 1821 after its period of neglect and decay and possibly with the help of his son-in-law the Rev. Joseph Ibbotson, Vicar of Ayton, also rebuilt the chapel. These are the fine buildings still standing today, although sadly the chapel has been neglected and is in disrepair. When Thomas Simpson died in 1848 the estate was sold to Isaac Wilson. With memories of his Lakeland childhood, the lovely views of the Cleveland Hills from the windows of the house must have made an instant appeal. He did not however take up residence until after the building of the railway. The census records reveal that Nunthorpe Hall was occupied by

William Simpson and his family. He was the son of Thomas Simpson and he gave his occupation as "Land Agent and farmer of 156 acres (the home-farm attached to the hall)". He is managing the estate for its owner, Isaac Wilson, until he is ready to move out to Nunthorpe but William Simpson died in 1853.

The occupations of the villagers are those which one would expect of a country community near a hall. Among the names is Thomas Barr, a gamekeeper who lived on his brother's farm. The village blacksmith was Thomas Waller whose household consisted of not only his wife and two children but also a journeyman blacksmith and his apprentice and the Land Agent's Clerk, Robert Clerk. This would suggest he had a prosperous business and lived in one of the larger houses. The village carpenter was named William Wright who lived with his wife and son in one of the cottages to which his workshop would be attached. The village shoemaker was George Ingledew who lived in another cottage with his wife and daughter and had served with the 61st Foot Regiment. He became a Chelsea Pensioner. Among the women in the village was Johanna Hutchinson, the village laundress or washerwoman, who lived on her own, while Ann Wood was the village dressmaker who lived in a cottage with her farm labourer husband and their three children. Seven other women were employed as "home servants" at the various large houses and farms.

There are seven men listed as farmers, working farms ranging from thirteen to two hundred and forty five acres. It is interesting to note that these farms did not belong to the Nunthorpe Estate and were probably owned by the farmers themselves. Except for the villagers quoted above, they employed the rest of the one hundred and twenty six inhabitants of Nunthorpe registered in this census. At this time the "township" of Nunthorpe with its farmland was only to the west of the present railway line for the eastern boundary of the parish was fixed along the beck which runs beside the railway. Not many years ago could be seen a boundary stone in what is now the Station Car Park. (It is now in Preston Park Museum). It marked the spot where the boundaries of the parishes of Marton, Ormesby and Ayton all met. As we have seen a thriving little town had been rapidly springing up around the Middlesbrough Farm in the Tees Valley but it is unlikely to have been of much interest to these country villages except as an added market for their farm produce.

Isaac Wilson was born in Kendal on 16th February 1822 so he was a comparatively young man when he came to live in Nunthorpe Hall. His father was a woollen manufacturer and a Quaker related to the great Pease family of Darlington whose members were engaged in developing Teesside. When only nineteen years of age, Joseph Pease recommended him to come to Middlesbrough where Richard Otley and John Davison were running Middlesbrough's first industry, the Middlesbrough Pottery Company, which had been in operation since 1834. So began his life-long career in industry and public service, for he was a founding father of the new town of Middlesbrough. His working life as enterprising industrialist, his public life as a director and later chairman of the first committee of the Tees Conservancy Commissioners, as one of Middlesbrough's first aldermen at the early age of thirty one, its second ever Mayor, its second M.P. all belonged to the growing town down by the river. Nunthorpe meant home to him and leisure hours.

In 1847 Isaac Wilson married Anna Dorothy Benson, a young lady from his native Kendal. They set up house in Sussex street in the new town of Middlesbrough, where Joseph Pease had built suitable private residences for industrial managers and owners. They were well built houses with gardens and orchards and views

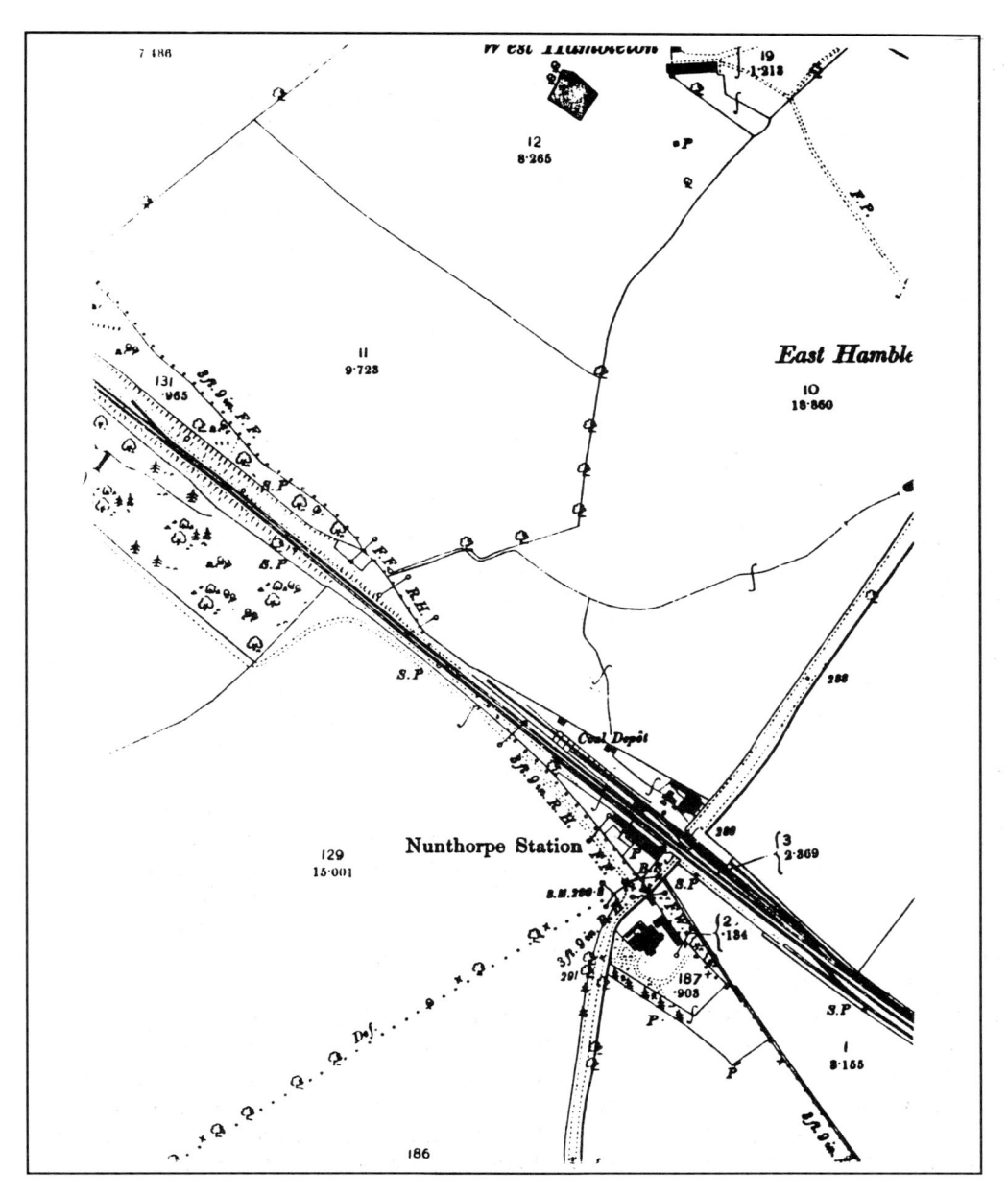

Nunthorpe Station 1894

The isolated Nunthorpe Station in 1894. Note B.S. boundary stone and boundary trees. (From Mr. Tom Pearce's collection).

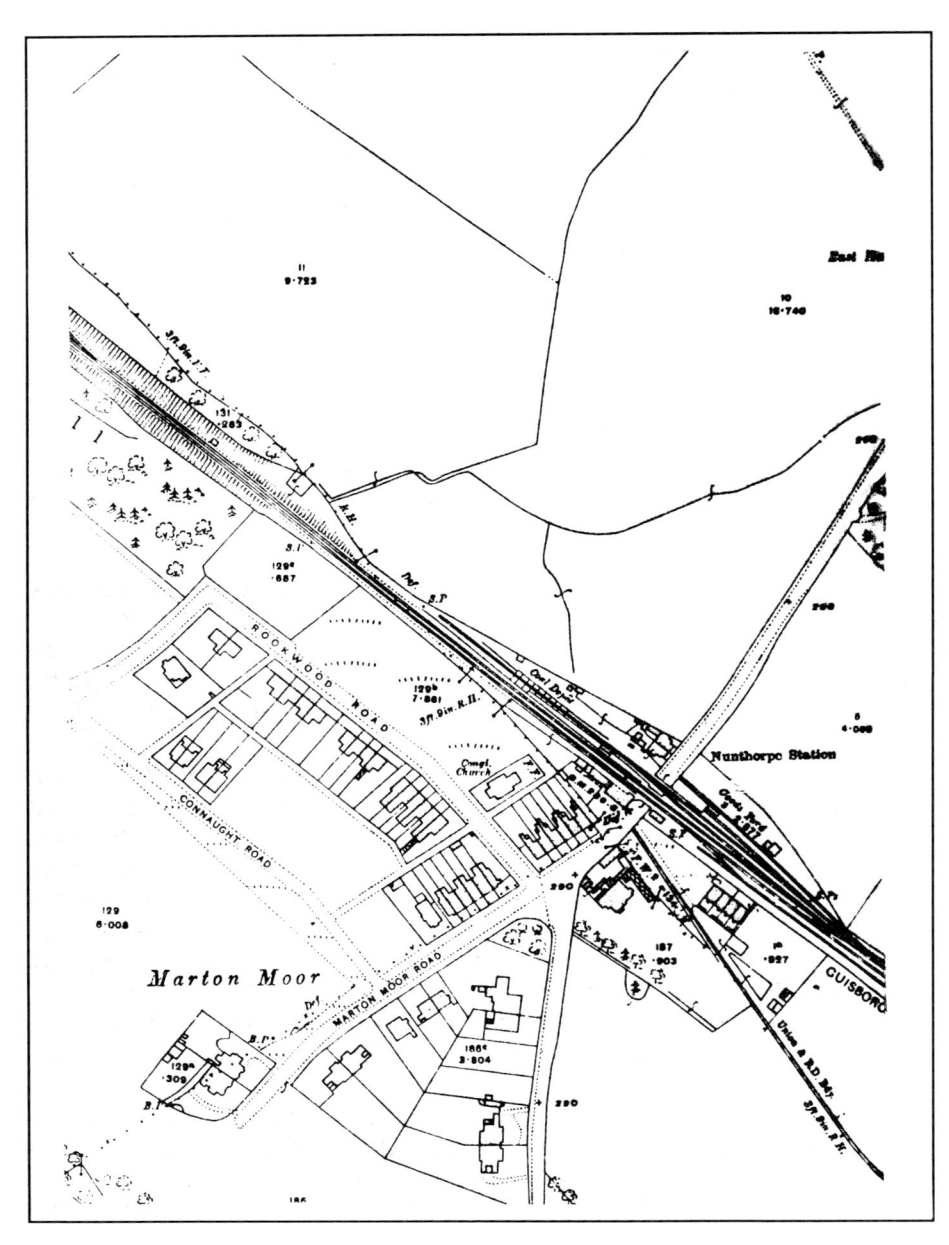

Nunthorpe Station 1915

This map shows clearly not only the busy station but the beginning of the Nunthorpe Station community as planned by Sir Arthur Dorman. (From Mr. Tom Pearce's collection).

of the pleasant slow flowing river. Before the vital year 1850, when thick seams of ironstone were discovered in Eston Hills, two daughters Mary (1849) and Helen (1850) had been born to the couple. He bought Nunthorpe Hall for his family but his shrewd business mind probably foresaw the necessity for railways in Cleveland to bring the ore from the mines to the ironworks on Teesside. He was one of the directors of the Stockton and Darlington Railway and probably helped to plan the routes of the Middlesbrough and Guisborough Line. Its use was to bring iron-ore from Joseph Peases' mine at Codhill (a hillside near Hutton) to the new ironworks by the river. He would take great interest in the building of Nunthorpe Station from which he would commute to his office in Middlesbrough. From this station which was opened in 1854 would come the coal for his household fires and the goods for his kitchen and farm. However he did not take up residence at the hall until after the birth of his third daughter Gertrude in 1854. In 1853 Isaac Wilson had been the Returning Officer for the first local elections ever held after Middlesbrough had been given its character as a Borough. This must have necessitated his presence in the town and on learning of his wife's pregnancy decided not to make a move until she was strong again. It was after the move to Nunthorpe in 1856 that his only son was born. In that year his wife gave birth to twins, Robert Theodore and Sarah.

No doubt his growing family made him turn his thoughts to education of the young and with his Quaker background, he was concerned with the education of the children of the rapidly growing numbers of working class people. Due to his influence a British School in Feversham Street, Middlesbrough was built. He did not forget the village children either, for he built the first small village school at Nunthorpe at the end of the village street opposite the hall.

In 1860 his youngest daughter, Dora, was born and in 1861 census gives us a picture of this busy prosperous household:

Anna Wilson aged 39, his wife.
His children, Mary aged 12, Helen aged 10, Anna Gertrude aged 7, the twins Robert Theodore and Sarah aged 5, Dora a baby of one year.

To look after the children they employed a governess Martha Gale Jackson aged thirty one from Hull and a nurse Hannah Marie Cooper aged nineteen of Darlington. With six young children to look after and only such a young nurse to help, Mrs Wilson must have taken a very active part in rearing her family. Unlike so many Victorian families they all grew up to be fine adults and to marry well.

To look after the house there were two housemaids, Eliza Janson from Sedgefield and Jane Ann Robinson from Glaisdale. In the kitchen were the cook Jane Cansfield aged twenty nine from East Cowton and the kichenmaid Caroline Graham from Richmond.

By the time of the next census in 1871 the status of Isaac Wilson in the community had risen considerably and his family was beginning to grow up. He is described as "Iron Master, Alderman and J.P.". Four of his daughters, now young ladies in their late teens and early twenties, are at home while the fifth Gertrude, is away, perhaps at boarding school. His son Robert, now fifteen, is also not at home and is most likely to be away at school. It would be interesting to know whether these children went to the Quaker school at Great Ayton or whether their father considered it too near home and sent them to another Quaker school. It is probable that Isaac Wilson and his wife attended the Quaker Meeting there and would know all connected with the school. Yet the census shows that the couple employed a governess Mary Grinton, aged twenty three, from Berwick-on-Tweed, so it seems as if the two younger girls, Dora and Sarah, were being taught at home. Hannah Maria Cooper who was the nursemaid in 1861 is still here as a housemaid and there is a seamstress, Mary Elizabeth Cooper, also from Darlington and probably her sister. Eliza Janson is still working for them but in the kitchen, the cook is now Mary Janes aged twenty seven, from Monmouthshire and her kitchenmaid Sarah Collingwood aged nineteen from Middleton Tyas. No doubt in view of their increased social status and the great amount of entertaining it now involved, the Wilsons employed a young butler, Angus Robertson aged twenty three, a Scotsman from Fort William.

In 1878 he was elected Member of Parliament for Middlesbrough, when its first M.P. Mr Henry Bolckow resigned, and he was re-elected again in 1880. But these were the days of industrial recession. His neighbour, William Hopkins, who had built Grey Towers, was bankrupt in 1880 after his bridge building company went into liquidation following the Tay Bridge disaster. Isaac Wilson was also a director of the company but survived for he had many other business interests. However, their standard of living as shown by the 1881 census was much reduced. None of the familiar names of servants are there and only two maids and a cook are employed in the house.

Mary and Dora are still at home. Helen was later to marry into the Pease family, (Joseph Beaumont Pease), and Dora died still unmarried in 1925 at Saltburn. Robert is now registered as an ironmaster and no doubt is running the day-to-day affairs of the family's business interests. Isaac now takes an interest in his farm and estate and being sixty years old begins to take things easy. Nevertheless he must have spent a good deal of time representing his constituency in Westminster for he returned unopposed again in the 1886 election.

Gradually he gave up his posts on his various committees in Middlesbrough and spent more time in Nunthorpe. In 1879 a Post Office in the village was opened and it was no longer necessary for villagers to go to Great Ayton or the station to post a letter of buy a stamp. In 1892 he was honoured by the people of Middlesbrough when he was given the Freedom of Middlesbrough, being only the third man to receive that honour. He just missed living into the twentieth century for he died aged seventy seven on 22nd September 1899. He was buried at Great Ayton.

Before he died he must have seen the first houses being built round the busy station and the beginning of the Nunthorpe we know today. This fine Victorian had shown the way to earn one's living in the smoke of industry but enjoy one's leisure hours in the country - a pioneer commuter.

From the coming of the railway in 1853 till after the Second World War when railway services nationally became restricted, the station itself was a great focus of interest in the community and until the increasing use of cars and buses in the 1920's the railway was the only means of travel, unless one was wealthy enough to own a horse and carriage. For all, it meant a good means of travel to work and shops. For this, the station catered well and became a regular meeting place for the community. When the line was opened in 1853 by the Stockton and Darlington Railway Company, its sole concern was to convey ironstone from the Guisborough mines to the ironworks and docks at Middlesbrough. Pressure for a passenger service was put upon the company by the people of Guisborough and at first only a few trains were running weekly from there to Middlesbrough. No doubt much greater pressure for a good passenger train service was exerted on the board after Isaac Wilson came to live at Nunthorpe Hall in 1856.

Nunthorpe Station 1992

Inset: Number Plate from D & S Railway

The Cleveland Hunt

The Hunt start off from Nunthorpe in 1938 led by Mr. and Mrs. Buckle and T. S. Petch.

149

Nunthorpe Station

Scene at the south end of Nunthorpe Station showing platform with incline down to the crossing, the porter-gateman's cabin, general office and small booking hall. Note the clock which served Nunthorpe for more than 100 years. Although the photograph was taken about 1960 the appearance of the station was unchanged since Victorian Times.

Tally-Ho Bob

Mr. Robert Brunton, born 1832, nick named "Tally-ho Bob", was the first member of the Brunton family to occupy Manor Moor Farm, Nunthorpe. This was situated at Manor Moor corner facing the old Stokesley Road. He earned his nick-name for when he had had "one over the eight" he could be heard shouting "Tally-ho" all the way home.

From then on the commuter services were improved and with the building of more and more new houses beside the stations and increasing demands of the industries growing up in Great Ayton and elsewhere, all stations, but Nunthorpe in particular, became very busy indeed.

The first regular passenger service was opened on 25th September 1854. Only one train each way, per day, was provided, leaving Guisborough at 8.10am and returning from Middlesbrough at 5.20pm. The building of the station was also completed this year. Included in it was the substantial stationmaster's house for he was on duty twenty four hours a day and regarded in the community as a person of importance and respect.

The rail services to Guisborough ceased in March 1964 and the station buildings there were demolished soon afterwards. On some of the station buildings two iron plates were fixed. One bore the initials "S and D Ry" and the other the number of the station, at Guisborough, it was B.12 and Nunthorpe B.3. Probably all except B.3 are now part of somebody's railway memorabilia collection. In 1864 the line was extended to Great Ayton to cope with the extensive mining and quarrying activities opening up there around Roseberry Topping. Great quarries also opened up along the hard Langbaurgh ridge for Whinstone which provided most of the hard cobbles for market places and setts for gutters and back streets in the local towns as well as Leeds and the growing industrial towns of the West Riding. Jet and alum were also mined on Roseberry while one particular outcrop was so hard that it provided hard whetstone so necessary for sharpening tools. All these mineral trains as well as those from Guisborough had to pass through Nunthorpe Station to the main line at Middlesbrough. This made Nunthorpe Station into a junction. The signal-cabin was built and the two signalman's cottages opposite.

Great rivalry existed among the businessmen in Cleveland in their bid to exploit its natural wealth and regarded railway building as such an essential part of that process. After much wrangling, a Parliamentary Bill was passed in 1858 for the building of a second railway in this area but to carry freight traffic only, known as the Cleveland Railway. Today its track can be clearly seen on the south side of the Cleveland Hills when travelling along the Guisborough valley, particularly near the Cross Keys Inn and as it passes under the road at Wendle Bridge. Its purpose was to link the ironworks and docks on Teesside with iron-mines being opened at Normanby, Scugdale near Guisborough, Brotton and Skinningrove. However this railway only lasted twelve years for in the following decade, all the small railway companies, including the Stockton and Darlington Company, merged to become the North Eastern Railway. In 1873 the Cleveland mineral line from Guisborough to Middlesbrough was deemed unnecessary and ceased to function.

Photography had been invented by this time and there are many photographs of country stations so it is not difficult to imagine what Nunthorpe Station would have seemed like while waiting for a train.

It is difficult for us to realise how very proud the Victorians were of the railway and its stations: Having bought our ticket in the small booking hall and stepping on to the platform we would see everything looking neat and trim. Hanging baskets and flower beds gave a festive air. We are standing on the down platform. Behind us is the station building, a long building consisting of the stationmaster's house, waiting rooms, office and porter's cabin. There is a slate roof projecting which protects the passengers from the rain and there are wooden seats below. As we look at our fellow passengers we see the ladies in crinolines (how did they manage to sit on the seats in the railway carriages?) and the gentlemen in "stove" hats and drain-pipe trousers.

One porter with his barrow is dealing with the luggage to go on the train, while the other is waiting for the signalman in the signal-cabin to tell him when to open the gates across the road. The stationmaster would be there in his top-hat and frock-coat supervising all the arrangements. We may not notice how low the platform was to accommodate the low trains but a century later the Nunthorpeans were very aware, as they leapt from the train for the platforms have now to be raised.

The next extension to the line reached Battersby Junction where it linked with the North Yorkshire and Cleveland Railway which ran to Stockton via Stokesley and Yarm and to Whitby via the Esk Valley. The coast route to Whitby via Brotton, Staithes and Sandsend, a most scenic railway also ran through Nunthorpe Station after it was opened in 1883 and was extended to Scarborough in 1885. This very picturesque line was closed in 1958. As all these trains passed through Nunthorpe and not Guisborough, Nunthorpe Station was a very busy station indeed.

For four or five years before my father died in 1967 aged ninety, he frequently had a visit from a fellow railway enthusiast. For hours they would pour over old photographs and magazines, speaking in railway jargon of the olden days when steam locomotives ruled the tracks. This spry little visitor was Will Huby. He was born and brought up in the stationmaster's house at Nunthorpe, for his father was stationmaster there for many years round the turn of the century.

Only recently did I discover that these memories had taken tangible form. He wrote a series of articles about Nunthorpe Station under the title of "Recollections of a Branch Line in the 1890s" which were published in the "North Eastern Express" a quarterly journal of the North Easten Railway Association, from November 1962 to November 1963. These give in some detail the lay-out and daily running of the station at the time. What a busy bustling place it was!

One peculiar difficulty of the station was the fact that it was at the top of a steep incline. He writes of this difficulty as follows:

"Owing to its position at the top of the steeply graded 1 in 39 and 1 in 44 bank, rising from the Middlesbrough direction, it was a compulsory stopping place for the numerous trains of ironstone from the mines in the Cleveland area and off the Stockton-Whitby branch (via Battersby Junction). The stop was necessary for the purpose of applying wagon brakes by the guard as they were drawn slowly over the bank head. The momentum over the falling gradient enabled the train to run by gravity some 3 1/2 miles to Pennyman's signal-box (which stands beside Marton Station) where the wagon brakes were released. Coming up the steep bank sometimes the heavy load had to be carried in two sections".

He describes the large station yard (now a supermarket car-park) as follows:

"The yard was in regular use by the carriages and conveyances of the local gentry, ironmasters and others travelling daily to Middlesbrough and the vicinity on business etc. There were some very fine carriages and when complete with coachmen and footmen in livery, presented an attractive appearance, enhanced by fine well groomed horses in well furnished harness".

Of the station itself he wrote:
"Generally speaking the station accommodation was

somewhat inadequate. At the main side there was a very small booking hall and general office, porter-gateman's cabin, general waiting and ladies room''.

Older readers who lived in Nunthorpe may remember sitting on the wooden bench which ran round the general waiting room with its large railway map over the fireplace. I am sure that they will remember too the cheerful blazing coal fire which the porter had lit there on cold frosty mornings. They may also remember the pump which stood outside. This unfiltered water, was the only water supply, not only for the stationmaster's house but for the two signalman's cottages at the other side of the railway tracks and the four houses in the Railway Terrace built in 1903 on the other side of the road. This state of affairs lasted till the mains water supply was connected for the nearby houses being built by Sir Arthur Dorman.

Coal there always was in plenty for in those days, the stationmasters were also the only coke and coal merchants. The coke and coal trucks tipped it into cells under the railway lines. These were situated at the station edge of what is now a supermarket car-park.

"The stationmaster received a commission at the rate of one hudredweight per ton of coal sold. The allowance had to cover retailing in cart-loads or small quantities and any other source of loss such as small unsaleable coal, losses due to rough shunting or pilferage en route etc., the one hundredweight being termed 'overweight'''.

Besides the handsome horses and carriages of the commuting gentry, all through the day there would be a procession of farmer's carts and gigs fetching and carrying all kinds of goods, great and small. As well as the ironstone from the mines, roadstone and whetstone from the Ayton quarries, there would be the carriage of the farm produce, not only from the Ayton and Nunthorpe farms but from the Guisborough valley. The carts would fill the waiting railway trucks with wheat for the millers, possibly at Thornaby, oats to supply the horses, so numerous in those days, barley for the brewers, hay for the ponies in the Durham mines, turnips and potatoes. The mention of potatoes brought to Mr Huby's mind a vivid picture of one aspect of station life in those days. The two porter-gatemen manned the crossing from 5am till 10pm and 11.15pm on some nights, which meant there would always be a good warm fire in the cabin there. This would be well known to the "locals" and provided a meeting place for friendly chatter.

"Potatoes were loaded loose or in sacks. Women from the Irish quarter of Middlesbrough arriving by train, went into the fields to "scratt", that is to gather the potatoes, all day and returning at night, each with an apron full of potatoes received from the farmer in part payment of their work. Potatoes which fell to the ground during loading operations were not always completely collected and those which remained usually found their way into the porter-gateman's cabin, where they were roasted in the oven and with a touch of salt made a very acceptable winter's evening snack. The station staff was often augmented in the evenings by farm lads and locals who came to the station to post letters, buy postage stamps, read or collect newspapers etc, take delivery of parcels or awaiting the arrival of livestock from market and an appreciable quantity of potatoes could be disposed of!"

On a dark and silent winter's night the oil lamps at the station must have shone brightly over the countryside. No doubt to one of the farm lads, an errand to the station would be most welcome and the busy farmer's wife, too would be glad to get him out of the farm kitchen from under her feet!

The position which the stations held at this time in the rural communities must have been like those in the Wild West of America so vividly shown in films. One wonders whether the signalman here in his cabin used to send urgent messages up and down the line on his telegraph as they did there!

Mr Huby relates another amusing story of how they dealt with a local farmer who had imbibed too freely and needed help to find his way home.

"A four-wheeled cart was in use for handling milk and mail traffic and, as necessary, in the goods yard. Occasionally this barrow was used to convey an elderly farmer, known as "Tally-ho Bob" from the station to his home in those cases when he returned from the market having had 'one over the eight' the trip was taken at a suitable interval between trains by the station staff who, if desired, could have liquid refreshment before returning with the empty barrow. If it was not convenient for the staff to leave the station, a message was sent for the farmer's 'carriage' to be sent to collect him; the carriage being just a farm cart with the end-door removed and two or three battens of straw placed therein in lieu of cushions!

Station life may appear to have been somewhat dull in those days but the country station was a centre of many activities, a meeting and a parting place for people in many occupations and walks of life and under so many varying circumstances, some gay, some grave. This being a junction station, passengers changed to await connections, farmers and/or their employees were waiting for the arrival of livestock from markets or shows, anxious to know what, if any, prizes had been awarded. Often a cross-section of the foregoing managed to congregate in the porter-gateman's cabin where in the winter, the fire may have been better maintained than in the waiting room and some may have been attracted by the smell of roasting potatoes. The result was that the waiting period passed more quickly and pleasantly for all concerned".

The station remained this bustling centre of activity for three more decades though to a diminishing degree until after the Second World War. When the ironmasters came to the station, the stationmaster would attend to their every need. The flower-beds at all times would be in an immaculate condition. In summer time the station would be gay with bedding plants and beautiful hanging baskets, demonstrating with pride the gardening skills of the staff. Until the out-break of World War II there was a keenly contested competition among the stations on the Eskdale Valley line to Whitby, for the most attractive station in summer. Hanging up in the Nunthorpe Station office before its demolition in the 1970's were two framed certificates which had been won in this way. The most successful station within living memory was Ormesby (now Marton) Station where during the 1930's the stationmaster was a keen gardener and made that exposed station bedecked with flowers in summer. He must have been following a tradition, for the office had its walls lined with certificates. Nothing of the buildings there remain but at Nunthorpe, the substantial stationmasters' house remains.

In their own first-class carriage the ironmasters and successful businessmen would meet. In Victorian times in the commuter train in the morning, there may have been Sir Joseph Whitwell Pease from Hutton Hall already on the train when the Nunthorpe gentry stepped on. At Ormesby Station they may have picked up James Pennyman from Ormesby Hall and Henry Bolckow and John Vaughan from their Marton residences. These men were the founding fathers of Middlesbrough and industrial Teesside. Who knows what momentous discussions took place as they travelled down the line to their Middlesbrough offices?

CHAPTER 11

The Coming Of The Iron-Masters

Following the discovery of ironstone in Eston Hills and the opening of mines all round the Cleveland Hills, the Middlesbrough "boom" period began. The mid-Victorian decades were years of great industrial change throughout the nation but it also meant a great deal of hardship for those whose traditional skills we no longer needed. Here, by the side of the river Tees, word went around that there was work in plenty. Miners came from Wales and Cornwall to open up the iron mines, not only at Eston, but Normanby, Loftus, Skinningrove, Upleatham, Skelton, Lingdale and all round in the Guisborough hills, even Roseberry Topping. In Ayton the population more than doubled and the coming of the railway meant, that not only the ironstone could be carried away, but the stone from the quarries. Because they were largely engaged in agriculture the change for the communities of Nunthorpe, Marton and Ormesby were not so dramatic as at Great Ayton or on Teesside, yet they were nevertheless hurled into the Industrial Revolution. The newly-rich ironmasters saw them as places of peace and beauty where they could build homes away from the smoke and dirt created by the ironworks.

During the 1850's and 60's workpeople flocked to Middlesbrough at a phenomenal rate - labourers from the farm lands and mills where machinery was taking over. Labourers in their hundreds fleeing from the Potato Famine in Ireland came here and in time built a cathedral for their Roman Catholic worship. Trades people of every description came to serve the growing community. Businessmen throughout Britain poured their money into the ironworks, mines, docks and shipyards when they became limited companies and investment made possible. The largest ironworks, Bolckow and Vaughan, became a limited company in 1864. All the time new ironworks were created, docks and ships were built as well as such amenities as brickworks, potteries and smaller manufactures serving the growing community. The troublesome river was dredged and deepened, its sandbanks and estuary bars were blown up. The river itself was contained in one channel, lined with stout walls made from the hard durable waste slag from the furnaces.

Of course social problems abounded, the greatest of which was housing: Large deposits of suitable clay for making bricks was found near at hand so that brickworks could be easily established. Far too quickly for health and comfort, street after street of small cottage homes were built and covered the marshy land at Newport (now the big industrial Canon Park). In the mid 19th century such was the pressure for accommodation that it was said that the beds were never cold, for as the day workers vacated them the night shift workers lay down to sleep in them during the day.

For centuries it had been the custom for craftsmen of all trades to live near their work, usually in workshops attached to their homes. Likewise the factory workers and the factory owners lived near their place of work. In early Middlesbrough too there were built streets of cottages for the workers and the owners lived in larger houses on the outskirts. In her "Story of Cleveland" Minnie Horton gives an interesting glimpse of the homes of the sisters, Mrs Henry Bolckow and Mrs John Vaughan as they lived side by side in Queen's Square before moving to the large sumptuous residences of Marton Hall and Gunnergate Hall. One suspects they may have looked back to those early years with some degree of longing. It is strange to relate that while their early homes in Queen's Square are still standing today, the great halls have long been demolished. Minnie Horton writes:

"Queens Square, which Joseph Pease had built was an elegant place and the two houses of H.W.F. Bolckow and John Vaughan on the north side of the railway, called Cleveland Buildings, were very handsome with their fruit orchards and gardens surrounded by poplar trees and having a clear view of the Cleveland Hills. The Cleveland Buildings are still in existence and a plaque stating they were the homes of Bolckow and Vaughan has been affixed to them.
The houses were three-storied and had beautiful rooms which were airy and spacious and the kitchen overlooked fields".

It should also be noted that the Royal Exchange (now Custom's House) is also in Queen's Square, so handy as a club and meeting place for the businessmen.

As the industries of Teesside prospered so did the fortunes of the industrialists and their ambitions rose. They saw the ancestral homes of the Pennyman's at Ormesby Hall, the Hustlers of Acklam Hall, the Chaloner's of Guisborough, all with their large inherited estates. They saw the somewhat more modest estates of the businessmen. Thomas Richardson of Ayton Hall and Ralph Ward Jackson at Normanby Hall and decided one after another they would do likewise. During the next three decades this "boom" period, before the industrial recession of the 1880's, Henry Bolckow had built Marton Hall, John Vaughan bought Gunnergate Hall and George Swann was at Upsall Hall.

Isaac Wilson came to Nunthorpe in 1856. In the chapter on Nunthorpe the story of his family life there has been told but in his capacity as business promoter and civic servant he proved himself a worthy Founding Father of the new town. He not only managed the first pottery works and was a director of the Stockton and Darlington Railway while still a very young man, but with the other businessmen of the town invested in the ironworks. First he went into partnership with Edward Gilkes to form the Tees Engine Works but in 1865 they were merged into the larger concern known as Hopkins, Gilkes & Co, which specialised in building iron bridges for the new railways, using circular iron columns. Later he became interested in the blast furnaces operated by Wilson, Pease & Co, at Cargo Fleet. But his greatest contribution to the people of this area was in his public life. The Tees Navigation Company had been set up in 1808 to improve the river for commerce. It had made cuttings through the loops in the river at Mandale and Portrack thus shortening it and by much dredging had eased the difficulties of the ships going up to Stockton. In 1852 this body was replaced by the Tees Conservancy Commissioners. It was realised that if the Tees was to become a good navigable river, necessary to the development of its ports of Stockton and Middlesbrough, drastic measures must be taken and a competent body with wide powers put in charge. The Tees Conservancy Commissioners (T.C.C.) consisted of fifteen members, five representing the Corporation of Stockton, five the town of Middlesbrough, two the ratepayers of Yarm and three the interests of the Admiralty, the latter as life members. Joseph Pease was one of the Admiralty representatives. The first work put in hand was the improvement of the navigation between Middlesbrough and the sea. In order to do this newly designed powerful dredgers had to be built to remove the great sand shoals which blocked the entrance and estuary of the river. Having accomplished this great work the Commissioners then set about building strong retaining walls of slag and concrete along the main channel. Though it took them twenty years to build them, they have remained largely intact to this day. As the chairman of the T.C.C. the man chiefly responsible for all this activity was Isaac Wilson. As early as 1855 the Admiralty Surveyor recommended that two breakwaters should be built on either side on the estuary but owing to considerations of cost and more pressing priorities the project was shelved. However in February 1861, a disastrous storm in Tees Bay caused the loss of between fifty and sixty vessels which had been sheltering there. The general opinion was that if the breakwaters had been constructed the vessels would have been able to ride out the storm in their shelter. Immediately plans were made and in August 1861 the construction of the two and a half mile South Gare Breakwater was commenced using the slag being produced in such quantities by the ironworks and the mines. The construction of the North Gare Breakwater was not started till 1882 and completed in 1891 when it was 3330 feet in length.

In 1853 Middlesbrough became incorporated and held municipal elections. On November 9th it installed its first mayor, Mr H.W.F. Bolckow and among its councillors Mr Isaac Wilson. The following year it was he who was chosen as its second mayor. When in 1868 boundary changes came into effect, Middlesbrough was able to send a member to Parliament and again the people chose Mr H.W.F. Bolckow to represent them. In appreciation he bought seventy two acres of land and had it landscaped in order to present the town with Albert Park, the open space it so urgently needed. When he died in 1878 his place was again taken by Isaac Wilson to represent the town at Westminster.

In 1865 Isaac Wilson was joined in Nunthorpe by another ironmaster and fellow railway director in the person of William Randolph Innis Hopkins (1866-1921). Very different in character from his neighbour, he was rather a flamboyant figure and loved the good things in life. He was Isaac Wilson's partner in the firm of Hopkins, Gilkes & Co. In 1864 he had married as his second wife, Miss Everald Catherine Elizabeth Hustler of Acklam Hall. This was a very prestigious marriage, lavishly celebrated not only by the families of all the gentry in the county, but publicly by the flying of flags from all public buildings. Only the best could be worthy of such a bride and he spared no expense when building "Grey Towers" with its beautiful extensive gardens, lake and park land.

The Hustlers had been the ruling family with its ancestral home at Acklam Hall for nearly three hundred years. Since Saxon times Acklam Church and its Manor House had been the centre of Acklam Parish which included the hamlets of Middlesburg, Linthorpe (or Leventhorpe) and Ayresome. During the Middle Ages the manor had been in the hands of the Boynton family but in 1612 William Hustler rented the Acklam estate from Sir Mathew Boynton and later bought it in 1637. In the Civil War which followed, like the Pennyman's of nearby Ormesby Hall, the Hustler family were on the side of the Royalists. In fact a letter has been found which suggests that King Charles I himself stayed at the hall when journeying through the country. Their loyalty was rewarded when his grandson, also William was knighted in 1673 by Charles II. Sir William rebuilt and enlarged Acklam Hall. Except for an attic storey added in 1850 the hall as it stands today is his creation. It is regarded as a splendid example of the Restoration Period especially its finely carved central staircase and superb plasterwork ceilings. Built 1683-4 it is believed that this plasterwork was done by a famous plasterer named Halbert, when he moved homewards after completing his work at Holyrood Palace in Edinburgh. From such a home came the first mistress of Grey Towers and the wife of William R.I. Hopkins.

He had come to Middlesbrough in 1850 to manage a patent fuel works. In 1853 with a Mr Snowden he had started the Teesside Ironworks which eventually merged to form the other half of Hopkins, Gilkes and Co. It was a horrific accident at these works which led to the founding of the first cottage hospital in the North. It, at last, brought to the notice of the ironmasters, who were largely the municipal authorities as well, the necessity for hospitals in the area. It must be remembered that it was not until the Crimean War broke out in 1858 that Florence Nightingale began her campaign for efficient hospitals in every town. In time the ironmasters responded well and they were responsible for building locally the Stead Hospital at Redcar, the Admiral Chaloner Hospital at Guisborough, and Eston Hospital at Eston, all of which were small but run efficiently and retained a homely atmosphere but now all closed. The first cottage hospital became the North Ormesby Hospital and was very well endowed, while in 1884 the firm Bolckow and Vaughan built the Infirmary which is the only one functioning today (1992). The others with their legacies of human kindness in their foundation have been sacrificed in the name of efficiency to be replaced by the large South Tees Hospital. Another small hospital, the West Lane Hospital, was the isolation hospital for cases of infectious diseases. This was very necessary as the overcrowding in the houses and the insanitary conditions of the hastily built streets of the town in later Victorian times, led to great epidemics of cholera and smallpox.

The heart warming story of the founding of the first cottage hospital is well told by Minnie Horton in her book "The Story of Cleveland":

"In 1858 there was a bad accident at the Snowden and Hopkins works, when a boiler supplying the steam for operating the rolling mills exploded at five o'clock, just before the men were due to leave work and the night shift were due to come in. The blast hurled a number of men into the river and some sixteen or seventeen were badly injured by steam and flying debris. Although Middlesbrough at this time had a population of 15,000, the nearest hospital was at Newcastle. Some of the badly injured people were taken there but died on the way. Others were taken to their homes and lodgings, but two men who had no one to care for them, were put into a stable in Stockton Street. They were in a shocking condition and were looked after by men who knew nothing of nursing methods. They had open wounds and were laid on straw until a lady provided sheets for them to lie on.

The sad state of these men so distressed Mr Jordison, who owned the printing works in the town that he appealed to Mrs Newcomen, a wealthy generous lady, who had inherited the Turner estates at Kirkleatham. She was the head of the Christ Church Sisterhood at Coatham and when the appeal for help came, she sent Miss Jacques an associate member of the Sisterhood back with him to Middlesbrough.

Miss Jacques who became known as Sister Mary had been trained at the Deaconess Institute at Kaiserworth in Rhennish Westphalia, where Florence Nightingale had also received her training. She rented a cottage where the injured men could be treated and afterwards her advice was sought regarding many sick cases in the poorer, overcrowded parts of the town. Eventually with the help of two nurses who received no salary, Sister Mary bought a house in Albert Road where she and her helpers lived and later, with financial help from Mr Del Strother and Mrs Newcomen, two cottages behind it in Dundas Mews. These cottages were converted into a cottage hospital, the first in the north of England. It was opened in March 1859 and contained eleven beds and a dispensary.

By the end of the year the little hospital had attended to fifty patients in the beds and four hundred and ninety people had attended as outpatients. The hospital was finally staffed by Sister Mary and a group of ladies who had taken religious vows (though members of the Anglican Church).

Eventually they became the Sisterhood of the Holy Rood, the first religious community in Middlesbrough since the Dissolution of the Monasteries in 1539.

Mr James White Pennyman (of Ormesby Hall) had laid out a new suburb in 1860 and called it North Ormesby. It had a church overlooking a spacious market place with streets and houses leading off this central square. Later when the Hospital at Middlesbrough proved to be too small, he built a large hospital near the square where it remained until demolished in 1983. In the early days the local workmen voluntarily contributed a halfpenny a week to the Hospital out of their pay. Four years later they increased it to a penny. The North Ormesby Hospital was opened in 1861. It had been the gift of Mrs Newcomen who also built a convalescent home at Coatham overlooking the sea where patients could recuperate. In 1888 the cost of each patient was 3s 1d (16p) per day. Mr Pennyman was a good friend for in 1875, he started a market at North Ormesby giving all the profits to the Hospital. Later he handed the market over to the Ormesby Urban District Council safeguarding the rights of the Hospital and in 1965 these market dues amounted to £4000 a year.

Towards the end of the nineteenth century all these hospital's resources were taxed to the limit by the epidemics of enteric fever, cholera and above all smallpox among the people living in such overcrowded insanitary conditions. The town had originally been built on a small hill by the river but it was surrounded by marshland. When this was covered hastily by streets of small houses, the problem of drainage was not tackled properly and with the use of earth closets very insanitary conditions ensued. Only when a proper sewage and drainage system was carried out was the town rendered healthy.

Before leaving the subject of North Ormesby Hospital mention must be made of what was up till recently a strong Nunthorpe connection with it. Older residents will remember Mr and Mrs Gerald Cochrane, who for sixty years lived in "The Box", (now a residential home for the elderly near Nunthorpe Station). Mr Cochrane was a member of the Cochrane family who owned Cochrane's Ironworks before all the smaller ironworks were merged and Mrs Cochrane was a member of the Del Strother family which was noted for its public service. They were lifelong workers and benefactors of North Ormesby Hospital and a large wing was named in their honour. The only reminder of the tradition of this fine hospital is the memorial windows which were formerly in the entrance hall of the old hospital and have now been placed in the new South Cleveland Hospital, Middlesbrough.

There is nothing to suggest that the terrible epidemics which befell Middlesbrough had a great effect upon the people living in the good country air of the parish of Ayton. However another great ill which happened to the young town certainly did. It was the great Industrial Depression of 1875-1888.

Like Isaac Wilson, William Randolph Innes Hopkins was a member of the Tees Conservancy Commission and a Middlesbrough Town Councillor from 1863-1874. He was elected Mayor in 1867 for two years runnning, and in 1868 he had the honour of being the chief civic dignitary to receive Prince Arthur (son of Queen Victoria) at the opening of Albert Park.

At Grey Towers he and his wife entertained a great deal and lived lavishly in their beautiful home and grounds until 1879 when disaster struck. William Hopkins was in financial difficulties and tried to sell the Grey Towers estate for £30,000 but failed to find a buyer. Then on 28th December 1879 the Tay Bridge disaster occurred; during a bad storm a gale blew down the central pillars of the structure just as a train was passing over it. The train plunged into the depths below and seventy five people met their deaths. This was regarded at the time as a national disaster. The Tay Railway Bridge had been looked upon as a marvel of engineering for it was the longest in Europe, it meant a great deal of prestige for its makers and it was built by Hopkins, Gilkes and Co. At the public inquiry the structure of the bridge was adjudged to be faulty - the very metal of the hollow tubular figures was not as strong as its specification. So its General Manager, William R.J. Hopkins, was apportioned the greatest blame. The firm was finished and its General Manager bankrupt in 1880 with his public life in ruins. Grey Towers was left empty and he with his wife and small son went to live at Norton, near Malton where they lived as highly respected members of society for the rest of their lives. By a strange twist of fortune their son, Mostyn Hustler Hopkins, inherited the Acklam estates and Hall when his uncle died in 1909. He sold Acklam Hall to Middlesbrough Borough Council in 1929 and they converted it into a Grammer School for boys which opened in 1935.

By 1875 the "boom" period of the iron industry was over and the whole industry, the life-blood of the new town was hit by an industrial depression for which it was totally unprepared. In any case the customers were no longer wanting iron but demanding steel. Cleveland ironstone was unsuited for the making of steel as it contained too much sulphur and phosphorus. The Bessemer furnace with its process of burning off the phosphorus and lighting up the whole area with its flames, had been invented in 1866. This was found to be successful in rectifying the fault and so by the 1890's prosperity had returned to Teesside industry.

Isaac Wilson at Nunthorpe Hall must also have been affected by the trade depression but he was a shrewd businessman and his interests were diversified. His style of life too was a more simple one. Nevertheless comparing the Census of 1851 and that of 1881 it is easy to see that he has reduced the number of servants and living more economically.

If the wealthy ironmasters had to adjust their lifestyles to the depression what about the poor workers living in the little houses in the streets of the new town? Many small factories closed, others only worked two or three days of the week and the largest employer of all, Bolckow and Vaughan, reduced the men's wages by ten per cent. In those days there were no trade unions, no Welfare State benefits to cushion the effects of the depression. There was only the soup kitchen and humility of accepting the very meagre parish relief. These are the cold statistics of this time as given in "The Story of Cleveland":

"At one time it was recorded that 7212 people were on outdoor relief, costing £800 a fortnight. Worked out this comes to something like 1s 1$^{1/2}$d (6p) a week for each person which, one would have thought, hardly keep body and soul together.

Over 5000 soup tickets a day were issued and in one week 8000 penny dinners were provided. Entertainments and races were held to help subsidise them. £50 was spent on supplying clogs for needy children. The average working man, no matter how well-doing, was rarely in a position to put away any money for rainy day".

Among the young couples living in the streets of Middlesbrough were my grandparents and my grandmother told me an interesting story of this time. In the sense that both of them had come from different parts of the country to find work and excitement in the new town, they were typical of their generation. Fanny was the eldest daughter of a well-to-do Lincolnshire businessman who owned several stationer's shops and a printing works. He was a typically strict Victorian father but when Fanny was twenty five years old, she quarrelled with him. Having an independent spirit she came to the new town of Middlesbrough. Here she earned her living by serving in a stationer's shop. Not long afterwards she met and fell in love with her future husband John George Ward. He was the eldest son of a prosperous farmer-innkeeper at Easington in County Durham. He had refused to follow his father on the farm, because he loved the steam engines and the railway. He was a fireman, soon to be promoted to an engine driver. So without any help from either family, for Victorian family quarrels were total, they were married in 1875 in the newly built St. John's Church and lived in one of the newly built terrace houses nearby in Hazel Street. They had to pay so much a week for furniture (that bill still exists) but they were very happy. Two years later their happiness was made complete by the birth of John William, their only child and my father. When the baby was about eighteen months old disaster struck, for in the general depression my grandfather was among those who were made redundant. There was no dole or state benefit scheme and they had no resources to fall back on. My grandmother told me how he tramped from place to place looking for work, even walking seventeen miles each way to Darlington but returned without hope. Soon the day came when after paying for the baby's milk, there was only bread and dripping to eat in the house. It was at this moment that a letter came - a letter most unexpected. It was from Fanny's mother, my Lincolnshire great grandmother, containing a £5 note, a fortune in those days! So unusual was the sight of a £5 note in that community that she could not spend it in a shop. She had to take it to a bank and convince the manager that it was hers.

Before the £5 was carefully spent my grandfather started work again on the railway and a few years later was driving an engine pulling trucks of material to build the South Gare Breakwater for which Isaac Wilson and the Tees Conservancy Commissioners were responsible. Better still, this opened the way for Fanny's truly wise and loving mother, to effect a family reconciliation and she saw her first grandchild when Fanny brought him home to her. This is all revealed in a treasured family souvenir letter written in 1880. It is a simple affectionate letter from a mother to her daughter but written on the deep black edged mourning notepaper of Victorian times. She had recently lost her youngest child, Fanny's brother Kirkham. It also reveals that Fanny, truly her father's daughter, is insisting on paying back the money a little at a time. Sadly this was possibly the last letter Fanny received from her mother and the reason it was kept. Not long afterwards her mother died suddenly from diphtheria, caught when she secretly took food to a poor family. My grandfather spent all his working life as an engine driver and must have been one of the first members of A.S.L.F. the engine driver's union. There was a photograph of him at a Union Conference when he went there as a delegate. He was essentially a man of peace and evidently spoke out against strikes. I remember as a small child standing on a railway bridge near Saltburn Station. I could not understand why Grandma looked so militant. There was evidently a railway strike on and she explained to me we were there to stop anybody throwing stones at Grandad as he passed underneath on his engine. Fortunately nothing happened.

After the departure of Mr Hopkins from Nunthorpe in 1880 Grey Towers was put up for sale but no buyers could be found. The mortgage was eventually taken up by his brother-in-law, Mr Hustler of Acklam Hall, who let the property to Sir Raylton Dixon. A few years later it was bought by yet another ironmaster. Again we find a man of integrity and strong individuality who was attracted to Middlesbrough at this time in the person of Arthur Dorman. He was to have a profound effect upon the development of Nunthorpe. He was born in Ashford, Kent and although educated at Christ's College, he was sent as a very young man to work in a small ironworks at Thornaby where a relative was a partner. In the belief that a young man should begin at the bottom, he had to work among the steel workers at the puddling furnaces. Today this process seems almost barbaric and certainly inhuman. Men with very long spoon-like rods stirred the red hot molten metal as it bubbled and spluttered in a huge cauldron-like furnace. It was very hot, very thirsty and dangerous work. He used to say that as a lad, one of his duties was to bring gallons of beer for these men. No doubt this experience was very valuable when in later years he owned and managed great steelworks. At twenty seven he went into partnership with Albert de Lange Long and they purchased the West Marsh Works from Sir Bernard Samuelson for the manufacture of iron bars and angles. Requiring further production they leased Samuelson's Britannia Works in 1879 and then bought them in 1882, where they commenced the manufacture of steel. To have prospered so well in a time of general depression must indicate not only the business ability of these two men but also a capacity for hard work and dedication. From this small beginning the name of Dorman and Long was to become world famous in the first half of the twentieth century. In 1902 it merged with Bell Brothers and in 1929 with Bolckow Vaughan and Co, thus Arthur Dorman was the co-founder of the greatest steelmaking complex in the country before nationalisation.

In his public life Arthur Dorman was a member of Middlesbrough Borough Council from 1880-1882 but he did not pursue his civic duties further. He had three sons and three daughters. One of his sons, Lieutenant G.L. Dorman was killed while serving with the Green Howards in the Boer War. As a memorial to him Arthur Dorman built the Dorman Natural History Museum beside the entrance to Albert Park. In recognition of his gift he was honoured with the Freedom of Middlesbrough in 1904. In Nunthorpe the dominant figure had been Isaac Wilson, with his death in December 1899, the turn of the century saw the beginning of the "squiredom" of Arthur Dorman who took an increasing interest in his Nunthorpe Estate.

Marton at this time also had its Squire. The year 1853 was a crucial one for the inhabitants of Marton. They woke up to find that not only were they to be connected to Middlesbrough by a railway but they were to have Henry William Ferdinand Bolckow, the wealthiest and most powerful eminent local Victorian, and his family in their midst. He had bought not only the burnt-out ruins of Marton Lodge but the whole estate which included the site upon which their village stood. On

John & Fanny Ward 1876 ➢

◂ *John & Fanny Ward 1884*

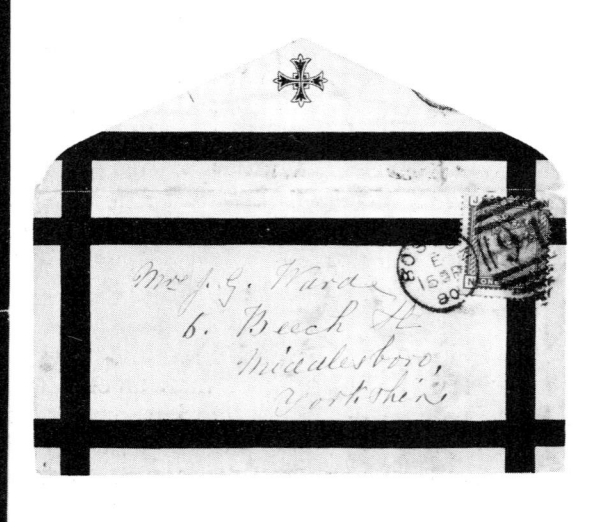

Dearest
       I'm sorry you have
had to send me the P.O.
I had not remembered it,
allthough it will be now
full. as Julia has to be
made ready for next week.
so I trust a mercifull God
will guard guide and
direct all her doings —
Fetty has been very poorly
I went in last night and
ill she looked — poor Child
Dad still continues going to
St Ignes. I came home
with him yesterday morning
early. I don't think it does
much good but a little

A black-edged Victorian Letter Sent at Time of Mourning.

that site he wished to build himself a magnificent home. He re-housed them in good cottages near the church and for himself built the most magnificent Victorian mansion in the area which only a millionaire like himself could afford to maintain. It had all the flamboyance of Victorian architecture in its heyday. Most memorable was the large glass dome in the centre. At the west side was a large heated conservatory for growing exotic plants - and that and a little of the south-facing terracing with rounded arches and its steps and terraces to the front, are all that remain today in the Stewart Park. The "squiredom" of the Bolckows in Marton, that is the founder and his nephew, to be followed by his son, lasted till just before the First World War.

The Bolckows moved into their new home, Marton Hall, in 1858 and maintained there an elaborate social life. As was the custom in Victorian homes it was filled with fine paintings and ornaments of all descriptions. Their guests would arrive at the station, if coming from some distance, to be met there by a fine carriage and liveried coachman. They would then be driven up the tree-lined Grove, which had just been built to link the village with the station. During the late Victorian and Edwardian period large prestigious villas were built along this road by prosperous businessmen from Middlesbrough who commuted each day to town. Once through the lodge gates the carriage would drive through the park to the impressive entrance to the great house. Should the visitors arrive in their own carriage they would enter the park through the entrance at Marton Cross-roads, where a lodge stood till recently. They would then drive up the fine carriage road to the terrace steps where their host and hostess would greet them.

One week-end in the 1890's Sir Gilzean Reid and Lady Reid were invited to stay in Marton Hall with the Bolckows. With them went Lady Reid's lady's maid and in old age she recalled what impressed her most: it was their arrival. They entered by the Marton Cross-roads and as they drove up the slope to the Hall she became aware that there were many people waiting to greet them at the entrance. As they came nearer they saw that not only were the Bolckow family waiting under the portico, but their full staff of servants, fifty two in all, and were lined up on either side of them. Had they but known it, this piece of ostentation was lost upon their visitors, for they were deeply religious and appreciated only a simple life. This young Lady's maid was my mother.

When Marton Hall was first built in 1858 it was a large mansion built on classical lines with a pillared portico and central octagonal tower capped by a glass dome. In 1867 Bolckow became Middlesbrough's first M.P. and presented the new town with Albert Park and in 1868 Prince Arthur of Connaught, Queen Victoria's son, came to open it. He stayed at Marton Hall with the Bolckows, and this was how it was reported in the local newspaper at the time:

"The inhabitants of Marton were all in their holiday attire meanwhile, and tuned out en masse to meet His Royal Highness Prince Arthur. Mr Bolckow very kindly allowed the whole of the people of the village and children and visitors from Ormesby to enter the Park, so that they might gratify themselves by catching a glimpse of the Prince. At half-past five o'clock the people were all expectation; and frequently, on carriages being heard on the road, they were mistaken for that containing the Royal visitor. About a quarter to six, however, the clatter of horses feet was heard, and up galloped a detachment of the Hussars, headed by Mr Bowes. Next came the Royal Carriage, drawn by four splendid horses, in which were seated His Royal Highness Prince Arthur, Mr H.W.F. Bolckow and his Grace the Archbishop of York. The second carriage contained Mrs Thomson, Sir George and Lady Wombwell and

Col. Elphinstone. In the third carriage sat Sir John Cowell, the Queen's Equerry, and Lady Cowell, Lieutenant Pickard and the Hon. and Rev. F.N. Clements. The fourth carriage contained Mr Carl Bolckow, nephew of the host. When the procession came along the road the Prince was loudly cheered. At the end of Marton Road and just opposite the main entrance to the Hall, there was a very fine triumphal arch, consisting of evergreens and heather, in the centre of which was the word "Welcome". On the other side of the arch were the words "God Save the Queen". The uprights of the arch were spacious and each contained a platform. On the right platform stood three little boys underneath a sheaf of corn, dressed as reapers in the Elizabethan style, and above them a sheaf of corn. The Royal procession was loudly cheered as the Hussars galloped up the carriage drive. His Royal Highness was received by Mrs Bolckow, who was introduced by Mr Bolckow. Afterwards the Prince was entertained to dinner, and amongst the guests were H.R.H. Prince Arthur and suite, his Grace the Archbishop of York and Mrs Thomson, the Right Hon. the Earl of Zetland, the Right Hon. Earl Vane and Countess Vane, Sir George and Lady Wombwell, Lady Cowell, the Hon. and Rev. F.N. Clements and Mrs Clements, the Mayor and Mayoress of Middlesbrough. Mrs Dundas, Mr & Mrs C. Bolckow, Miss Bolckow, and Mr. Mrs and Miss Barclay. The sleeping apartment of the Prince and his dressing room are magnificently furnished, blue silk and velvet being used in the upholstery work".

The report continues with a description of the mansion and some history of the estate and the last paragraph is rather interesting:

"A little further to the south, and opposite the croquet ground, is an old pump, carefully preserved in its primitive state; it is called Capt. Cook's pump, and supplies the hall with the finest water that can be procured in the district".

He also bought Capt. Cook's manuscripts and had honoured the great explorer in 1858 by erecting a large granite vase on the site of the cottage where the explorer was born. This is there today.

In 1878 Henry Bolckow died and he was succeeded by his nephew Carl. Carl was not a real businessman like his uncle had been and in any case the "boom" years of the iron industry were over. The industrial depression of the 1880's forced Carl to sell his manuscripts in 1888. Nevertheless the extravagant entertaining went on for the next twenty years till in 1907 furniture and books had to be sold to pay off the debts. The money had run out and the family were forced to leave their mansion. It remained empty till the 1914-18 War when troops were stationed there. It was never lived in again. The estate was bought in 1925 by Thomas J. Stewart who presented the hall in its magnificent grounds to the people of Middlesbrough as a Park. The great glasshouses and conservatory were restored to form a valuable asset to the Parks Department but the hall was a veritable "white elephant" for which no viable use could be found. By 1960 it was seen to be deteriorating rapidly so the decision was made to demolish it. The men had just begun their great task of demolishing the roof when it accidently caught fire. On June 4th 1960 the whole night-sky was lit up as the great building was reduced to ashes. History had repeated itself for in 1832 Marton Lodge had burnt down on the very same spot! After the debris had been cleared away its fine conservatory was restored and the beauty of its flowers has given great pleasure to its thousands of visitors ever since.

Not long after Henry Bolckow came to Marton his partner John Vaughan bought the neighbouring estate and Gunnergate Hall. John Vaughan had married, for

Marton Hall

Gunnergate Hall

Old Eston

An old photograph showing the stone cottages of Old Eston and the road leading up to the hills which used to be known as Woodgarth. This may have been the Eston end of an old road across the hills shown on Graves' map of 1803.

From "Teesside & Old Cleveland re-visited in old picture postcards" - Zaltbommel/Netherlands

Ormesby Hall

Ormesby Hall was built in 1740 though the kitchen wing was built in Tudor times. It was the ancestral home of the Pennyman family for 300 years. Now it is the property of the National Trust.

Ormesby Hall by Alec Wright

his second wife, Henry Bolckow's sister but his disposition was very different from that of his brother-in-law and partner. He was a Welshman, a clever engineer specialising in the manufacture of iron, a very good managing director of the ironworks, liked and respected by all his workmen. He bought Gunnergate Hall which had been built by a Quaker banker named Charles Leatham in 1857 but he died a year later and his widow sold the estate to John Vaughan in 1860. The estate ran between the Yarm road and Gunnergate Lane. He had two sons, John and Thomas. The eldest son, John, was clever and full of promise but he died at the age of nineteen. His father was heart-broken and his health began to suffer. By 1864 he began to lose interest in his business. Suffering from paralysis, his doctor, ordered him to go to London and he died there in 1868. He was buried in Marton Church yard in the Vaughan vault beside his beloved son John.

His fortune of over half a million pounds, a huge sum in those days, and the estate was left to his remaining son, Thomas. Perhaps influenced by the extravagance of the Bolckows, Thomas began to squander his fortune. He doubled the size of the house and fitted it up lavishly. The local Evening Gazette noted (30th August 1870) "a complete revolution. Magnificent dining, drawing and billiard rooms, pillars of polished Aberdeen granite. The gardens, greenhouses, vineries etc have been greatly extended. Gunnergate Hall will take its place among the stately homes of England". It was said that the billiard room cost £40,000 and a bedstead cost £1,500. But the plans to make Gunnergate Hall into such a stately mansion all came to nought, when his firm crashed in 1879. The Hall was bought in 1881 by Carl Bolckow who had succeeded to the Marton Hall estate. But this was the time of the industrial depression and he sold it to Sir Raylton Dixon, another industrialist and shipbuilder in 1888.

Sir Raylton Dixon was born in 1838 at Newcastle and moved to Middlesbrough as a young man to manage a shipyard on the river Tees called Richardson Duck Co, when the owner retired he bought the yard and gradually, with partners acquired other yards. They pioneered many processes in the making of steel ships. He served on the boards of many shipping lines. In those days the shipyards along the Tees were famous, making ships for the Navy and P. and O.

He and his family came to live in Gunnergate Hall in 1888 and there was great excitement in Marton when his daughter Miss Bessie May Dixon married the son of Carl Bolckow, Mr Henry W.F. Bolckow, in July 1890. The Dixon's lived at Gunnergate Hall until Mr Raylton Dixon died in 1901. His widow then left the hall and it was never lived in again. It was occupied by the Army in both World Wars and demolished in 1946.

As we look back today, about a century later when three great halls stood round the small village of Marton, what do we find to recall that time? The sites and grounds of Tollesby Hall and Gunnergate Hall have been covered by housing estates. Only the Lodge, which stood beside the entrance gatehouse to Gunnergate Hall is still there. It is much restored and modernised as it stands on the corner to remind us that along that road, carriages of famous people drove up to the great hall. But what of the greatest of the Victorian mansions, Marton Hall? It is now Stewart Park to be enjoyed by all and especially by the young families coming up from Middlesbrough. The trees which they planted in Victorian times are now grown to full maturity and glorying in their seasonal beauty throughout the year. The creatures of the wild, the birds, the squirrels, mice, voles and so on, have found a sanctuary. They have been joined by other animals and birds from many lands. Young children delight in seeing the antics of the wallabies, monkeys, peacocks, parrots and so forth.

This brings to mind an eerie experience my friends and I had about twenty years ago. It was the Friday night before the Teesside Show, now Cleveland Show, which is held there annually on the last Saturday in July. We had been preparing stalls in the large marquees but stayed on rather late. When we were ready to go, we found the gates of the car-park had been locked. The car was then driven along to the Marton Road entrance but when there, found that the gates were not only closed but the gardener and his wife, who lived there, were not at home. By this time it was pitch dark and we had to drive right across the Park to the Grove entrance. The great trees meeting overhead seemed to form a dark tunnel and as the beams from the car's headlights passed along, they woke up all the animals. The night became alive with alarming sounds - screeching from the monkeys, bleating from the goats, alarming sounds from the kangaroos, squawks from the parrots and piercing cries from the peacocks. A primitive fear of the jungle, a scary experience seemed to overcome us, as we sped along. When we reached the lodge gates, facing the Grove, to our great relief a man came out of the house and unlocked them.

The plants and flowers from the extensive greenhouses now fill the flower-beds in the squares in the town and the hanging baskets in the streets. They and the skilful gardeners working in them were largely responsible for Middlesbrough enjoying the honour of gaining the Britain in Bloom Award to become the best kept industrial town in the country. The restored conservatory is filled with beautiful plants and flowers at all times of the year, giving pleasure to thousands of visitors. The granite vase erected by Henry Bolckow has been joined by a very prestigious Captain Cook Birthplace Museum, and restaurant. The foundation stone was laid in September 1978 to mark the 150th Anniversary of his Birth. In a unique way it traces his birth, life at all stages, the voyages of discovery he made and the countries he discovered. It was opened by the Prince of Wales and earned his enthusiastic approval. It has also received many awards for its architecture.

How ironic and yet satisfying to realise that which was conceived in a spirit of pride and privilege should in the end become a source of pleasure to so many thousands of people, not only here at home but also overseas. A little reflection makes us aware of how ephemeral are the great designs of even eminent men, compared with the quiet workings of the natural world. Yet we must not forget the generosity and fore-sight of the few who made this possible.

What about the other buildings which Major Rudd was responsible for? The School's foundation stone was laid in December 1849 and ever since it has served the children of Marton. The building of the large housing estates round Marton village necessitated the building of a large modern school further along the main road in the 1960's but the fine old school is still being used now as a kindergarten. Incidently a parade of shops and large garage also came into being at this time.

After World War I an old army hut was bought by the villagers and converted into a village and church hall. Until that happened the school was also used as the village hall as was usual in villages at that time. Held there, the Parish Magazines reveal, were meetings of a Marton Mutual Improvement Association and members were encouraged by their employers to study for a government examination. Those who passed were congratulated by having their names published in the magazine. In 1888 we read they were Messrs C. Robinson (Tollesby Farm), Robert Brunton (High Farm), William Brunton (Marton), William Humphrey (Acklam) which says much for the state of farming in the area, even in a time of depression.

Since Major Rudd was responsible for restoring the Parish Church of St. Cuthberts in 1843, it has faithfully served its parishioners ever since. As more and more houses have covered the surrounding fields, the Vicar, Rev. Gordon Fisher and his Committee embarked on an ambitious project to build a suitable Parish Centre. A large hall with all the modern facilities has been built and it was opened on 5th July 1991.

In the 19th century and beginning of the 20th century businessmen from Middlesbrough were building houses in Marton and with the population ever increasing a small Wesleyan Chapel was built at the top of the Grove. Further down the road lived a widow who was to greatly benefit it and help so many other chapels and churches in the area in our present time. Agnes Spencer Whitwell was born on a farm in Marton in 1868 and eventually became headmistress of the Blue Coat School in Stockton. She met and married Thomas Spencer the founder of Marks and Spencer. After his death in 1905 she returned to Marton and lived in the Grove, a very wealthy woman. She lived quietly and was very well liked. She used to say with a smile "Do not expect too much of me for my initials are A.S.S.". When she died in 1959 at the age of 98, her grandchildren being provided for, it was found that she had left the bulk of her fortune to found the Spencer Trust. This was to be used to promote youth work in Stockton and to help to build churches and chapels in the new housing estates springing up all around Middlesbrough at this time. A new vestry was her gift to St. Cuthbert's. The whole cost of the St. Agnes Church at Easterside was defrayed by the Spencer Trust. Marton Methodist Church was extended and generous donations were made towards the building of new Wesleyan Chapels at Nunthorpe and Ormesby.

Since the 1950's the building of housing estates both private and municipal has extended so far southwards from Middlesbrough that the erstwhile rural villages of Marton, Ormesby and Nunthorpe are all joined together, swamped by a great mass of urbanisation called suburbia.

Captain Cook Birth Place Muesum, Marton

Photograph by Arnold Kidson of pupils of Captain Cook's Memorial School, Marton, in the old vicarage garden.

May Pole Dance

In ancient times May Day (1st May) was heralded with great celebrations to welcome the beginning of summer. Everyone would rise very early and go "A-maying". They would gather branches and flowers and decorate the May Pole with wreaths and ribbons. It was then carried in a procession and set up for the day. In many places it is still the custom for a young girl to be crowned May Queen and for dancing to be held round the May Pole on the village green.

The following is from the Marton Parish Magazine June 1888:

On upon a time there were gay doings in Marton, and is testified by the following inscription taken from an old memorandum book of the Parish Clerk of Marton: "There was a may-pole which stood upon a plane whose end broke off and struck the ground 20 feet distant. The broken piece was 40 feet long".

Query: What was the length of the may-pole?   What a wonderful may-pole it must have been.

CHAPTER 12

The Twentieth Century

To those who were born in the first decade of the twentieth century to look back on childhood days seems like entering an alien age, so much has the pattern of living from babyhood to old age, changed. Human nature may be the same but the outer appearance of social life and attitudes differs greatly. The Ward family lived in Newtown, near Eston, where a small estate of houses had been built beside Church Lane, opposite to the little by-road which led to Eston Cemetery and the ancient Eston Parish Church, St. Helens. This lane probably followed the old path to the church where parish registers go back to Tudor times. In this early twentieth century the old church was only used for funerals and it was to the large red bricked Christ Church built in 1884 beside the main road through Eston, we went to worship as a family. Though now a busy road between Eston and Grangetown, Church Lane in my childhood was indeed a country lane with tall hedges each side. Beside it were two farms - Eston High Grange Farm, a large farm with many old outbuildings owned by Mr Ingledew. He was a friendly man who did not mind the children playing in his fields and later on was a real friend to the teenagers in the depression years of the late "twenties and thirties". The other farm was owned or rented by a Mr Bacon, who appeared to us as a grumpy old bachelor who did not like children around the place. He had only a few cows and sold milk so probably had difficulty in making a living. The small estate was surrounded by fields and orchards so we enjoyed a country childhood full of interest and quiet excitement. The changing seasons meant sliding, sledging and skating in the winter, for there always seemed to be plenty of snow and ice. In spring there was the joy of picking the abundant wild flowers, especially the cowslips and violets. In summer we played in the "Fifty acre" hayfield where the farmer left a special corner of hay for us and in autumn there was the gathering of brambles for eating and jam-making. Crab-apples for jelly making and elderberries for making delicious elderberry syrup and for the boys - conkers. At Easter we climbed up the hills to roll our coloured "paste eggs". All the year round were trees to climb, railings to test our balancing skills as we walked along them on our way from school and above all becks (streams) to jump! The becks were always a fascination to us. The jumps were graded by us, beginning at the narrowest part and as our legs grew achieving some quite wide jumps of six to eight feet. There was always an added incentive in this game for, if we missed the far bank and landed in the stream, we knew we would be spanked when we got home! We must have played near the becks at a very early age for I can remember the fuss made of me, when it was alleged that I had saved my brother's life. One rainy day we had been walking down Church Lane near the beck opposite Ingledew's farm when my brother fell in. The beck was in flood and I, being only two years older than him, caught hold of the toddler's petticoats and saved him from floating through the open culvert where he would have undoubtedly drowned. A passer-by helped to pull him out and told my parents what had happened. The authorities immediately placed an iron grid over the open mouth of the culvert. My brother was put into trousers and not long afterwards joined the Babies class at Normanby Council School. Going to school meant going through Eston Cemetery and up Normanby Road, a distance of about two miles. Nobody regarded it as a hardship that children under five had to walk six to eight miles a day, backwards and forwards to school for there was of course, no provision for school dinners. All I can remember is the fun we had going backwards and forwards. Eston Cemetery was more like a park with its numerous seats, beautiful shrubs, fine trees and flower-beds. For this the people of the area had to thank the first chairman of the Burial Board the Rev. William Ward-Jackson of Normanby Hall who, with the help of his gardeners planted and laid it out in 1881 and since then it had been maintained. In the spring time masses of daffodils bloomed around the old graves and the flower-beds were gay with tulips and wallflowers. Down one side of the cemetery was a path known as Tinkers Alley which ran between the wall and a beck but our parents did not like us using it for it was the haunt of tramps and Gipsies! Sometimes we came the longer way home via Old Eston. At the beginning of the path across the fields from there, was a very old blacksmith's forge where we could watch Mr Snowden shoeing a horse or fitting an iron rim to a wooden cart wheel.

When not at school most of the time out-of-doors was spent in the large allotment where, like most of the neighbours, my father grew vegetables and kept domestic animals. It provided good fresh vegetables for growing families by the bucketful, especially suppers of mushy peas or onion porridge. Of extreme interest to the children were the animals kept there - hens, rabbits, pigs, some having names, but being country-bred children we did not seem to mind them ending up in the cooking pot! What a boon these allotments were in time of wartime rationing!

Annual holidays except for a week spent with grandparents or at the homes of aunts and uncles were almost unknown, nobody having considered the possibility of paid holidays for workers of any kind. Most men, like my father, working in the steel-works or mines worked in shifts, seven days a week, six to two mornings, two to ten afternoons and ten to six, night shift. This made outings for the family rare and exciting events even walks to another village. By working an extra shift one Sunday in three, the men could arrange to have one Sunday in three off work. Father's "week-end off" meant that he cycled home at six o'clock on Saturday morning and did not go back till six o'clock on Monday morning. In this way it was possible to have such an exciting treat as going to Middlesbrough Market on a Saturday night. Teesville had not yet been built so we walked over the field path to North Ormesby, a distance of about four and a half miles. At North Ormesby we sat on top of an open-decked tram which banged and clattered its way to the Town Hall. From there we walked down Albert Road under the railway bridge to the old Market Place which surrounded the old Town Hall. The stalls were bright with fruit, vegetables and flowers, as we clutched the hands of our parents as we mingled with the unaccustomed crowds of busy people. Noise was everywhere, the brass band, probably Salvation Army, playing in the background mingled with the

An Edwardian Childhood (the Ward Family)

175

Middlesbrough Market

shouts of stall-holders and the barkers selling their patent medicines. My father used to listen to these latter as they amused him with their antics but I did not like to watch the man who pulled out teeth! In the winter there was an added gaiety to the scene for each stall was lit by a flaring naphtha lamp hanging from its roof - all most exciting! At the end there was a thrilling journey home. By train we went to South Bank where we were met by Tommy Metcalfe's horse-bus. Its owner had a well organised carrier business and went regularly between Eston and South Bank station. On Saturday nights benches were fixed inside ready for passengers from the trains. Sitting on that bench with my hand in my father's hand and leaning against him, there was a feeling of sheer joy and contentment after a tiring happy day.

Sometimes on fine summer evenings we would walk across the fields either to Ormesby Church or still further via Lackenby and Lazenby to Wilton Church. We must have been small when we began to go to Ormesby Church for I can remember the difficulty my parents had lifting my brother's pushchair over the stiles! Other Sundays, before she came to live with us, we would visit my Victorian grandmother for the afternoon and stay for tea. She was strict with us but I have happy memories of playing with my Sunday doll. When I was a little older I sat reading "Arthur Mee's Children's Encyclopaedia" which she had collected in parts and had had bound, thus laying the foundation of a good general knowledge. After tea in the evenings, we children often played with toys and children's games like snakes and ladders but also we played as a family at card games. Whilst we learned to play very early and when old enough, bridge, so that we could always help to make up a four-some if necessary, when our parents' friends visited. As teenagers there was a great deal of singing the popular songs round the piano. Scouts and Guides, meeting once a week in the Church Hall, meant, perhaps a week's camping in the summer. All social activities of the village were based round the various churches and chapels - Whist Drives and Dances in the Church Hall being very popular if the family attended church and socials if a chapel.

Two memories of World War I, I share with Mr Maurice Wilson, the Eston local historian. In his book "The Story of Eston" he describes in detail how, while we were getting ready to go to school on Wednesday 16th December 1914, all at once we heard "sudden reverberating, booming thuds". This frightening experience went on for about half an hour and then came the news that the Hartlepools had been bombarded! Later an aunt came to visit and gave us a vivid first-hand account. Indeed Hartlepool did suffer severe damage to property, one hundred and twenty seven people were killed and more than five hundred injured. The second memory of World War I also concerned Hartlepool. Zeppelin attacks on the north east coast took place from time to time as the munition manufacturing plants on Teesside and at Skinningrove could have been regarded as legitimate targets. On a clear moonlight night the noise of its engines could be heard and the beams of searchlights would focus on the zeppelin which looked like a great silver cigar hanging in the sky. One night as we watched from a field near our home, we saw the zeppelin suddenly burst into flames and the burning pieces tumbled from the sky; fortunately for the people of Hartlepool into the sea. One of our early aeroplanes had flown above it and dropped a small bomb on it, igniting the gas inside. This was in the autumn of 1916 when aeroplanes were very fragile affairs and this was a very brave thing to do. The pilot was awarded the Victoria Cross. After this the zeppelin raids ceased.

Perhaps we were too young to appreciate the full impact of this war and were shielded from the great anxiety of those who had loved ones "at the front" and the horror of the long casualty lists. This fell mainly on the women for the men were working full out in the mines and steel works to produce the munitions. My own father, of military age, had a responsible position in the power-house of the steel works and so was exempt from conscription.

Then there were the smells and tastes of a childhood home. In those days any woman who bought bread and did not bake it at home was regarded at best as a poor housekeeper or at worst a slut. Coming home hungry after our long walk from school on baking days, the house was pervaded by that most evocative smell of baking bread. Our special delight on those days was "ovenbread". For this the dough was rolled out about half an inch thick till about a foot or more square, set to rise a little and then baked on a floured oven shelf. It emerged in time for our homecoming golden, very crisp, crusty and delicious. It was still warm and the thick butter melted into the holes. This was topped by a thick layer of golden syrup. No wonder it provides a delicious memory! The side oven in the Yorkshire range was heated by coal and sticks and perhaps this made the bread more crusty. The old folks always maintained that bread baked in a gas oven never tasted so good.

Then there was the jam making which seemed to take place during August holidays. Plum jam making with Mother and Grandmother is my most vivid memory. Near to us was a large orchard. It produced the finest plums and apples which we bought not by the pound but by the stone (14lbs). Victoria and green-gage plums were the ones made into jam. Grandma's Victoria plum jam was her special pride and joy. The large luscious plums were cut in two and the stones taken out. Each stone was cracked and the kernal extracted - that was my job! Grandma said the kernals helped to set the jam. The fruit and sugar were put into a large copper jam pan with an iron handle. This was set on the wide bar over the fire in the grate which was giving a good heat but no smoke. Knowing when the jam was set without the aid of controlled heat or such refinement as a jam thermometer must have been tricky and perhaps Grandma's pride in her skill was justified. Cooking apples were made into apple pies, apple dumplings and roasted with sugar and raisins tucked in the centre. All through the autumn and winter were plenty of ripe apples in the pantry for hungry children to eat. Before Christmas all the family except the men folk, sat round the table preparing the fruit and nuts for the Christmas fare on one whole or even two evenings. Little stones from the large raisins had to be taken out - a sticky job, the sultanas and currants had to be cleaned, the almonds had to be blanched, the lemon and orange peel cut up and the walnuts cracked. Another messy job was chopping up the suet from the butcher's for the plum pudding. Next day all the family would be invited to stir the plum pudding with a large wooden spoon and wish a wish. Into the basin or basins went the rich mixture smelling faintly of brandy, covered with greaseproof paper and cloth, to be boiled over the fire or in the boiler house for hours and hours. The Christmas cake and mincemeat making were equally exciting events. We might even be allowed to scrape out the baking dish and lick the spoon afterwards!

Christmas Eve, in Grandma's time was a somewhat solemn affair. We were put to bed early, woken up later and taken in the dark to Grandma's house. Here we found the table covered with her best lace trimmed linen cloth on which was the large Christmas Cake, on a glass stand, and flanked on each side by a large rice cake and ginger cake which seemed traditional in our family. On a cheese dish sat a large chunk of Wensleydale cheese. For drinks was sherry for the adults and homemade lemonade for the children. At twelve o'clock as the grandfather clock struck, my father cut a large wedge out of the Christmas Cake with his mother's hand on top. He would wish us all a happy Christmas and hope that we would all be together again next Christmas. He then gave each member of the family a piece from that first wedge - surely a symbol of family unity! With the piece of cake went a thin slice of cheese. Visitors to the house during the Christmas period were always given a mince pie, for a lucky month in the year, a piece of Christmas Cake, a piece of cheese to eat with it and a glass of wine. In the households which originated from County Durham and further north, more was made of New Year than Christmas. In our household a similar cake-cutting ceremony took place when the "first-footer", usually my father, came in. It was important that he should bring in with him a sixpence for prosperity, a piece of bread to represent food, a piece of coal, to represent fuel and a piece of greenery for good health for the family during the coming year.

Wash day, usually Mondays, was another family ritual and it too had its special dinner. Unusually for those days, my father took a great interest in the laundry process and when he was on the right shift, which was two weeks out of three, he took things in hand himself. While Mother was getting us ready for school, he lit the boiler fire. We were very fortunate in having a boiler in the scullery. This was a brick structure with a chimney and in the middle was a large iron boiler with a wooden lid, built in the corner of the room. On wash days, although there was hot water in the tap at the sink, this was where most of the gallons of hot water was obtained and the white clothes boiled snow-white. During World War I and afterwards when rationing made food scarce, this boiler was used almost daily to cook the food for the animals on the allotment especially the pigs and the hens. The food consisted largely of "pig" potatoes, that is, little ones which were considered too small for human consumption and obtained from neighbouring allotments and farms. To them were added special meal and household scraps, for nothing edible was ever wasted. For the hen food, barley meal or something similar, a little of this food was mixed with water to produce "crowly". The hens certainly thrive on it for there always seemed to be plenty of eggs to gather.

In most households the actual washing was done in a wooden wash tub and the clothes beaten up and down with a "dolly stick" but my father had bought for us what was then regarded as the latest in washing machines. There was a wash tub and on the top was fixed a sort of mangle or wringer with large wooden rollers. At one side of the machine was fixed an iron bar with a wooden handle. This bar was vigorously pushed back and forth so that the clothes were well swished round. They then were pushed through the rollers so that the soapy water fell into the tub below. The rollers were worked by turning round the large iron wheel at the side by its handle. So effective were these rollers that dry sheets could be pressed through them and need not be ironed. After the clothes had been washed and mangled, the tub was drained of its dirty water by means of a tap at the bottom and a bucket. Now rinsing could commence in the fresh clean water now put in. After being mangled once more, they were ready to be pegged out on the lines in the garden, that is, all except those that had to be starched and blued. There were a great many of these white starched articles in those days for, not only were there white linen tablecloths, napkins, tray cloths, tea towels, sheets and pillow-slips, but also the underwear of the girls and ladies which was made of white calico and the shirts of the men with their stiff collars and fronts. Then of all the senseless garments, there were the white starched pinafores of the schoolgirls which were a pride to their mothers and such a misery to their lively daughters!

Meanwhile in the oven was cooking the special "washing day dinner" and the special dish we called "dad's dinner" but is known in other circles as "panackity". It was made in a large dripping tin and consisted of layers of sliced potatoes and sliced onions alternating with layers of slices of cold meat left over from the large Sunday joint, usually beef, of those days. Over the top was spread beef dripping and leftover gravy so that the top layer of potatoes emerged hours later, golden and crisp. This dish was followed by a large homemade rice pudding which had also been creaming in the oven for hours. After dinner the washing process continued but by the time we came home the clothes were hopefully dried, or about to be, and with the kitchen floor washed and all cleared up.

After tea, the ironing on the kitchen table began and in this all the girls were expected to take their share, beginning with handkerchiefs for the littlest ones. What a boon it was to the housewife when in the 1920's electric irons became the vogue. Before that flat irons were placed on a stand immediately before the bars of the fire grate. When ready the iron handles were very hot and had to be carefully grasped when holding a thick pad round them. If the surface of the iron was rough, there was a bar of yellow soap at hand on which to rub it. Somehow the work got done each week but whether she had domestic help or not, washing day was always a tiring day for mothers.

In those days in almost every home, whether working class or in the kitchen of farmhouse or mansion was a large clip rug. In the corner of the home you would have seen a large wooden frame of flat boards in which were burned numerous holes with wooden pegs in some. Round two of these planks would be wrapped a partly made clip rug with the piece in the making, stretched inbetween. The base of the rug so stretched was stout canvas or hessian or in some poorer homes, sacks could be used. Clothes in those days when outworn or unliked were not sent to Oxfam but made into clips. The clips were made by cutting the garment into strips about half an inch wide. These strips were then wrapped round a piece of wood to be cut into pieces so that the clips would all be the same size. Each clip was taken separately and pressed double through the canvas with a "prodder". The prodder was made at home by a very ancient method. One prong of a wooden peg was broken off and the peg pushed into the glowing embers between the bars of the grate. As the prehistoric people had already found out, if you remove the woodash you have left a strong sharp point. If the cloth used was suitable and colourful quite pretty patterned rugs could be made. "Hookey" mats were another method of making rugs on canvas but you needed a special hook. The material used had to be much thinner than that of the clipped rugs and they were usually more colourful. Sometimes stencilled canvas was used to form pretty patterns. Whether the material was thick or thin, none was ever wasted by the economically minded housewife.

As well as her white lace crochet work another craft my mother practised was quilting. Now known as Durham quilting and being revived it was done there in Eston at that time. It was practised by a group of ladies from the church for the Church Bazaar and they met at our house. This quilt too was worked on a frame but a much bigger one for these quilts were double-bed size. Cotton wadding was placed between large pieces of coloured satinette cloth and firmly tacked down. This "sandwich" was tacked down with tacks on to the two side pieces of a large frame and pegs put in to the holes so that a strong tension between was obtained. As the work progressed, it was wrapped round one end and let out the other by altering the pegs but always keeping the firm tension. Patterns were marked out on the material by means of templates. The ladies sewed right through the quilt with firm running stitches along the lines.

They chatted as they sewed and for them it made the afternoon a friendly social occasion. If at home, I threaded the needles for them.

No holidays abroad, no expensive toys, no swimming baths or sporting facilities, no radio, much less T.V., yet how grateful one should feel at being able to record such a happy childhood. One thing is sure that without the so-called advantages of today, we enjoyed our days and were NEVER bored!

The children being brought up in Nunthorpe, Ormesby and Marton at this time must have enjoyed a similar childhood, playing in the woods and fields as they made their way backwards and forwards to the village school near the church. The farm children would help in the daily work of the farms, feeding the animals, riding the horses and later tractors and so forth. The meet of the Cleveland Hunt with its horses and hounds nearby would be a special occasion and perhaps following on foot. When not at school there would be the weekly trip to Stokesley Market. In September the animals would be made ready to enter one of the classes at Stokesley Show and perhaps win a prize. Traditionally the school was given a holiday on this day and after the Agricultural Show they would all enjoy the fun of the fair.

The Nunthorpe estate of Sir Arthur Dorman included the land up to the west side of the station, the old boundary running along the railway line, then as now. It was around the station that he planned a small suburb. Roads were laid out with trees planted on either side. The large terrace houses in Marton Moor Road were intended for his employees with the end house being used as the estate office. The railway company had built the two Victorian cottages on the other side of the railway to house the signalmen needed for the busy signal cabin. In 1903 four more railway cottages were built on this side of the railway not far from the signal cabin. Plots of land bordering on these roads and the main Guisborough road were sold during the 1890's and early years of this century to Middlesbrough businessmen who, as previously mentioned, commuted by train to town. Most of these were large villa type houses with large gardens, for to live in Nunthorpe was regarded as a status symbol, a token of esteem. Sir Arthur however laid down certain stipulations for those living in his village. The roofs of all buildings must be of slate. There must be no public house or shop. However he was keen to provide sports facilities.

During the 1920's and 1930's, as in so many villages, in Nunthorpe, Marton and Ormesby there was an almost passionate interest in sport, especially the summer sports of cricket and tennis. On the cricket field all social barriers were forgotten as the sons of the great landowners played side by side with the farmer's sons and labourers. Skill with bat and ball was applauded by all and the winning of a local match was of vital interest to everybody. The greatest rivalry was between Nunthorpe and Marton. At Nunthorpe the matches were played on the cricket ground in the grounds of Grey Towers and supported by the Dorman family. After the death of Sir Arthur Dorman in 1931 and Grey Towers was sold, Mr O'Neil, who lived at Nunthorpe Hall, gave the cricket club the field which is now the upper part of the sports field. Then a fine wooden pavilion was built where the ladies provided refreshments of sandwiches, homemade cakes and teas during the interval between the two innings. About 1952 when the Polo field came up for sale Lady Kathleen Harrison who at that time lived in Red Cottage, which almost faced the field, bought it and presented it to the inhabitants of Nunthorpe as a sports field. It was then that the Sports Club was inaugurated and the present pavilion first built. It has been greatly extended in recent years.

At Marton the cricket matches were played on a large

field beside the village pub "The Rudds Arms", this site was used continually for cricket, at least since the 1880's, until a few years ago when the Parkway road was built and the cricketers were given a suitable field set further back. The Parish Magazines reveal what an important recreation cricket was at the turn of the century and reported regularly of its achievements, and the village pride and dedication is very clear. Mr William Brunton was the owner of the field and presented it, in 1947, to the Marton War Memorial Playing Fields Trust with a condition that the Trustees must take care of and maintain the War Memorial Garden. As the end of the field reached the main road, there was danger when the ball was given a mighty swipe to score a six. One ball narrowly missed a passer-by and it was alleged that another ball hit a passing bus. So a very tall wire-netting fence was erected by the side of the main road.

Opposite Captain Cook's Memorial School is a delightful garden, a war memorial established in 1947. The elegant stone cross was a gift from Sir William Crosthwaite to the people of Marton. Also in this beautiful setting is a plaque, mounted on a big boulder which was brought from Point Hicks Hill, near Cape Everard, the first point on the east coast of Australia which was sighted from the Endeavour in 1770, and stating that Captain Cook died at Ohwyehee on 14th February 1779. It is still looked after by the Trustees of the Marton War Memorial Playing Fields Trust, and was established for the residents and the immediate surrounding area. The land was given by Mr H.W.F. Bolckow.

On looking back it would seem that the summers were warmer and sunnier then. Certainly we each had our face tanned by the sun without going to Spain and sunburn could be a problem. Every year we used nivea cream to protect our skin. For those without access to a tennis court were the public tennis courts provided at the end of Rookwood Road, as shown on the schoolboy's map. These disappeared when the land was sold for building. As the large houses each employed a gardener to maintain their large gardens the mowing and care of these lawns was no problem.

For the older men was the Bowls Club which functions to this day on its ground beside the railway at the end of the lane beside the Railway Cottages. It was bought for the community by Mr John Ackroyd who lived in Connaught Road. He was a Methodist and ardent teetotaler, so he charged the club a peppercorn rent on condition that no alcohol was consumed on the premises. This stipulation stands to this day. It has always been a very successful club both socially and the standard of its play.

It may be asked if, during Edwardian/Victorian times there were any places where young people could meet and perhaps dance, in the area. Mr Clifford Brunton used to tell his son, Jack, stories of when he was a young man at the turn of the century. At that time the young villagers used to hold dances in one of the barns at High Farm, which was situated on the site where now stands the Avenue Junior School. The lads cleared the barn and then waxed the floor by scraping candles onto it and then rubbed it in to make a slippy surface. That the floor must be slippery was essential for all the young ladies must be swung off their feet while dancing "The Lancers".

In the 1930's the Middlesbrough Golf Club bought farmland which backed on to Brass Castle Lane and laid out an eighteen hole golf course with clubhouse and steward's accommodation beside the road. This has flourished ever since and today enjoys a reputation as a first-class course.

Photograph-Arnold Kidson

Dedication ceremony of the Stone Cross War Memorial erected in the memorial garden 1947, a gift from Sir Wm. Crosthwaite to the people of Marton. (Note Captain Cook's memorial School in the background)

A winning Bowls Team in April 1954.

Nunthorpe Sport

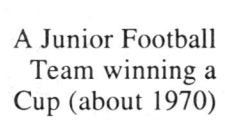

A Junior Football Team winning a Cup (about 1970)

Marton Cricket Team 1907

Showing three members of the Brunton family, a few years earlier nearly the whole team was made up of Bruntons.

Tennis Parties

Were a regular event on an area adjoining the Cricket field at Marton (about 1917).

High Farm (Coach Horse field about 1960).

This was the scene before Nunthorpe Junior School took its place together with all the surrounding development. The crest of Ormesby Bank can be seen quite clearly.

Farming more than 50 years ago.

One of the first prototype Combines in the area owned by Mr. Jack Brunton, called a Grain Marshall. Driver Mr. Robert Lightfoot. Tractor driver Mr. Kenneth Burnicle.

Before the building of the post-war housing estates which began in 1957, there was a village community spirit round Nunthorpe Station and all the social life was centred on the "Institute", now known as the Community Centre, in Connaught Road. Its foundation was due to the initiative of the local inhabitants after World War I. They formed themselves into a limited company with a chairman and executive committee issuing two thousand £1 shares. With the money they bought an ex-army wooden hut from Marton Hall in 1920. The hut was re-erected on its present site, leased from Sir Arthur Dorman for which they paid a nominal sum of one shilling a year as rent, on condition that no alcohol was consumed on the premises. These consisted of a large dance or concert hall with a stage and toilet facilities. Leading from it at the side was a supper room with kitchen. Beyond the hall was a billiard room and with its own door at the back, a library room where the books were changed once a month when boxes arrived from the Yorkshire County Library. The billiard room was strictly for men only, for they formed themselves into a club with a subscription of ten shillings a year. There they played their games of billiards, snooker and cards free from feminine company. Weekly Whist-drives were held in the supper room but in the years between the Wars, the most popular social functions were the Whist-drives and Dances. Once a year the Police Federation of the district held a Whist-drive for charity which was occasionally held here. Wonderful prizes such as a suite of furniture could be won so a large crowd of players was attracted.

The great social functions on the Nunthorpe social calendar were the Whist-drives and Dances connected with the Sport's Clubs which went on till 2am. Especially so was the Cricket Dance where the young people of all classes, employer and employee, danced together, the men in evening dress and the ladies in their best finery. As the four or five man band with piano, violin, saxophone and drums pounded out the lively tunes of the period, the dancers began their programme with a grand parade. The gentlemen walked down one side, the ladies on the other, to meet in the middle and parade down together. Again they went round the room in couples and came down in fours. Yet again they went round and down to form rows of eight. These then formed themselves into squares, ready to dance a set of "Lancers" or "Courtelians". Then would follow a programme of Waltz, Foxtrots, One-steps, Military-two-steps, St. Bernard Waltz, and probably a dance which was a current craze such as the Charleston, the Palais-glide or the Hokey Cokey. This scene of village dances in the wooden "Institutes" of the period seems to have been common throughout Yorkshire, James Herriot in his books writes of those in Thirsk and the Dales where very similar functions were held but without the drink. Locally there was "Marton Bungalow", another wooden army hut situated at the corner of Marton Crossroads opposite the Garage. In Ormesby, the present Community Centre was then the village school but there was another "Bungalow" where dances were held over where the garage now stands in the village centre.

After 1926 the women had their own Women's Institute which met on Wednesday afternoons once a month with their yearly Flower and Produce Show and Christmas Party to which their husbands were invited.

Public meetings of all kinds were held in the Institute hall and smaller gatherings such as adult classes and childrens' parties were held in the supper room. It was a focus of constant activity.

In the 1930's before the average man drove his own car, the male population with a few exceptions, commuted back and forth by rail to Middlesbrough and elsewhere.

For this the railway provided a very good half hourly service by "Sentinal" cars or coaches. A "Sentinal" train was like a large bus-coach with a steam engine in the middle and it was "push and pull", that is, was able to go up or down the line without being turned round. They functioned very well until the outbreak of World War II. There were about forty trains a day going through Nunthorpe Station at this time.

As the men met each other so regularly this gave rise to what was a uniquely Nunthorpe phenomenon - "The Ten-to-One Minstrels", the name deriving from the train they regularly used. This Concert Party exploited the talents of men everybody knew and many were the jokes and topical songs about characters and local events. This concert was followed by a dance and the profit given to charity. As can be imagined this was a very popular social occasion enjoyed by all.

At this time the cluster of houses round the station were surrounded by fields and woods which added to its truly village atmosphere. There were no pavements or grass verges beside the unmade roads which were jokingly referred to as the "hills and the dales". This atmosphere was especially felt at night when the owls were hooting and the darkness only broken by the rays of a single lamp on "The Tree". Again, there were times when the Cleveland Hunt met at this corner and the place seemed full of horses and hounds and their followers.

Though traditionally the Meet of the Foxhounds gathered at the Hall where maids handed each rider a stirrup cup, as time went on more and more farmers and their families joined the Hunt and it met regularly during the season at several convenient places.

The most notable farming family in the Nunthorpe and Marton area this century has been the Brunton family. It was on their land that the modern estates of Nunthorpe were built when the housing authorities decided to develop South Teesside in the housing boom after World War II. The process of covering the fields of farmland with new houses and roads has been going on ever since.

The most prominent member of this family living here now, is Mr Jack Brunton whose family has been farming here for over one hundred and fifty years; originating in the Peebles area of Scotland. The first Robert Brunton, early in the 19th century, became a shepherd to the then Lord Zetland and worked on his estate at Upleatham. Sometime between 1841 and 1851, with his wife and son, he moved to Marton and his descendants have been prosperous, hardworking farmers, butchers, innkeepers there ever since. They figure prominently in parish records as Churchwardens and other officers serving the community. In the early years of this century when Yorkshire was synonymous with cricket and rivalry was intense, not only between the county teams but even more so between the village teams, the Brunton family produced great cricketers to play on the fine playing field then situated adjacent to the village pub, the then cosy little Inn, "The Rudds Arms". It is said that at one time no less than twelve of them played for their village team, one of whom being good enough to be chosen for the Yorkshire second team.

Mr Jack Brunton was born at Marton but was brought up at Marton Moor Farm, Nunthorpe, where his parents lived after taking over the farm in 1916. This farm was previously tenanted by various members of this family for many years including his great grandfather "a character" known as Tally-ho-Bob. The farmhouse stood at the junction of Stokesley Road and Guisborough Road, facing Stokesley Road. After the death of Sir Arthur Dorman in 1931 the Grey Towers Estate was put on the market and split up. As has been previously

Original Drawing by Mr. Barry Wright

St. Mary's Church, Nunthorpe

stated this was a time of great industrial depression. Agriculture, nationally, was in the doldrums and so farmland was comparitively cheap. Thus as in the days of the yeoman farmers centuries before, a chance was possible for a tenant to buy his own land. This the thrifty Brunton family at Marton Moor were able to do. The outbreak of World War II made the nation realise the value of its farms and the produce it provided. As in the 18th century modern methods and modern machinery brought prosperity to energetic young farmers.

Marton Moor Farm prospered and was extended southwards when High Farm was acquired, members if this family had been tenants there since about 1880. The fields of both these farms are now covered with houses to form the estates in the Marton Moor area bordered by Dixon's Bank and Gypsy Lane. The Avenue Junior School is built on the site of the High Farm, house and outbuildings. Later Jack Brunton acquired three small farms bordering Brass Castle Lane; Ryehill Farm, South Ryehill Farm and Sunny Cross Farm. Together they form a farming estate which borders on the western boundary of the Poole Hospital grounds. The farm on the north side of Brass Castle Lane was the one acquired by Middlesbrough Golf Club in the 1930's.

Before selling the Marton Moor Farm he had earned for himself a reputation nationwide as a cattle breeder by establishing a pedigree herd of Ayrshire cattle. He founded it in 1939 and his animals won many top prizes at shows all over the country including London Dairy Show. This herd of cattle was then sold when Marton Moor Farm had to go for development in the early 1960's. Another project he undertook was to reclaim an area of the steep slopes of the Eston Hills (Swans Corner). These hills were mined for ironstone in the 19th century and since the mines closed were badly neglected and covered with trees, dense scrub and thick undergrowth. He hired caterpillar tractors, tackle etc, in order to clear the area. The work being done in the winter when his staff were not so busy with farmwork. It was not long before his cattle were grazing peacefully on those slopes won from that hillside waste.

Marton Moor Farmhouse was featured on radio. Before the days of television on Christmas Day the B.B.C. radio network celebrated with a Commonwealth Round the World broadcast. Families living in the lands of the various members of the Commonwealth were linked together and messages of goodwill were broadcast from each until Buckingham Palace was reached where King George VI gave his Christmas message. Marton Moor Farm, technically within the boundary of the Marton Parish, the birthplace of Captain Cook, was linked with a farmer's family in New Zealand and Christmas greetings were exchanged. In the background were heard the bells of Nunthorpe Parish Church.

Having sold his cattle and home farms this enterprising man, six years later, in 1969 acquired a new type of land to develop and expand his growing hobby of trees. Part of the Feversham Estate having come on the market, he bought Urra Estate, a great track of moorland, woodland and valley in Bilsdale, with many tenanted farms. He took over several of the farms as they became vacant, developed a good Beef herd of cattle and the hillsides carried his large flocks of sheep. He has created there a beautiful landscape with tree planting and lakes with both conservation and profitability in mind.

In early Victorian times the most prominent family in Marton was the Rudd family and the village inn was named "The Rudds Arms". Perhaps it is appropriate that the pub in the Nunthorpe and Marton area is "The Brunton Arms" in Gypsy Lane.

Sir Arthur Dorman was a keen Anglican churchman

Sir Arthur Dorman and Lady Dorman

Sir Arthur Dorman and Lady Dorman lived at Grey Towers, Nunthorpe, for more than thirty years. He was responsible for building St. Mary's Parish Church and the School. He planned the roads of the village round the Station and planted trees in the Avenue and Connaught Road. He built the terraced houses in Marton Moor Road and Rockwood Road in 1913. His sons played polo in the Polo Field – now Sports Field and he encouraged all sport.

Grey Towers

and it was probably he who pressed for what was now in fact becoming a necessity. Great Ayton was no longer a small country village. The mining and quarrying industries had brought in an influx of workers so that its population now numbered more then two thousand. It had built its new church in 1877. Nunthorpe too was no longer a hamlet dominated by a large house but was beginning to develop into a suburb for commuters to Middlesbrough. Parish boundaries were changed so that the new Nunthorpe parish comprised of Nunthorpe Village with its surrounding fields and farms and also that part of the Ormesby parish which included the former hamlet of Morton. Plans were also put in hand for the building of a parish church.

The Non-Conformists however forestalled them in building their church. At first it was known as the Congregational or Free Church and its foundation stone laid by Sir Arthur Dorman in 1911. It later became part of the Methodist Circuit and had its own Minister and Manse. This first building is still standing in Rookwood Road and now known as Rookwood Gospel Hall which is a mission church. Recently its appearance has been greatly improved. The original building was lighted in the middle by a large glass box-like structure which made strangers at first think it was the Baths!

In connection with the founding of the Methodist Chapel in Nunthorpe, mention must be made of the Dodds family. In a newspaper report by the Stockton and Darlington Times in 1962, Mrs Dodds, then eighty years old, was interviewed. She had lived in Nunthorpe more than fifty years and brought up her family here. She first came to Nunthorpe in 1907 at the age of twenty five, and said in those days there were no buses and the only shop was the tiny shop in the old village one and a half miles away. There were only two houses near the railway (excluding the railway cottages for employees) and all the surrounding land was being farmed. At that time Nunthorpe was a happy family and they had no policeman. Being a staunch Methodist she recalled how at first, they held services in private houses before the Chapel was built. In it she sang in the choir every Sunday for fifty years. She not only was a founder member of the original little chapel, but lived to see its beautiful successor built on the corner site of Connaught Road and Marton Moor Road. The foundation stone for that was laid on 29th February 1961.

Meanwhile in those early years before World War I plans were going ahead to build a parish church for Nunthorpe. As early as 1912 Lady Dorman was instrumental in founding a Mother's Union holding monthly meetings. She and her ladies set about raising funds for the new church. There is still in existence copies of a recipe book compiled by these ladies, to be sold for church funds and it makes fascinating reading. What a contrast to our eating habits of nowadays! For example a recipe for a nourishing "Working Man's Lunch" begins with 6lbs of steak! - but when one thinks of the manual labour exerted, without today's modern machinery, no doubt such "stoking up" was very necessary.

In 1914 negotiations for the actual building took place for a church to be set up on a site donated by Sir Arthur Dorman. A design by the well known ecclesiastical architect Mr Temple Moore based on the early English type of architecture was on the point of being commissioned when World War I broke out and all building stopped.

After the end of hostilities the development of the village round the station went apace. Main services were brought in and laid under the rough, though tree lined roads. The main sewers brought drainage and there was no longer need for septic tanks which the large houses had used up to this time. The mains water

"Grey Towers" became Poole Sanatorium

Nunthorpe Village School

With Vicarage and Parish Church in 1950.

Infant Class 1946/7

Teacher Miss B. Greenwood

pipes replaced the wells and pumps as a water supply. The pump in the railway yard which supplied the water for the stationmaster's household and the families in the railway cottages was a feature of the railway station till after World War II. The town gas from Middlesbrough was pumped up and finally the electric cables. Now it was possible to have street lighting - one single lamp placed on "The Tree", that is, the tree which stands at the junction of Marton Moor Road with the main Guisborough Road. Inter alia, it is astonishing to see the complex mixture (if that is the right word) of the pipes and cables buried beneath the metaled surface of our roads today. Over many weeks the writer watched a road being prepared before becoming part of a housing estate. First very deep down went the huge pipes to carry the sewerage and main water drains with smaller earthernwarepipes to each housing site. After these were buried the other services followed in turn, the gas mains and individual pipes, the electricity cables, the telephone wires and after that they were covered up the gutters. All these amenities are now under the roads of the original Nunthorpe Station complex, except for the telephone wires, but they only came very gradually in the years before World War II.

As more and more houses were built along the roads the necessity for a parish church became more urgent. New tenders were considered for the same church design by the famous architect, Temple Moore, and specifications as before but owing to the increased costs of labour and materials after the war, the lowest tender received was about two and a half times that received from the same firm in 1914.

The contract was let to Messrs John Thompson & Sons of Peterbrough and the foundation stone was laid by Sir Arthur Dorman. Building proceeded throughout 1925 and it was finally consecrated by the Archbishop of York on 20th July 1926.

On this occasion, a small boy, a farmer's son was there with his mother in the crowd of parisioners. He recalls how the great man looked southwards towards that glorious view of the Cleveland Hills and said "*I will lift up mine eyes to the hills from whence cometh my wealth*".

Since then various features have been added and the most notable being the Lych Gate at the entrance to the Churchyard. It was erected in memory of all the men of the parish who were killed in the Second World War and built in the same Temple Moore style. The stone was obtained from Gunnergate Hall which had been demolished just before in 1947. The oak wood framework, gates and panelling were made by Robert Thompson of Kilburn the "mouse man".

Nowadays the site of the church seems a strange one, being isolated from the houses in the greater part of the parish. It is said that Sir Arthur Dorman envisaged that the housing development would grow round Nunthorpe Village but no doubt, he was also influenced by its nearness to his own home at Grey Towers.

When Sir Arthur Dorman built the village school in 1903, as was customary then, he built the headmaster's house next door. For the vicarage it was decided to enlarge the schoolmaster's house next to the school and the headmaster to live in one of the new houses being built near the station.

As the horse and carriage gave way to the motor car as a means of travelling to church, the need arose for a car park. Mr Jack Brunton undertook this task and arranged that his workers from Marton Moor Farm should bring and spread brick-rubble, after clearing the site first, and also arranged for a council steam roller to flatten it. Thus the first church car park came into being. In order to allow the convenience of the modern hearse vehicles access to the Church door he made a further gift of a gate, situated by the side of the existing Lych Gate, made by Thompson of Kilburn, as a memorial to his parents.

In the 1950's it was realised that a Church Hall had become a necessity. In response, Mr Jack Brunton gave a site of land at the end of Rookwood Road for the purpose. However while still considering how to raise the funds for the new building, in 1960, the building firm of Wimpey's made a very good offer for the site for housing. This sale enabled the church authorities to buy another site in Morton Carr Lane and have money towards the cost of the building. An appeal was made for funds to complete the project and the two main contributors were the Spencer Trust (founded by Mrs Agnes Spencer of Marton) and Mr Jack Brunton as a memorial to his parents.

When Sir Arthur Dorman died in 1931 Grey Towers once more became vacant though his son Mr Charles Dorman and his Irish wife continued to live at Ryehill House off Brass Castle Lane for many years. Mrs Charles Dorman became very well known in the village as a popular president of the flourishing W.I. during the 1930's. They had no children and it is strange to reflect that none of the ironmasters who were the founding fathers of Middlesbrough and who built the "halls" in the surrounding villages left behind sons to succeed them in their enterprises as the Pease family had done. Even the Pennyman family who had lived at Ormesby Hall since Tudor Times ran out of male heirs. Mr James Pennyman who built North Ormesby at the end of the Victorian era had three sons but one was drowned in the garden lake as a child and the other two died young also and without issue. It was the son of one of his daughters who succeeded him and took the family name. He married Ruth Pennyman, a distant cousin, and a talented writer for the stage. Some of her plays were performed in the West End of London and it was due to her influence that famous actors from London came to Ormesby Hall to perform plays, mostly Shakespearian, in the stables.

After the death of Sir Arthur Dorman on 14th February 1931 Grey Towers was put on the market together with seventy seven acres of parkland. It says a great deal for the depth of the industrial depression at this time that in October 1931 a syndicate of businessmen were able to buy it for £4,500 as a speculation! However soon afterwards a Middlesbrough Alderman, Lieutenant-Colonel I. Gibson Poole, bought it from them, together with a further thirty seven acres, for £7000 and generously presented it to the town to be equipped as a Sanatorium. Tuberculosis (T.B.) was a great scourge at this time especially among the poorer classes. Its treatment was mainly bed rest for a long period, fresh air and graduated exercise. "Grey Towers" or Poole Sanatorium as it came to be known, with its beautiful surroundings and wide lawns was ideal for this. On June 2nd 1932 it was formally opened by Alderman Cooper, Chairman of the Sanatorium Committee. The hospital at this time consisted of the house only being adapted for the nursing of forty patients. This time of depression with its low standards of housing and nutrition was causing great concern regarding T.B. throughout the medical circles in the North East and it was decided to form a Joint Board which would provide a centre where surgical treatment could be given to T.B. patients and further research into treatment of the disease could be undertaken. Poole Sanatorium with plenty of land for development and its ideal situation was chosen. The Poole Joint Sanatorium Board consisted of representatives from the Councils of Middlesbrough, Sunderland, Darlington, South Shields, Gateshead and West Hartlepool, under the chairmanship of Alderman Cohen of Sunderland.

Plans went ahead for the building of a Sanatorium of three hundred and twenty beds, the foundation stones being laid in October 1938 by Lady Poole and Alderman Cohen. It was hoped that the project would be completed by 1942 but with the outbreak of war in September 1939 all building stopped. With conscription into the army of all young men and women, it was revealed how prevalent T.B. was among the population so government permission was granted for the completion of the hospital buildings and of the hospital facilities for research into the treatment of the disease. The "Children's Block" of sixty beds was the first to be completed and adult patients admitted there towards the end of 1943. The main building was completed and occupied by early 1945. In August 1945 the new Poole Sanatorium was opened by Princess Marina, Duchess of Kent, and mother of the present Duke of Kent.

With the implementation of the National Health Service Act in 1948 the Poole Joint Sanatorium Board ceased to exist and it was taken over by the Cleveland Management Committee. Happily the post-war years have seen the introduction of new drugs and new treatments so that the requirement of a Sanatorium for the dreaded T.B. no longer exists. Known as Poole Hospital it was necessary only to reserve twelve beds exclusively for T.B. patients. Its two hundred and sixty four beds were mainly used by patients with respiratory diseases. Very valuable work was done with geriatric patients and medicine to help their condition.

For some reason Sir Arthur Dorman forbade the building of shops on his estate and specifically in Marton Moor Road. Ward's shop, the newsagent and general store being at the corner, used Roodwood Road as the address of the shop and Marton Moor Road for the house, though the same building. Incidently the addresses of all houses in Nunthorpe were of names only and not numbers until about 1938. Mrs Ward, my mother, being somewhat superstitious like most people of her generation, received quite a shock when she discovered that her home, Dolvean, Marton Moor Road, where she had lived happily for five years, was numbered "13" in the road!

In the 1920's there were two house-shops where it was possible to buy a few groceries but in 1932 two shops were built on the east side of the station next to the two railway cottages and over the estate boundary. Robinson's was a sub post office which also sold groceries etc. Up to now, without going on the train to Middlesbrough, it was only possible to buy a stamp or post a parcel at the village post office, one and a quarter miles away. This tiny post office remained in business till the mid 1960's. The second shop to open was Griffith's the chemist, but in 1935 it became Tate's the greengrocers and is now Lloyd's Bank. The Ward family came in 1933 to the corner site previously mentioned to take over a small house-shop business. The shop was really the dining room in which an outside door opened onto the path. Up to this time the newspapers had been sent up from Middlesbrough by train and sold at the station. This business was transferred to Ward's, who from then on for almost forty years, delivered them to the houses and in this way a viable newsagency and general store was established. As the size of Nunthorpe grew and developed so did this business with its reputation for friendly service and good delivery. It also became a focus for neighbourly gossip and where the new residents met the old ones, that is those who were already established here. Before the family retired in 1972 the whole house had been converted into a proper shop and store-rooms. It became a mini-supermarket which delivered and was one of the first shops in the area to become part of the Spar grocery group. Mr Purvis, the shop manager was chairman of the local group of small grocers trading under its management. As the estates were built so did the number and length of the newspaper rounds till in the end twenty boys and girls were employed. The Ward family being so well known were prominent in public affairs during the 1940's and 1950's. Mr and Mrs Ward Senr. actively supported and were prominent members of the weekly Old-fashioned Dance Club and the Whist Drive, both held weekly in the Institute. Mr Donald Ward and his wife both served as Parish Councillors for many years and Mrs Rosalind Ward was well known in Women's Institute circles, as a member of the Yorkshire Federation Executive Committee and a cookery demonstrator. She once demonstrated cookery at the Yorkshire Show before no less a person than Princess Mary! It was not until several years after the war that the present parade of shops was built on the other side of the railway.

All this time the garage opposite had been a simple converted wooden structure selling petrol and doing motor repairs by the Anderson family. In recent years it has been modernised to become the large establishment it is today selling motor cars.

During the Second World War the steel works of Teesside worked night and day producing munitions and as such, here a likely target for enemy bombing attacks. By the same token, it was a well protected area. From the first days of the war silver barrage balloons floated overhead and there were numerous anti-aircraft guns, some in batteries of sixty four guns which fired simultaneously. There was a large one with its crew stationed near Nunthorpe Village in a field at the junction of the Stokesley Road and Ayton Road. There were numerous searchlights placed strategically around Teesside and when warships were anchored off the Tees their lights added to the display, as they ranged around the sky. Billingham with its chemical works, on the other hand, was surrounded by great barrels which if ignited could provide a smoke screen for the works.

The air-raids took place mostly during the early period of the war before the policy of intense bombing of cities was carried out by both sides. As Nunthorpe was situated so high above Teesside, it was possible to watch a raid from a suitable vantage point such as from Westwood Avenue. On some still moonlit nights towards the end of the war, a most sinister sound from high up in the air vibrated on all sides like the buzzing of millions and millions of angry bees. It was the gathering of the allied bombers setting off for a thousand bomber raid over Hamburg and other north German cities. Some of us felt great sorrow for the toll of death and destruction that night's work would bring. How great that death and sorrow was we did not know until after the war.

In houses, shops and halls the black-out regulations were very strict. Cars, vans and buses drove along the roads with masked lights which showed only a veritable chink. Street lights of course were out from the first day for the duration of the war. Trains were blacked out at night with blinds over the windows and the stations so faintly lit that it was sometimes difficult to get out at your right destination. If at home the curtain slipped and a chink of light appeared, there was soon a knock at the door or a shout from the Air-raid warden. These brave men and women paraded the dark streets every night whether there was a raid or not and they and the firemen were the civilian heroes of the war. The great problem for Teesside munition works was how to keep working at night without being a prime target for enemy bombers. In those days when an iron-furnace was being tapped the whole sky lit up. In the general black darkness it was surprising how even a small chink of light showed up. Yet such was the efficiency of our military intelligence, that every time an enemy force of bombers came to attack the area, all the lights at the works were out and only a general darkness pervaded. The enemy dropped very bright flare lights. These gave

Wards

The village shop from 1933 to 1972 at Nunthorpe Station – and a customer.

Connaught Road, Nunthorpe in the 1950's

Scene at Nunthorpe Station February 1940

One line has been cleared by snowploughs and was the only means of communication. The concrete pillars were an anti-tank defence device.

a stage-like effect when viewed from on high from away, as from Nunthorpe. Together with the searchlights, the flack from the anti-aircraft guns, the blazing of burning oil tanks and perhaps an aircraft falling in flames gave an unreal effect such as one might see at a great firework display.

In spite of the black-out, rationing, Home Guard and wardens to say nothing of its one bomb which fell harmlessly in a field, Nunthorpe was not so much affected by the war as those in more congested areas or along the coast. The shoreline between Saltburn and Coatham was considered a possible place for an enemy landing and all the beaches were heavily mined. Regulations in the towns and villages along the Yorkshire coast were very strict. Here, at Nunthorpe, we saw plenty of preparation for war in the form of army manoeuvers. During the war-time winters and especially in 1942 the roads were often blocked by snow. Only along the railway with its snow-ploughs running up and down continuously along the lines was communication maintained. On one snowy day at such a time two tanks stopped outside Ward's shop. The men were so hungry that we saw Guards' officers clutching a loaf of bread in their hands as they stood outside and eating it whole. It was all the shop could supply and they had lost their rations - presumably in the snow!

On another occasion towards the end of the war two divisions were on manoeuvers with the object of defending and capturing Guisborough. An army soup kitchen was set up on a vacant plot of ground at the corner of Bedford Road. A group of soldiers appeared in the evening and when they were asked what they were doing, they replied "We are the 'dead' coming for our supper!".

One day in early May 1944 a whole armoured division passed along the main road. Hundreds of tanks, large and small, a huge tank recovery vehicle with a crane capable of lifting a tank, trucks and vehicles of all kinds travelled along the road, hour after hour all day long. Night fell before they had all been through and when darkness fell the tanks made their way through the hedge and lined up round the cricket and polo fields - (now the recreation ground) burning the ground. The men slept under the hedges and on the pavements, until day came and they could go on. Behind them came a gang of men to repair the ploughed up roads so that they were fit for ordinary traffic.

"Digging for victory" was a great wartime slogan and a necessity for supplementing the rations. In Nunthorpe, allotments were made on waste ground and a small field beyond the railway yard and behind the two shops where among other things, grew wild raspberries in profusion, which made a welcome addition to our meagre diet. The writer tried to keep bees. One warm summer's day in 1942 a neighbour's bees swarmed and hung in a great bunch from a lower branch of the first lime tree in Connaught Road. On making enquiries the owner of the bees said she could have the swarm if she could get it. Having made suitable preparations for housing the new swarm in a hive, she and her sister set off. Face protected by a hat and bee-net she mounted a pair of household steps while her brave sister held a large basket below to catch them. With a hooked walking stick she shook the branch violently and then plop! the swarm fell mostly in the basket - but not all. hundreds of bees were flying everywhere. However the Queen was in the basket and after some ten minutes or so of bee panic, they too joined her there. We carried the basket to where the hive was prepared. The Queen sent out her scouts to see if the hive measured up to their requirements and then we watched in wonder as the whole swarm marched in order up the white sheet to their new home. Miraculously neither of us nor any of those watching received a single sting.

After the war came a period of readjustment on all levels. For a time the rationing of food and clothing was even more severe. Men and women from the forces had to adjust once more to civilian life among their families. Industry had to readjust to peace-time needs and especially to the repair in the towns of the war-damaged buildings. In the cities such as London, Coventry and Plymouth, large areas lay totally ruined where the Rosebay willowherb and Ragwort bloomed in wild profusion. But in Nunthorpe there was no damage and the interrupted programme of building houses and roads was resumed. At last the roads were metalled and paths of paving stones and grass verges ran down each side of them. Cherry trees were planted down the top end of Rookwood Road to form an avenue to the Methodist Chapel. Then there was the street lighting! Now it was no longer necessary to carry a torch when paying a visit at night to a friend or delivering a newspaper on a winter's evening.

Town planning became the order of the day, towns and villages were no longer to be allowed to develop in a haphazard fashion. Such things as ribbon development of houses beside the roads as had happened before the war, was no longer to be tolerated. The plans of every building must be carefully scrutinised before being given planning permission. Land-use of the area must be scrutinised too and as with other councils the Middlesbrough Borough Council and the North Riding County Council employed professional town planners. They it was who decreed that Middlesbrough must develop southwards. Since the last war no matter what boundary changes there have been made or under what name - North Yorkshire, Teesside or Cleveland, the process of urbanisation in the area has gone apace until now the three separate communities of Marton, Nunthorpe Station and Ormesby have all joined up.

With this urbanisation has come certain advantages. It was inevitable that the village shops should be replaced by supermarkets and the Marton Parade of shops is particularly fine. Each place has now a fine library to replace the monthly box from the County Library. Recreational societies such as the Gardening Club and the Bridge Club have come into being but above all, instead of the little village school which in 1962 had three teachers and sixty pupils, there are now three primary schools and a very large Comprehensive School at Swan's Corner, with facilities for going on to the Sixth-form College in Flatts Lane. Also at Swan's Corner is the Rural Centre for mentally-handicapped teenagers, in the former Upsall Hall. Each year they hold an Open Day to demonstrate the surprising skills of which these pupils are capable. The Upsall Hall with its splendid view of the Cleveland Hills, was built in Victorian times, by the Swan family who were ironmasters.

The churches too have responded to the need but perhaps not to the same extent. St. Mary's is still the only Anglican Church in Nunthorpe but they have built a new church hall situated off Morton Carr Lane, where services are held every Sunday in addition to those in the church, and the old St. Cuthberts is the only Anglican Church in Marton. Now beside it is a fine building - The Marton Parish Centre. As has previously been noted the Methodists built a beautiful new church to replace its tiny chapel. This latter building has been greatly improved lately and is now a mission church known as Rookwood Gospel Hall. The Roman Catholics built a fine dual-purpose building in Gypsy Lane which serves admirably as church and hall and is known as St. Bernadettes. In response to the great housing development around Gypsy Lane in Marton and Nunthorpe, they built a Primary School. The newest church to be founded, also just off Gypsy lane, is the United Reformed Church whose foundation stone was laid by Mrs Margaret Blakey in 1972. The initiative for this entirely new venture for this area was given by a group of about a dozen local residents who met fortnightly in the Institute for a service conducted by the Minister of the Park Presbyterian Church in Middlesbrough. In 1963 the Presbyterian authorities decided to establish a Preaching Station to take advantage of a site donated by the building firm of Yuill's who were building a large estate on land bordering on the Marton end of Gypsy Lane. As leader for the venture, the Presbyterian authorities sent Miss Margeret Taylor who had lately qualified as a Minister. She was soon to be well known to listeners of Cleveland Radio, which began broadcasting a few years later. A wooden hut was erected not far from the site of the present church and the hard working and enthusiastic band of workers equipped it with the best second-hand furniture they could find. This enthusiasm had a distinctly Scottish flavour. Its first secretary Lennox Williamsom and his wife Norma, as well as Mrs Blakey, who took the place of her husband, George who died soon after his appointment as a first elder, were all of Scottish descent. Others gathered round all equally enthusiastic, such as Ian Macintosh who for many years acted as handyman to the emerging church. In 1971 came the crucial meeting when it was decided they must build a real permanent church on the corner site that Yuill's had reserved for them. Once it was decided to go ahead offers of free professional help both within and without the church came from all sides. It was to cost the church £25,000. Looking back one realises the timing was just right for only two years later came decimalisation and mounting inflation which would have made such a venture impracticable. On 12th May 1973 it was dedicated for worship by the Moderator of the United Reformed Church, for by this time the Presbyterians and Congregationalists had joined forces. Right from the beginning the church flourished and has provided a much needed venue for youth organisations such as the Boys Brigade as well as church and social events ever since. For obvious reason it was named St. Andrews.

But what has happened to the oldest church in the area, where Christianity began here a thousand years ago and whose chancel dates back to the twelfth century? It is a happy thing to be able to record it has not only been preserved but is still loved and cherished by the inhabitants of Ayton. It has a custodian and with his willing band of workers sees that all is as it should be. It has almost become a shrine for visitors from Australia and New Zealand who visit the Cook family grave in the churchyard as part of the Captain Cook tour; Marton, Ayton, Staithes and Whitby. They and other visitors are asked to contribute to the fund which maintains it. As there is no electricity in the church for heating and lighting, it is closed during the winter months. In May there is a special opening service when the church is beautifully decorated with spring flowers and lit by candles. From then on during the summer it is open on Sunday afternoons from 2pm to 4pm. At other times it can be viewed with permission of the custodian. At the end of the summer is another special service when the church is again decorated with the fruits and flowers of autumn and aglow with candles. To take part in these services is an unforgettable experience enjoyed by so many - especially when one remembers the hundreds of Aytonians who have sat and worshipped on those very pews.

Great Ayton still remains a beautiful Yorkshire village with its green and riverside intact under the lovely Cleveland Hills. Its new buildings and renovation of old ones have been discreet and the modern estates on its boundaries not obtrusive. In the summer it attracts many visitors and tourists so that there are now new shops of good quality to cater for their needs. The flourishing Quaker School which dominates the green still retains its eighteenth century facade and the original Meeting House. A peaceful atmosphere is still retained which is in keeping with its quiet religious reputation. It has escaped the urbanisation which has engulfed its northern neighbours in Cleveland.

What of Nunthorpe village, the original Nunthorpe? For most of this century there appeared to be two Nunthorpe villages, which only had the church and school in common. Nunthorpe Village being a farming community built four agricultural cottages after the war and was regarded as being allied to Great Ayton and Stokesley while Nunthorpe Station with its commuting population felt itself to be a new identity faintly connected with Teesside.

Gradually all that makes community life viable in the old village has been withdrawn. Its hall now an old people's home, its "Grey Towers" once a large hospital but now stands empty like an abandoned ship, its only shop and post office closed and even its school no longer echoes with children's voices, so it lies forgotten or perhaps its atmosphere is like that of a retired but kindly old lady full of memories.

Since the building of the by-pass road, little traffic has passed down its one street, except the farm tractors and cars and the Ayton bus which passes hourly during the day. For the most part it just sleeps.

The twentieth century flows on. It has seen the three local villages of Ormesby, Marton and Nunthorpe each with its "Squire", large Hall and farming community change into one large urban sprawl of council estates and suburbia. The age of horse and carriage travelling along country lanes has been exchanged for the motor car, speeding along wide straight roads while aeroplanes zoom overhead.

Our television screens bring us pictures from all over our planet and beyond; and computers calculate with the speed of light. One asks oneself "Whatever next!". Looking ahead one wonders also how people living here a hundred years hence will view US. One hopes it will at least be with toleration. Secretly one wonders whether all the problems which seem, at the moment, to beset us on every side will have been resolved by then. But, if they have managed to resolve OUR problems, I suspect they will have just as many of their own - for that's life! But - the eternal verities will always remain. Arnold Toynbee, the greatest historian of our time came to the view *"that the core and meaning of history turned upon a slow and painful clarification of the true relation between God and man"*.